THE MIGRATION PROCESS IN BRITAIN AND WEST GERMANY

Research in Ethnic Relations Series

Reluctant Hosts: Europe and its Refugees
Danièle Joly and Robin Cohen

Democracy and the Nation State
Tomas Hammar

Antiracist Strategies
Alrick X. Cambridge and Stephan Feuchtwang

Ethnic Minorities and the Criminal Justice System
Robert Waters

Pacific Migrant Labour, Class and Racism in New Zealand
Fresh off the Boat
Terrence Loomis

Migration, Socialism and the International Division of Labour
The Yugoslavian Experience
Carl-Ulrik Schierup

Race and Public Policy
A Study of Local Politics and Government
Shamit Saggar

Race, Discourse and Power in France
Maxim Silverman

Paradoxes of Multiculturalism
Essays on Swedish Society
Aleksandra Ålund and Carl-Ulrik Schierup

The Migration Process in Britain and West Germany

Two demographic studies of migrant populations

HEATHER BOOTH

Avebury

Aldershot · Brookfield USA · Hong Kong · Singapore · Sydney

Published by
Avebury
Ashgate Publishing Ltd
Gower House
Croft Road
Aldershot
Hants GU11 3HR
England

Ashgate Publishing Company
Old Post Road
Brookfield
Vermont 05036
USA

A CIP catalogue record for this book is available from the British Library and the US Library of Congress.

ISBN 1 85628 058 6

Printed and bound in Great Britain by
Billing and Sons Ltd, Worcester

Contents

List of tables: Part I

List of appendix figures

List of appendix tables

List of tables: Part II

Acknowledgements

The bulk of the work involved in writing this book was carried out at the ESRC Research Unit on Ethnic Relations, the forerunner of the ESRC Centre for Research in Ethnic Relations (CRER) at the University of Warwick. The study on West Germany was first published separately in 1985 in the CRER series, Monographs in Ethnic Relations. The British study was completed in 1986, and has been placed together with the German study in this book as two case studies of the same migration process.

I am grateful to the staff of the CRER, and to Ashok Bhat, for comments on an earlier draft of the British study; and to the statisticians and others in the various government departments in Britain and West Germany who assisted me in obtaining relevant data. I am also grateful to Lillah Freeman, Rose Goodwin, Matilda Imamaeva and Francoise Laubreaux, who typed this manuscript in its various stages and to those who assisted in its publication, including John Wrench of CRER.

1 Introduction

The migration process

When members of a population leave that population in sizeable numbers for residence amongst another population from which they are demographically distinguishable, there begins a process of formation of what might be termed a 'new' population, or migrant population. Of course, this population is not new in any sense other than the fact that its members have broken away from their parent population to form a separate group or population resident elsewhere. The migration process involves the formation and development of the new migrant population from the fact of migration through to the stage at which it can no longer be said that the development of the population is significantly affected by migration, either directly or indirectly. When this stage has been reached, the population would no longer be described as migrant and the migration process would be complete.

A first requisite for the migration process is, of course, migration. But no sooner has the migration of the first migrants occurred than the natural demographic development of the migrant population begins through the course of birth and death. These two aspects of the migration process, the flow of migration and the natural demographic development of the population, take place simultaneously. At first, the flow of migrants is the more significant factor in the growth and character of the migrant population, but as the flow declines and the population takes form, births and deaths become the more significant factors in the population's development. This is always the case, since for various reasons, all migration flows become reduced and eventually cease to have any direct significance in the demographic development of the population in question. Once this has occurred, the development of the migrant population continues through natural increase alone, but the rate of natural increase is determined by the indirect effects of migration on the structure of the population and on its vital rates, as discussed below. When such indirect effects cease to be of significance, the migration process may be said to be complete and the population would no longer be described as migrant.

Migration itself is of course a demographic event, and one which is of fundamental importance in defining the migrant population. The aspect of migration that is of most significance in determining the demographic character and development of the migrant population is not the size or volume of the migrant flow, whether net or immigrant, but the pattern of migration. By this is meant the demographic characteristics of migrants, principally in terms of sex and age but also including marital status and dependency status, as well as the relative timing of their migration. The pattern of migration is concerned with issues of who migrates, when and with which family members. These various facets of migrant characteristics and behaviour determine the demographic composition or structure of the early migrant population resident in the country of destination. This structure is typically irregular since the majority of early migrants are males of young adult age who migrate for work. As migrant labour, these constitute the main flow of primary migrants on whom later migrants depend. Whilst this primary migrant flow may include some women who migrate as labour in their own right, the majority of women migrate at a later stage as the dependants of male labour, along with their children. Thus the composition of a migrant population in the early stages of the migration process is heavily biased towards young adult males.

As the migration process progresses, and more women and children migrate, the population develops a more balanced structure. The number of older male children in the migrant population may initially increase, as the process of family reunification begins. Such children often precede their mothers who remain with the female and younger children until sufficient funds have been accumulated to pay for the passage of the remaining members of the family. In general, however, given the characteristics of the dependants of most migrant labour, the reunification of families progresses towards a population consisting of young adult males with fewer adult females of a slightly younger average age and with younger rather than older children. Older children and older adults usually make up a very small proportion of a migrant population in the early stages of the migration process.

These irregularities in the age structure of the migrant population are very important in determining the development of that population. Whatever the demographic rates of fertility and mortality in the population, the structure of the population may be even more important in determining its development, especially if that structure is irregular. This is because it is the structure of the population which determines the base to which the demographic rates apply. This is easily seen by way of example. If a population consists entirely of males, then whatever the rate of fertility, the number of births will be zero, and the population will decline as deaths occur. Similarly, a population composed entirely of children will experience no births until those children reach puberty. Since puberty is reached at different ages, the number of births will initially be small but will increase rapidly before declining again as fecundity declines and menopause is reached. This will result in a 'wave' of children in the population, which will grow up to produce another wave.

This effect is seen clearly in migrant populations in the early stages of the migration process. Of course, given the span of years over which women bear children, these waves run into one another, become merged and indistinguishable. The structure of thus becomes more regular, and with time these structural effects are lost all together.

It is through both the direct effect of migration and the indirect effect of irregularities in the population structure that the migrant population is subject to rapid change in its demographic character. Such change is inevitable in so far as its indirect causes are concerned. The irregularity of the age structure of a recently migratory population ensures continuing change merely through the process of ageing. Thus, a large cohort of infants will progress through childhood and adulthood to old age as a permanently large cohort, passing like a wave through the structure of the population. In addition, though fertility rates may remain constant, for the reasons discussed above an irregular age distribution results in a fluctuating number of births per year, giving rise to continuing though usually less marked irregularity in the age distribution. If fertility and mortality rates were to remain constant and migration were to cease, such irregularity would, over generations, eventually disappear.

Constant rates of fertility and mortality rarely occur, however, especially in a migrant population. As the structural effect becomes less significant, and as migration ceases so that it is not continually reinforcing the structural effect, changes in fertility and mortality rates begin to play the dominant role in the determination of the population's structure. Indeed, in the absence of migration the structure of any population is ultimately determined by the two inevitable demographic events of birth and death.

The levels and patterns of fertility and mortality of a migrant population are initially determined by the norms prevailing in the population from which the migrants come. This does not necessarily imply that those members of a population who migrate have the same fertility and mortality rates as those members who do not migrate. Where mortality is concerned, it is often the case that migrants are amongst the healthiest members of the population from which they migrate, and in some cases this extends to their being healthier than the general population in the country to which they migrate. Such a differential in mortality is often due to a self-selection process whereby only the fit successfully cope with the upheaval of migration, but it may also be due to more formal selection procedures in Which health checks form an official barrier to the unfit. In general, such health factors apply only to the primary migrant whilst the health of dependant migrants is not taken into account.

Though the basic norms determining initial fertility and mortality behaviour remain with the migrant, the experience of migration generally has some effect on demographic rates. In the case of fertility, migration may have a significant effect on the pattern if not the level. The disruption of family life by the migration of different family members at different times, sometimes stretching over many years, obviously disrupts family building, often at a time when women are the most fertile. On the reunification of husband and wife, there is often a period of high fertility

3

during which time lost in family building is made up. This distorts fertility patterns and, to the extent that time lost regarding childbearing can never be regained, reduces fertility levels.

Quite apart from the effects of selection and migration itself, the demographic behaviour of a migrant population generally changes as a result of adaptation to the conditions and norms prevailing in the new country of residence. The usually better health facilities and environmental conditions of the new location result in improved health and hence lower mortality rates amongst the migrant population than would have been the case if migration had not occurred. With time, however, there may be counterbalancing effects if the migrant population adapts to a lifestyle with associated higher risks of diseases of affluence such as heart disease. In general, the mortality of a migrant population will tend towards the levels and patterns prevailing in the country of destination, since mortality is determined by external and environmental conditions including housing, working conditions, nutrition and lifestyle.

Where fertility is concerned, the initial norms of the migrant population are often eroded as migrant women adapt to the situation in which they find themselves in the country of destination. The extent to which this change occurs, and the speed with which it is achieved, varies significantly between migrant populations and is heavily dependent on cultural factors. Whilst the norms of women who have themselves migrated may not change appreciably, there is often a marked difference in fertility rates between these migrant women and women who either migrated as small children or were born in the country of destination. This difference is usually in the direction of reduced fertility rates since contemporary migration generally flows towards the developed countries where fertility rates are low. This is not to imply that the fertility of a migrant population will necessarily tend to the same level as that of the population in the country of destination. Fertility differentials are maintained more or less permanently between different groups in almost all populations, and are based on a variety of factors including religious and cultural norms. The continuing existence of a difference in fertility does not therefore indicate that the migration process has not been completed.

It must, of course, be recognised that no migrant population remains closed to the possibilities of marriage with members of the population in the country of destination. Again, the extent to which this occurs varies according to cultural factors. Though such intermarriage is not of relevance per se in the definition of the migration process, it is generally to be expected that marriage to a member of the population in the country of destination is associated with more rapid changes in demographic behaviour.

The various component parts of the migration process are, of course, interrelated. This is clearly evident in the effect of migration on the irregularity of the population structure, and its effect on the demographic development of the population. Less in evidence is the reverse effect of population structure and demographic development on migration. Though it may be taken for granted, the migration of family members as

4

dependants can be regarded as determined by the population structure. Furthermore, the migration of fiances, both male and female but particularly in the case of females, is a direct result of imbalances in the structure of populations. Such imbalances in the numbers of young adult males and females are particularly felt in populations which traditionally marry amongst themselves and are relatively closed to intermarriage with the population in the country of destination.

As long as primary migration occurs, the population will continue to be subject to renewed irregularity. The migration of dependants, however, has a regularising effect on the structure of the population, and the same is clearly true of migration caused by the irregularity of the structure. Whilst changes in fertility and mortality also have an effect on the age structure of the population, these effects are more gradual and regular in themselves and are usually much less significant in the short term.

The migration process continues to occur whilst these irregularities continue to affect the structure of the population. In sum, since these effects are due to migration, the migration process continues while ever the effects of migration, whether direct or indirect, are felt.

Terminology

It should be clear from the above description and definition of the migration process, that the term refers to populations and not to individuals. The members of a migrant population may or may not be migrants in the true sense of the word, that is persons who have migrated from one location to another. Rather, the population encompasses migrants and their progeny. Even amongst true migrants, distinctions are drawn between primary migrants or those who migrate for employment, collectively referred to as migrant labour, and secondary migrants or those who migrate as the dependants of primary migrants. Secondary migrants include wives, dependant children, elderly parents and other dependant relatives, and fiances.

Where the migrant population is being discussed in terms of stocks rather than flows, the children are often referred to as 'second-generation migrants'. This term includes both the children of primary migrants who have themselves migrated and those who were born in the country of destination who, strictly speaking, are not migrants at all. Occasionally the idiosyncrasy embodied in this term is continued into 'third generation migrant', but more often the word migrant is dropped. In the two studies presented here, it has been necessary to draw a distinction between the terms 'immigrant' and 'in-migrant'. This is due to the ideology involved in terms of the political status of migrants within the country of destination, as discussed in the relevant chapters, and the distinction has no demographic significance.

The studies

The two studies that appear in Parts I and II below detail the migration process which has occurred, and which continues to occur, in two countries of Western Europe, namely Britain and West Germany. Both countries have received substantial flows of migrants since the Second World War, and both have taken steps to stem these flows such that today migration has virtually ceased. The broad similarities in the migration processes experienced by these two migrant populations do not extend to the philosophies under which migration took place. In the case of Britain, migrants entered as immigrants and were always regarded as permanent. In contrast, migrants to West Germany were viewed as temporary guestworkers who would never gain permanent status.

These different philosophies are necessarily reflected in the foci of the two studies. The first study, on Britain, does not address the issue of status, since it is irrelevant. Rather, the study discusses in detail the pattern of migration to Britain and the factors which determined that pattern. The study shows how the pattern of migration has determined the current demographic characteristics of the migrant population and how the demographic development of the population continues to be influenced by past migration. The migrant population in question is the population of New Commonwealth and Pakistani ethnic origin composed mainly of migrants from the Caribbean and from India, Bangladesh and Pakistan.

The second study, on West Germany, addresses the question of the status of the migrant population. In particular, the study shows that contrary to their temporary dejure status the majority of the migrant population in West Germany today are behaving demographically as if they were permanent. The study details the differences between six different migrant populations, particularly in terms of their migration patterns, and shows how each population is at a different stage in the migration process. The six populations included in this study are those of Italian, Greek, Spanish, Portuguese, Turkish and Yugoslav nationalities, which together made up 73 per cent of the total foreign population resident in West Germany in 1981.

A common theme in these two studies is the importance of the influence of economic and political factors in shaping the pattern of migration. Whilst the initial impetus for migration to both Britain and West Germany was economic, the migrant flows were soon curbed by legislation based on political considerations. In both countries, this early legislation had the result of accelerating the establishment of migrant families, though later legislation has been aimed at limiting the entry of dependants to a minimum.

This similarity in the migration patterns of migrants to the two countries is continued in the significance of those migration patterns in the demographic development of the migrant populations. In both studies, it is shown how the demographic characteristics of migrants, the different

6

timing of their migration and their relationship to earlier migrants have determined the structure and development of today's migrant populations.

Part I
DEMOGRAPHIC DYNAMICS:
ETHNIC MINORITY POPULATIONS
IN BRITAIN

2 The British study

Over the centuries, Britain has received a good many migrant groups into her shores, groups that have long since become demographically indistinguishable from the population which they joined. The most recent episode of migration to Britain, and the one of interest in the present study, involves people from the countries of the New Commonwealth and Pakistan, people who are commonly termed 'black'.

The presence of black people in Britain dates back over several centuries (File and Power, 1981; Fryer, 1984), though the majority of the two million black people living in Britain today owe their residence to post-war migration. The black population has been met with considerable hostility from the white, predominantly racist, population; and numerous issues have been raised which, though they have been debated in the political arena, have often been directly related to demographic factors. In the present century, early hostilities were heightened by the fact that some black men courted and married white women (Joshua and Wallace, 1983, ch.1): these 'unusual' demographic events arose in part from the near absence of black women (or in demographic terms, from the exceptionally high sex ratios) which in turn arose from migration patterns. More recently, the debate about immigration and the resultant legislation not only concerns a basic component of population growth but has had a significant effect upon it. The so-called 'numbers game' at first involved the 'interpretation' of immigration data, but soon progressed to include another demographic factor, fertility. And, as if demographic concepts were only just being mastered, growth due to the age structure was belatedly brought into the debate in the guise of concern about future concentrations of the black population in the inner cities.[1] These issues have received greater attention than their actual significance, in demographic terms, has deserved. This fact alone points to the need for a better understanding of the demographic processes that are occurring in the black population. It is important to understand these processes and to recognise their significance not only in the study of migrants (Booth, 1982) but in the provision of facilities and services.

Data sources

In Britain, knowledge about the demographic characteristics of the black population is fragmented and incomplete. It is fragmented because it is of necessity based on several different sources of data, sources which refer to different points in time and different groups of people, and which use different definitions. It is incomplete because various groups of people are omitted from various data sources, and because in some areas of demographic interest, such as nuptiality, data on ethnic origin are not produced. Most of the research that has been undertaken in this field has concentrated, not surprisingly, on census data (for example: Eversley and Sukdeo, 1969; Rose et al., 1969; Lomas, 1973). Such large volumes of data as the census provides are necessary to allow analysis where several dimensions are of interest or where base data are necessary to calculate rates of relatively rare events, such as death by a particular cause. Census data, however, do not generally provide information concerning migration flows and research into these has been based on specific sources of migration data (for example: Peach, 1968). Other information is obtained from surveys both within government and without, which though not specifically demographic do provide information of use in demographic analysis.[2]

These various sources of information are, of course, published in as many different reports. In the late 1970s an attempt was made to gather the main findings together in one publication (Runnymede Trust and Radical Statistics Race Group, 1980). Shortly afterwards, a conference on the demography of minorities was held and its proceedings published (Coleman, 1982). Since then, a great deal of additional information has become available, most notably from the 1981 Census, but also from surveys such as the Labour Force Survey.

The information available from these various sources form the raw materials of the demographic analysis that follows. Such materials are widely regarded as objective, but this is rarely the case. When the population in question is an ethnically–defined minority group of a largely racist total population, objective data are hard to find. The history of data production on the ethnic minority population in Britain shows how selective data have been produced to meet the needs of government mostly in response to racist concerns (Booth, 1988). Despite their dubious origins, these data are useful in that they contain information about the development of the population which has been largely determined by political factors. Thus, the demography of the ethnic minority population in Britain cannot be divorced from the political context in which its development has taken place. The analysis that follows aims to demonstrate the influence of political factors on the demographic development and structure of the population.

The population

The ethnic minority population in question is that of 'New Commonwealth and Pakistani ethnic origin'. The definition has itself been developed according to political criteria. Official statistics are grouped according to a variety of criteria including historical and legal factors and the social and political concerns of the day. Thus people from the Commonwealth have long been distinguished in statistical terms from people from elsewhere in the world. More recently, statistics concerning the Commonwealth have been divided into the Old Commonwealth (OC) and the New Commonwealth (NC), a division on implicit racial grounds following immigration law. The OC comprises Australia, New Zealand and Canada whose citizens are mostly white. The NC comprises the remainder of the Commonwealth, including the Caribbean countries (popularly referred to as the West Indies), India, Bangladesh and certain African countries, most of whose citizens are black. It also includes other territories such as Hong Kong, Singapore, Cyprus, Malta and Gibraltar. Until 1 September 1973, the NC also included Pakistan.[3] After Pakistan left the Commonwealth, it became necessary to refer to the New Commonwealth and Pakistan (NCWP) so as to maintain the same grouping for social and political purposes. The term 'New Commonwealth and Pakistani ethnic origin' has been coined to define people from the NCWP and their descendants.

A distinction should be drawn here between the terms 'NCWP ethnic origin' and 'NCWP born'. The former includes all people of NCWP ancestry regardless of birthplace, whilst the latter includes people born in the NCWP regardless of ancestry. Thus, the term 'NCWP born' includes white people born in the NCWP, but excludes people of NCWP ancestry who were not born in the NCWP but in, for example, Britain. The term 'NCWP ethnic origin' was introduced to overcome these imprecisions in defining the ethnic minority population. In quantitative terms, however, many imprecisions remain in the definition and measurement of this population and its characteristics. These biases and errors are discussed in Chapter 4 where the data on the population and its demographic characteristics are themselves presented.

Though the population of NCWP ethnic origin is often referred to as 'black', it includes people, such as Cypriots, who are by no means black in terms of colour. They are, however, discriminated against by society at large and to some extent share much the same social and economic experiences as those members of the population who might more accurately be described as black. To single out only the two largest ethnic groups, West Indians and Asians (a term which comprises many groups) would be to ignore the smaller ethnic groups which in 1981 comprised 20 per cent of the total, though in some cases datalimitations do in fact have this result.

Notes

1. Enoch Powell, 24 September 1981, speech to Young Conservatives, Cobham, Surrey.
2. Government survey sources include the Labour Force Survey, the General Household Survey and the National Dwelling and Housing Survey. Non-government surveys include the PEP survey reported in Smith (1976), and its successor reported in Brown (1984).
3. Countries are referred to by the names by which they are known today, regardless of date. Thus 'Pakistan' refers to present day Pakistan, formerly West Pakistan, and the former territory of East Pakistan is referred to as Bangladesh.

3   Black migration to Britain

Though small black communities existed in Britain prior to the 1950s,[1] the majority of today's population owe their residency to the migrants who came here after the Second World War in search of work. In 1951, there were 256,000 people living in Great Britain who were born in the New Commonwealth and Pakistan (NCWP). These migrants and those who followed in later years form the basis of today's migrant population in Great Britain, the population of NCWP ethnic origin. This chapter details the migration patterns of these migrants.

Early migration: informal control

The post-war wave of black migration to Britain began in the late 1940s, and gathered strength in the 1950s and 1960s. It occurred in response to various factors including economic and demographic conditions in the countries concerned (push factors) and economic conditions in Britain (pull factors). Indeed, economic factors dominated other considerations. The Royal Commission on Population, for example, dismissed black immigration as extremely problematic in terms of assimilation: it was important that immigrants should be 'of good human stock and were not prevented by their religion or race from intermarrying with the host population and becoming merged with it' (Royal Commission on Population, 1949, p.124). And though the UK government considered as early as 1950 the control of black immigration on political grounds concerning fears of non-assimilation,[2] they were prevented from doing so by the economically determined political situation surrounding decolonisation.[3]

The pattern, though not the level, of this early migration can be seen in Figure 1 (Appendix Table A1) using data from the 1971 Census on birthplace and year of entry to the UK (Lomas, 1973).[4] The relative timing of the three main migratory flows from the West Indies, from India and from Pakistan and Bangladesh can be seen. Migration from the West Indies was generally earlier than that from India, which in turn was earlier than that from Pakistan and Bangladesh (and, in fact, migration from Africa, not shown here, was later still (ibid.)). This relative timing is

15

explained by the policies adopted by the ruling bodies of the countries or colonies concerned, and to a lesser extent by the actions of British employers. London Transport actively recruited labour in Barbados from 1955 to 1965, and though only ten thousand men found employment in this way, many others from the West Indies also came to Britain in response to advertisements and the general demand for labour. Despite efforts on the part of the UK government to informally restrict migration from the colonies, West Indians were generally free to emigrate (Duffield, 1988, ch.2). Jamaica, for example, imposed only the restrictions that criminals could not migrate, and that those under 18 or over 50 could only do so if they were to be supported and cared for. Indeed, Mr Norman Manley, Chief Minister of Jamaica, reaffirmed during a visit to the UK in September 1958 that Jamaica would not voluntarily restrict migration but that any controls would have to be imposed by the UK, in which case help with unemployment in the West Indies would be sought (The Times, 12.9.58). Migration from the West Indies thus increased during the 1950s, checked temporarily by the recession of the mid to late fifties.

In contrast both the Indian and Pakistani (including Bangladesh) governments 'voluntarily' imposed restrictions on emigration in response to pressures from Britain. In india, these were introduced in 1954. Before then, Indians were coming to Britain at a greater rate than other groups from the NCWP, often as students or professionals, though some less educated Indians also came at this time. In order to stem the flow, the Indian government introduced controls on the issuing of passports, requiring a financial guarantee of 1,500 rupees ($112 in 1958) and a medical examination.[5] The Intelligence Bureau routinely investigated anyone applying for a passport, and those emigrating to Britain were required to pay a deposit to their government to cover their return air fare (ibid). Though these measures may have curbed the potential flow, they also led to a black market in passports. Of the 17,300 Indians entering Britain between 1955 and 1957, an estimated 70 per cent had forged passports and had paid up to four times as much to get to Britain than they would have paid had they been able to go through official channels (Duffield, 1988, ch.2). The pattern of Indian immigration is thus much lower in the 1950s than that of West Indian immigration, but it is clear from Figure 1 that the recession had the same effect on both flows. The higher level of Indian immigration in the 1940s and early 1950s and the fact that many Indians were prepared to pay the high costs of coming to Britain on forged passports suggest that in the absence of these informal controls, indians may well have come to Britain in equal if not greater numbers than West indians during the later 1950s. Indeed, when passport restrictions were lifted in 1960, because of the problems created by invalid documentation and because of the opposition by the Indian Workers Association (ibid., ch.2 and 6), there was a sharp rise in the flow. But this was very short-lived because formal inmigration control in Britain began in 1962.

Migration from Pakistan and Bangladesh began rather later, and was also subject to voluntary restrictions. Emigrants had to have a knowledge of the English language and to have either an offer of a job in the UK or good prospects of securing one. In addition, a paper guarantee was required that repatriation costs would be net, but when in the spring of 1958 many Pakistanis (and Bangladeshis) in Britain were found to be destitute or at least unemployed, a financial guarantee was introduced in the form of a repatriation deposit of 2,500 rupees (£187 in 1958) (The Times, 12.9.58). Even so, the flow from Pakistan and Bangladesh continued to increase after the recession, and Figure 1 even shows an increase in 1962 despite the fact that British controls were introduced on 1 July of that year.

Migration under formal control

The Commonwealth Immigrants Act 1962 was a major influence on the pattern of inmigration from the NCWP. Not only did it reduce the flow, but it also created the earlier rise in immigration in 1960 and 1961. This period was in fact one of recession during which immigration levels would have been expected to decline, but the impending controls caused migrants to hasten their entry to Britain. Once the Act came into force, immigration fell to levels in keeping with the demand for labour in times of recession and the employment voucher system that the Act introduced meant that levels could not rise without limit when the demand for labour was high (Peach, 1968). This effect is seen most clearly in Figure 1 for West Indians, and also for Pakistanis and Bangladeshis. For Indians, the effect is less clear because of the simultaneous effect of the removal of passport restrictions.

On an individual level, the 1962 Act closed off the option of working in Britain for a few years at a time. Much of the migration from India, Pakistan and Bangladesh had been of this circulatory nature, and male members of the family often took turns to come to Britain. For them the Act meant choosing between more permanent employment in Britain or remaining in their country of origin. Those choosing to work in Britain usually brought in their families.

At first there were no specific quotas for the employment voucher system, but levels were to be adjusted according to economic and social conditions in the country. In practice this meant that about 33,000 vouchers were issued to West Indians, Indians and Pakistanis and Bangladeshis during the first year of operation but only 9,500 of these were actually used during that time (ibid., p.54). In September 1964, however, category C for unskilled labour was suspended and in 1965 a White Paper (1965) abolished the category all together and limited the total number of A and B category vouchers (for those with jobs and with skills or qualifications, respectively) to 8,500. The entry of labour was thus severely restricted. By then, however, and as a direct result of the 1962 Act which forced migrants to make a decision about remaining in Britain and bringing in dependants, the flow of dependants was gaining strength. Though labour migration decreased it is not discernible from Figure 1, nor from Figures 2 and 3 below, because of the increased flow of dependants.

The data shown in Figure 1 are only indicative of immigrant patterns, since they include only those people resident in Great Britain in 1971. The actual levels were somewhat higher. The annual number of West Indian arrivals, for example, fell from 26,000 in 1956 to 17,000 in 1958 and rose to 62,000 in 1961 (Peach, 1968, pp.41 and 47). With the introduction of the 1962 Act, the Home Office began to administer immigration and produce statistics.[6] Figure 2 (Appendix Table A2) shows the number of acceptances for settlement from 1963 to 1983. Whilst black immigration has decreased over that period, other immigration has increased. By 1980, the immigration of aliens was only 2–3,000 lower than immigration from the NCWP, and the subsequent decline in alien immigration was probably due to the economic recession of the early 1980s. Signs of an upturn in alien immigration were already apparent in 1983.

Data from a second source, the international Passenger Survey (IPS),[7] shown in Figure 3 (Appendix Table A3) suggest that alien immigration has been higher than immigration from the NCWP since 1980, but they also suggest a much higher level of alien immigration since 1965 than do the Home Office data. Migration from the Old Commonwealth is also higher according to the IPS data, but much of this difference arises from the fact that many migrants from the Old Commonwealth are patrial [8] and therefore excluded from immigration control.

Though these two data sources do not entirely agree on the level and pattern of immigration from the NCWP, they do both show the increases in 1967/8 and 1972 due to arrivals from of East Africa. These migrants were of Asian origin and as holders of UK passports,[9] were entitled to settlement in Britain. Prior to 1967, very few exercised this right,[10] but the policy of Africanisation adopted by the Kenyan government in the mid–1960s led many Kenyan Asians to seek refuge in Britain. The flow increased during 1967 but was purposefully stemmed in the following year by the introduction of the Commonwealth Immigrants Act 1968. This Act introduced the concept of patriality, restricting the entry of non–patrials with UK passports, including the East African Asians, by a special voucher system. Only 1,500 special vouchers per annum were issued to heads of households, entitling them and their dependants to entry to the UK. The effect of the Act is seen in Figure 2 in the flow from the NCWP, in Figure 3 in the flow of UK passport holders (UKPH), and (partially) in Figure 1 in the flow from india where many East African Asians were born. (For more details, see below.)

The effect of the Immigration Act 1971, which came into force on 1 January 1973, on the entry of NCWP citizens was not numerically great. Figure 3 shows a slight downward trend to mid–1974, and if UK passport holders are excluded from the Home Office data these too show a decrease from 1972 to 1973. In later years, however, there is an increase due partly to the speeding up of processing of dependants' applications for entry clearances in India, Pakistan and Bangladesh. More recently, changes in the Immigration Rules in the direction of more restrictive control have reduced overall flows. These effects are discussed in detail below.

All immigration to the UK is to some extent offset by emigration, and black immigration is no exception to this. Figure 4 (Appendix Table A4) shows the levels of emigration from the UK. While not great, there has been an almost constant flow of NCWP citizens leaving the UK since 1965. Old Commonwealth and alien flows have also remained fairly stable; and it is only UK citizens who have tended to emigrate less, though temporary increases, such as in the early 1980s, do occur. Net migration is shown in Figure 5 (Appendix Table A5). In overall terms, net migration has been generally negative since 1965, though the trend is towards a positive balance and this was in fact achieved in 1978/9 and 1982/3 – 1983/4. This overall trend is dominated by the UK citizen pattern, which is in turn dominated by emigration. The net migration of NCWP citizens and of aliens has remained positive and until very recently was generally declining. In 1983/4, the balance of migration of NCWP citizens was 25,000.

The changing character of migration

While the original reason for migration from the NCWP to the UK was economic, the composition of migration changed over the years from mainly labour and male to mainly dependants and female. This was already occurring prior to the introduction of immigration control in 1962, most notably among West Indians. Figure 6 (Appendix Table A1) shows the patterns (but not the levels) of entry for females and males living in Britain in 1971.[11] In comparison to total entries shown in Figure 1, these separate data show more clearly the patterns of immigration. Before 1960, when economic factors prevailed, the entry of males followed a similar pattern for all three groups, and the peak in male entries at the time of the introduction of control is also more visible.[12] In terms of sex differences, female migration from the West Indies closely followed the male pattern but with a lag of about a year. Some of these early women migrants were in fact single female labour. From as early as the late 1940s, the British government had recruited nurses in Barbados and this continued through the 1950s though the numbers involved were very small. Other women also came in search of work but many more came as dependants of male labour.[13] The decline in female entries at the time of the recession in the mid to late 1950s is therefore due partly to the low demand for labour, both female and male, and partly to the fact that fewer males could afford to bring in their dependants in times of recession. Nevertheless, the entry of dependants at this time was much less severely affected by recession than the entry of male labour (Peach, 1968, ch.4).

It is not entirely clear why female immigration from the West Indies should have been greater than male immigration in the year before controls were introduced. The impending control of labour would suggest a greater proportion of male immigration than female. In 1961 and the first half of 1962, however, this was not the case [14] and it seems that the reason was the fear of general immigration control, though the 1962 Act did not in fact restrict dependants (Peach, 1968, p.48). After the Act came into force, the pattern of female migration was roughly similar to that for males, but at a higher level. By then, male immigration included a large proportion of male dependant children and the demand for employment vouchers was low, with only 2–3,000 vouchers per year being used from 1963 to 1965 (ibid., p.59).

Female immigrants from India and Pakistan and Bangladesh were almost all dependants rather than labour. Those from India maintained a fairly low level,[15] but increased in the late 1950s and again in 1961 after passport restrictions were removed. There is little evidence of any hurry to come to Britain prior to the 1962 Act, but levels increased during the mid–1960s as family reunion took place, exceeding male entries by 1965. Female migration from Pakistan and Bangladesh remained at a very low level until the mid–1960s when dependants began to enter the country in greater numbers. It was not until 1970, however, that the number of females equalled the number of males.

Immigration control data from the Home Office provide extra detail according to legal category of entry to the UK. Though millions of people enter the UK each year (including visitors, students and returning UK residents), only a small proportion are 'accepted for settlement' as residents of the UK. These are divided into two broad groups. The largest comprises those people who are "accepted for settlement on arrival' in the UK. Such people have already obtained the necessary documents entitling them to legal residence in the UK. The second group comprises those 'accepted for settlement on removal of time limit'. Such people are allowed to enter the UK only on a temporary basis at first, and obtain permanent settlement after a specified period, depending on their reason for entry, provided certain conditions are met. These two groups are shown separately in Figure 7 (Appendix Table A6) by reason for entry.

Acceptance for settlement on arrival

Acceptance for settlement on arrival is confined almost entirely to the dependants of people already settled in the UK. This includes children under age 18 and elderly relatives as well as wives and husbands,[16] but it is seen in Figure 7 that the majority are wives and children. The acceptance of husbands on arrival has been subject to several changes over the years, because it has been regarded as a source of primary immigration in that husbands both form part of the labour force and increase the number of male household heads. They were originally barred from acceptance on arrival in 1969 and this restriction was reaffirmed by the 1971 Immigration Act. In 1974, however, the Immigration Rules were changed to allow husbands to join wives already settled in the UK, and in 1975 and 1976, less than 2,000 husbands were accepted each year. In 1977, this Rule was again changed in response to fears of 'marriages of convenience' solely as a means of gaining entry to the UK. Recently married husbands were allowed to enter only temporarily and permanent settlement was granted only if, after twelve months, the Home Secretary was satisfied that the marriage was genuine. Thus acceptance for settlement on arrival was no longer possible for recent marriages, and the 1977 to 1979 statistics refer to the entry of husbands of long-standing marriages only. Husbands of recent marriages entering temporarily appear in the statistics on acceptances for settlement on removal of time limit, discussed below. Despite the fact that this 1977 Rule reduced the number of husbands accepted on arrival to about 500 per year, with no increase in the number of recent husbands and fiancés accepted on removal of time limit, further changes were made in the Rules in 1980 restricting the entry of husbands to those of patrial women only. Since most women from the NCWP are not patrial, this new Rule reduced acceptances on arrival to 110 in 1981 and to only 20 in 1982 and 1983. The Rule has resulted in considerable hardship, and in May 1985 the European Court of Human Rights ruled that it was unlawful because it discriminated against women. Further changes in the Rules were thus made: both husbands and wives seeking to join their spouses in Britain must now prove at entry clearance that the purpose of their marriage is marriage and not to gain settlement in Britain. They must also prove that they will not be a burden to the State.

Non-patrial UK passport holders are also accepted for settlement on arrival. Only heads of households, that is holders of special vouchers, are shown separately in Figure 7, and their dependants are included with all other dependants.[17] The original quota of 1,500 vouchers per annum has been increased several times in response to factors in East Africa. The quota was insufficient to deal with demand and a queue developed which by 1970 exceeded 7,000. In recognition of this, the quota was doubled to 3,000 in 1971 and an extra 1,500 were available in that year only to reduce the waiting list. There was thus an upturn in the flow, continued in the following year by the expulsion of Asians from Uganda. The quota of vouchers was increased in 1972 to 3,500 and in the same year 35,000 UK passport holders (including dependants) entered Britain, about 25,000 of them from Uganda. Those who could not gain immediate entry to Britain went to India where they waited to come to Britain under the special voucher allocation for future years. Many are still waiting. Entries to Britain fell after the immediate crisis had passed, as both Figures 2 and 3 show, but the quota was increased in 1975 to 5,000 to ease the pressure on those still in East Africa. In mid-1976 the estimated number of UK passport holders remaining in East Africa was about 38,000 including dependants (Home Office, 1977), though they were not necessarily on the waiting list or intending to leave. By 1978 the queue in East Africa had disappeared and vouchers were available on demand to those eligible. At the same time, however, the waiting list in India has grown, and stood at 4,930 at the end of 1981,[18] as a result of the low priority given to people temporarily living in India, for whom only 600 vouchers per annum were available in the early 1980s. It is not known whether this allocation has been increased (or decreased), because allocations to particular countries are kept secret in order to allow for 'flexibility' (Home Affairs Committee, 1982). Thus, though in total the quota could be fully issued, it is in fact under-issued because of the scheme's administration.

Table 1 shows the annual number of vouchers used (that is acceptance on arrival) in relation to the annual quota and the number issued. The proportion used of those issued is high but it is only in the early years of the scheme that the quota was fully issued. Surprisingly, only 60 per cent of the quota was issued in 1972, the year of the expulsion of Asians from Uganda. The increases in issues in 1974 and 1975 reflect efforts to deal with the backlog of applicants, and this is also seen in the increased number of acceptances in Figure 7. More recently, the issue rate and hence the number of acceptances on arrival have been very low despite the backlog of applications in India.

Acceptance for settlement on removal of time limit

Acceptances for settlement on removal of time limit include a variety of groups for whom the length of time between temporary entry to the UK and permanent acceptance for settlement varies considerably. For this reason the trend in the total annual number of acceptances on removal of time limit bears little relation to current immigration patterns. The possibility of acceptance for settlement on removal of time limit was introduced on 1 January 1973 by the 1971 Immigration Act. In the first years the largest category comprised those people exempted from deportation by virtue of the fact that they had been resident in the UK for the last five years and were resident here on 1st January 1973. Since this includes most of those people who came to this country in the 1950s and 1960s, before immigration controls were imposed, these numbers do not represent real acceptances for settlement in the same sense as acceptances of recent immigrants. Rather, this is merely a case of government putting its house in order by officially accepting people who were allowed to settle long ago. The effect on the statistics of this five year residency rule was short-lived because only those resident on 1st January 1973 are eligible. Evidence of this began in 1978 when only 3,400 people were accepted compared to about 7,000 per year in the previous four years. By 1983 there were at most 90 such acceptances; these people and their dependants appear in the statistics as 'other' acceptances on removal of time limit. In 1983, the total number of those exempted from deportation and all dependants (i.e. 'others') was 3,010.

The number of acceptances for settlement on completion of four years in approved employment increased to 2,300 in 1979, and has remained at about that level until 1983. Since the time limit involved is four years, these figures reflect the number of work permits first issued at least four years ago.

Table 1: Special vouchers issued and used by East African Asians

Year	Annual quota	Issued no	%	Used no	%
1968	1,500	1,470	98	1,054	72
1969	1,500	1,510	100	1,672	111
1970	1,500	1,560	104	1,644	105
1971	1,500/4,500	3,820	85	2,956	77
1972	3,000/3,500	2,090	60	3,260	156
1973	3,500	2,280	65	1,994	87
1974	3,500	3,520	101	3,379	96
1975	5,000	5,000	100	3,789	76
1976	5,000	3,590	72	3,708	103
1977	5,000	1,890	38	2,032	93
1978	5,000	1,820	36	1,752	96
1979	5,000	1,650	33	1,604	97
1980	5,000	1,350	27	1,390	103
1981	5,000	1,456	29	1,360	93
1982	5,000	n.a.	n.a.	1,290	n.a.
1983	5,000	n.a.	n.a.	1,540	n.a.

Source: Home Affairs Committee, Immigration from the Indian Sub-Continent, Minutes of Evidence; London: HMSO, 1981.
Home Office, Control of Immigration Statistics, annual; London: HMSO.

Note: Control began on 1 March 1968. The 1971 quota increase occurred on 1 June and the 1972 increase occurred on 1 May. Percentages are calculated using the higher quota in these years. The 1971 quota of 4,500 includes 1,500 vouchers available for that year only.

The need for a work permit for employment or business purposes in the UK was introduced for non-patrial Commonwealth citizens by the 1971 Immigration Act. Such work permits are issued by the Department of Employment for specific posts and are generally restricted to certain professions in which the demand for labour exceeds the UK supply.[19] Until 1 April 1985, doctors and dentists were not subject to this work permit system, but new entrants are now required either to obtain a permit or to have $150,000 at their disposal to invest in their practice, which must be shown to be needed.

Acceptances on removal of time limit by reason of marriage applies to people coming to the UK in order to marry a UK resident. Female fiancées are admitted temporarily for three months, during which time the marriage must take place if the woman is to be accepted for settlement. The annual number of acceptances of females from the NCWP increased slowly to about 5,500 in 1978, but has since fallen to 4,000 in 1981 and increased again to 5,000 in 1983. Since the time limit involved in acceptance by marriage for women is only three months, the number of fiancées entering the UK and the number of women accepted for settlement by marriage in any one year are virtually the same.

Males were first accepted for settlement by marriage (after entry as fiancés) as a result of the 1974 change in the Rules, already mentioned in relation to husbands, and the three month time limit applied.[20] In 1977, however, the time limit was extended from three to twelve months causing a temporary decline in the level of acceptances. In 1978, therefore, there was a rise in acceptances to the previous level of about 4,300. More recently the level has fallen to 2,200 in 1983, as a direct result of the 1980 change in the Rules restricting entry to fiancés of patrial women. The 1977 Rules also subjected recently married husbands to acceptance on removal of time limit, and these are included with fiancés from 1977.

Acceptances from India, Bangladesh and Pakistan

During the last decade or so, most of the immigration from the NCWP has been from India, Bangladesh and Pakistan.[21] Acceptances for settlement of people from these countries combined are shown in Figure 8a, and data for the separate countries are also given in Appendix Table A7. Dependants account for all of those accepted for settlement on arrival,[22] and wives and children for all but a few per cent of the total. It is seen in Figure 8a that acceptances on arrival in all categories increased in the mid-1970s. The reasons for the increase in the number of husbands accepted is the 1974 change in the Immigration Rules already discussed. For the remainder, increases at this time were also due to administrative factors. In order to reduce the queues and waiting times after application, the processing of applications was quickened resulting in the increases in 1975 and 1976. These increased acceptances from India, Bangladesh and Pakistan made up most of the increases in the same years in acceptances from the entire NCWP. This temporary increase was followed by a general decline in all categories of acceptances on arrival, especially from Pakistan. The slight increase in the early 1980s was due to the increased entry of people from Bangladesh, especially children.

In 1983, acceptances for settlement by marriage accounted for 70 per cent of the 6,500 acceptances on removal of time limit from India, Bangladesh and Pakistan (see Figure 8b and Appendix Table A8). For both women and men, the numbers of these acceptances increased (with the exception of men in 1977) until 1979 and have since declined, though the number of women has increased recently. In 1983, 3,400 women and 1,400 men were accepted. The restriction of settlement by marriage cuts across the traditional practice of arranged marriage, forcing many Asian families to seek marriage partners for their daughters and sons from within the Asian community living in Britain. The intention behind the restrictions is not so much to reduce the already small flow of young females as to cut down the even smaller number of young males entering the country. Males are generally regarded by the immigration authorities as primary migrants because of their role as household heads and breadwinners, whereas females are regarded as secondary migrants because they are usually dependent on the breadwinner. This distinction bears no relation to the fact that both female and male fiancé(e)s or recent spouses are equally (un)related to the population in Britain, but it is now embodied in the law in the form of the 1980 change in the Immigration Rules. This discriminates against women from the NCWP. Though this is indefensible, it should be noted that because of the imbalance in the sexes, it is relatively easier for single Asian women to find an Asian marriage partner than it is for males. It is doubtful, however, that such considerations as sex ratios entered into the decision to restrict male entrants.

Acceptances from the West Indies

Acceptance on arrival from the West Indies are also mainly women and children. The main feature here, however, is the small numbers involved (see Appendix Table A9). In 1974, there were only 1,600 acceptances on arrival, a flow which has steadily declined to a trickle: in 1983 there were only 240 such acceptances. The numbers of West Indians accepted for settlement on removal of time limit is also very small: only 500 such acceptances occurred in 1983. The low level of migration from the West Indies is a reflection of the fact that for West Indians the migration process has reached a natural conclusion, though this has taken place within the increasingly restrictive framework of British immigration law. Thus, after labour migration was controlled in 1962, dependants made up almost the entire flow and these by now have mostly come to the UK. Indeed, the flow of West Indians leaving Britain (mostly for the West Indies) has recently exceeded the number entering.

Migration and the migration process

The above discussion of black migration to Britain has shown how the various economic, social and political factors have determined the pattern of that migration. It has already been stated that all migrant flows eventually come to an end, for whatever reason, and black migration to Britain is no exception to this. Indeed, the period of migration has been short in relation to other migratory flows to Britain, such as the Irish migration, and has quickly reached the point where it is no longer the main direct determinant of the growth and development of the population. It has been seen above that this has been largely due to the imposition of political controls on immigration, but the recent excess of West Indians leaving the UK highlights the influence of negative factors within the UK.

The dependence of the later stages of the migration process on migration itself underlines the importance of the pattern of migration for the demographic development of the population. Through this dependence, the factors that have shaped the pattern and character of black migration to Britain continue to influence the development of the black population. Thus, it is the political factors which led to the informal and formal control of migration that have helped to determine the demographic development of the black population and which continue to have some influence today.

The demographic process through which this influence continues is discussed in detail below. It is of relevance here, however, to emphasize that in discussing the importance of the pattern of migration it is not the size of the flow that is significant. Rather, it is the demographic characteristics of migrants that are important. Thus, through their effect on the demographic characteristics of the migrant flow, political controls on migration have shaped the demographic structure of the immigrant population in Britain and hence have considerable effect on the structure of the entire ethnic minority population.

Notes

1. Notably in seaports such as Cardiff, Bristol, London and Liverpool where black seamen settled, but also due to the settlement of men who had fought voluntarily for the mother country in the First and Second World Wars.

2. Cabinet Office files for 1951 show that the control of black immigration was considered as early as 1950. See The Times, 2 January 1982.

3. See Duffield (1988) for a discussion of migration and decolonisation.

4. The levels of migration shown in Figure 1 are too low because they include only those immigrants still living in Great Britain in 1971. In addition these data are subject to reporting errors and differential rates of loss (emigration and death) by year of entry so that the patterns shown are approximate.

5. That health checks were regarded as an informal means of immigration control was made clear by Mr R.A. Butler, Home Secretary, during the Conservative Party Conference, 11–13 October 1961.

6. Published annually and quarterly by the Home Office.

7. Published in OPCS, Series MN. These data are subject to large standard errors arising from the small sampling proportion. The survey samples between 0.1 and 4 per cent of passengers, only a fraction of which are migrants. In 1981, only 823 migrants and 128 emigrants with NC citizenships (excluding Pakistan) were included in the sample giving an estimate of 28,900 immigrants and 15,800 emigrants. The standard errors of these estimates are 1,600 or 5.6 per cent of the estimate for immigrants, and 1,500 or 9.4 per cent for emigrants. For net migration, estimated at 13,000 the standard error is even greater at 2,200 or roughly 17 per cent. In practice, these errors should always be taken into account. For example, the estimate of 28,900 NC immigrants has a 95 per cent confidence interval of approximately 25,800 to 32,000: this means that we can be 95 per cent certain that the true number of NC immigrants in 1981 was somewhere between 25,800 and 32,000. Obviously, such wide intervals or margins of error render these data very unreliable. For subdivisions of the NC, the errors are even larger proportions of the estimates because of the smaller sample sizes. For West Indian migrants, of whom there are very few, the errors are particularly high. For this reason, data by individual citizenships within the NC are not published. See OPCS, Series MN, no.8. In fact, these published standard errors are underestimates because they are based on the assumption of simple random sampling, whereas a weighted two-stage sampling procedure is actually carried out. In addition, there are other unestimated

non-sampling errors due to non-response, possible differences between sampled and unsampled flights at airports, possible concealment of migration intentions and the fact that intentions may not be realised. Efforts to reduce both sampling and non-sampling errors were introduced in 1979. See OPCS, Series MN, no.7 and earlier issues, especially nos. 2 and 4.

8.   Under the 1971 Immigration Act, a patrial is a person who has the right to live in the UK. This includes (a) those born in the UK, (b) Commonwealth citizens settled before 1973, (c) UK citizens by registration or naturalisation, and (d) Commonwealth citizens with a UK born parent or grandparent. Patrials thus have close ties with the UK either by birth or heritage. The concept was first introduced under the Commonwealth Immigrants Act 1968, and amended under the 1971 Immigration Act and the 1981 Nationality Act (effective from 1 January 1983).

9.   Not all Asians and East Africans had UK passports. When Kenya, Uganda and Tanzania became independent, Asians were allowed to choose between citizenship of their country of origin, their country of birth, or Britain. In Kenya, many Asian men obtained Kenyan citizenship by naturalisation in order to be able to continue in business after the restrictions of business activity to Kenyans. In many cases, their wives chose British citizenship to safeguard against continued hostilities in Kenya.

10. Data for this period do not actually exist because the 1962 Act did not apply to UK passport holders. See Smith (1981, ch.4).

11. Lomas (1973) uses separate cumulative proportions for females and males to illustrate their different patterns of entry, but this does not allow for the differing total volumes of migration between the sexes by 1971.

12. The peak in 1963 for Indians is not borne out by other data and is probably due to reporting errors.

13. In a 1973 non-random sample of 110 West Indians living in Britain, 26 per cent of women had migrated for economic reasons compared to 73 per cent of men. 70 per cent of women and 9 per cent of men came to join a spouse or relative. See Foner (1979).

14. Not for Jamaicans, at least. See Peach (1968, p.48).

15. The higher female rate during the mid-1940s (Figure 6) may indicate that this early migration was mainly professional people, but it may also be due to differential mortality (since these data are of migrants alive in 1971). Male migration prior to 1962 was probably higher relative to female migration because of the rotation of family labour. Passport restrictions also discouraged the migration of dependants.

16. Procedures for obtaining permission to enter (entry clearance) as dependants are lengthy and difficult and must be completed prior to entry.

17. Dependant children of UK passport holders include those under 18 plus fully dependant unmarried children aged 18-24. Children aged 18-24 who are not fully dependant must apply for a special voucher as head of a separate household.

18. About 20 per cent are expected to refuse a voucher when offered one. Including dependants, the queue thus represents fewer than 10,000 people. Estimates of the number of UK passport holders and dependants in India of 39,000 in 1976 and 34,000 in 1982 are speculative and misleading.

19. Data on work permits refer to all permits issued to NCWP citizens and aliens, and are published by the Department of Employment in the Employment Gazette.

20. A very small number of male fiancés were accepted in 1973, but these were exceptional cases.

21. Excluding UK passport holders, Sri Lankans are not included: in 1983, 100 Sri Lankans were accepted for settlement on arrival and 820 on removal of time limit.
22. Those with a grandparent born in the UK are not included in these data because. they are mostly white. Such people account for a very small number of immigrants from NCWP countries (see Appendix Tables A6 and A7).

4 Demographic development

Britain's black population is undergoing a period of rapid demographic change. Such change is an integral part of the migration process, and its rapidity and degree are indicative of the stage reached in that process. In general, rapid and significant changes are characteristic of a population in the early stages of the migration process, whilst a population at the end of the migration process no longer undergoes changes due to either the direct or indirect effects of migration. The black population is thus in the early stages of the migration process. Indeed, in demographic terms and hence in terms of the migration process, post-war migration to Britain from the NCWP is a relatively recent event. It is because of this recency that migration has a highly significant effect on the demographic development of the black population. This effect continues in the absence of further migration, a situation that has all but existed in Britain regarding the black population for some years, largely through the irregularities, either directly or indirectly due to migration, in the demographic structure of the population.

The changes that occur as the demographic development of the population progresses are manifest in the structure of the population as measured by, for example, its age and sex distribution, its marital status characteristics and the dependence of the elderly and very young on the working-age population.   Thus the structural irregularities in the population assume a changing significance: today's children, for example, are tomorrow's parents and tomorrow's labour supply.

In general, the shorter term demographic changes in a migrant population are due to irregularities in the age structure, whilst the more gradual and longer term changes are due to modifications of demographic behaviour with respect to fertility and mortality.   In the absence of migration, it is these rates of fertility and mortality that determine the structure of the population, and whilst their effect may initially be masked by more immediate fluctuations due to structural irregularities, their underlying effect is of greater significance.

The levels of fertility and mortality are also instrumental in determining the size of the population and its rate of growth.   In the absence of migration, any population in which annual births exceeds annual deaths is increasing. Such is the case for the black population, and in 1980-81 its estimated annual rate of growth due to natural increase was 2.5 per cent. This relatively high rate of natural increase is bolstered by the population's structural effect: on the fertility side, there is now a more balanced proportion of women of childbearing age, and on the mortality side the population is generally too young to die. These effects are disappearing with time such that the rate of increase is slowing significantly. The level at which it stabilises will be determined by fertility and mortality rates as and when these rates themselves stabilise.

Discussion of the demographic development of the black population is, of course, dependent on the existence of demographic data. The statistical definition of the black population has changed over time, in response to the changing adequacy of the various proxy variables in use. As discussed below, all of the definitions and methods of measurement employed have their problems, with the result that considerable biases exist in the data. The difficulties in obtaining accurate and meaningful data stem, of course, from the sensitive nature of the subject: classification by ethnicity is by no means a simple exercise as is detailed below.

In terms of the migration process, it is important to distinguish between the various ethnic minority populations which constitute the black population of Britain. Demographically, these populations are distinct and the stages which they have reached in the migration process differ. It has already been seen how the migration patterns of the main ethnic minority populations have developed individually over time, and the effect of these patterns is seen in their demographic development, as discussed below.

Though not a main area of interest in the discussion of the migration process in Britain, the settlement patterns of migrants determines the local development of the migrant population. The concentration of the black population in certain inner city areas is of course a result of the settlement patterns of migrants and the preponderance of black youth in that population is the result of the demographic development of the population, especially in the case of the current West Indian population. Though the physical location of the black population may be a long-term reality, the existing irregularity in the structure of the population is not.

Population definition and measurement

Measurement of the black population resident in Britain has never been a straightforward exercise. This was at first due to the difficulty in defining the population by surrogate variables, and later due to the inacceptability of more direct questions. The resulting data are biased, and the extent and nature of such bias varies both between ethnic minority populations and between data sources. This makes the interpretation and comparison of the data difficult.

Early estimates of the size of the black population were made using census date on birthplace. The use of such data involves errors due to the fact that data are biased by their inclusion of white people born in the NCWP, mostly during the period of British colonial rule. This bias is substantial, especially for the population born in India, Pakistan and Bangladesh, though it has decreased over time. In 1951, 72 per cent of the enumerated Indian born population in England and Wales were estimated to be white; 50 per cent were white in 1961, and 30 per cent in 1966. For those born in Pakistan and Bangladesh, 55 per cent were estimated to be white in 1951, 19 per cent in 1961, and 7 per cent in 1966. Thus, for England and Wales, 86,000 people in 1951 and 82,000 in 1961 were estimated to be 'white Indians and Pakistanis', that is white people born in India, Pakistan and Bangladesh. By 1966, this group was estimated at 74,000 (Rose et al., 1969, pp.96–7 and Appendix III.3). Secondly, birthplace data exclude black people who were born in Britain, and though parent's birthplace has been used to identify the children of immigrants, their British born grandchildren are excluded. This bias increases with time as more grandchildren are born, and affects the West Indian population estimates the most because of their earlier migration to Britain.

By 1971, the proportion of UK born people in the black population was substantial and a census question on parent's birthplace was introduced to identify these people. It was thus possible to identify the population born in the NCWP and their descendants, that is the population of NCWP ethnic origin. People with only one parent born in the NCWP were usually included in this exercise. White people born in the NCWP were excluded, most of whom were identified by the fact that both parents were born in the UK or the Old Commonwealth. Where parents' birthplaces were not sufficient indicators of ethnic origin, estimates were made by means of a 'surname analysis', involving the examination of surnames to determine ethnic origin (OPCS, 1976, 1977).[1] Of those enumerated in the 1971 Census as born in the NCWP, about 24 per cent or 271,000 were estimated to be white and were therefore excluded from the estimate of the black population. In addition, 480,000 people were estimated to be black and born in the UK, and these were included in the estimate (OPCS, 1977).

It was in recognition of the temporary usefulness of parent's birthplace to identify the black population that a direct question on ethnic origin was proposed for inclusion in the 1981 Census (White Paper, 1978, paras.24–5). Tests on the format of such questions were already underway (Sillitoe, 1978a,b,c,d), but later tests met with considerable opposition from the black community, and in the event the question was not included in the census (OPCS 1980a, b). This meant that birthplace was once again the only data available on which to base population estimates, and birthplace of head of household was adopted as the criterion by which the majority of the population of NCWP ethnic origin could be identified. This surrogate for ethnic origin avoided neither of the biases inherent in the use of place of birth. Birthplace of head of household does not necessarily indicate ethnic origin, and in any event other members of the household may not be of the same ethnic origin as the household head. Thus some black people are omitted, whilst some white people are included. It has been estimated that the surrogate definition covers only 90 per cent of the total population of NCWP ethnic origin, and includes about 15 per cent who are not of NCWP ethnic origin (that is mostly white British people) (OPCS, 1982a). As for future censuses, it has already been recommended that a suitable question on ethnic origin be included (Home Affairs Committee, 1983).[2]

Apart from biases arising from the use of surrogate questions for ethnic origin, further inaccuracies have been shown to exist in census estimates of the size of the black population. Underenumeration has been a source of error throughout. It has been variously estimated that the 1961 Census underenumerated the Jamaican born population by 13 per cent (Rose et al., 1969, pp.97–98) and the West Indian born population by 20 per cent (Peach, 1968, p.114). The 1966 Census is estimated to underenumerate the black population born in the NCWP but excluding Cyprus and Malta, by 16 per cent with Pakistanis underenumerated by as much as 38 per cent (Rose et al., 1969, p.98), and there is evidence to suggest that the 1971 Census is also underenumerated (Peach and Winchester, 1974). One reason for this underenumeration is undoubtedly the reluctance of some members of ethnic minorities to give information about themselves, fearing that it could be used to their disadvantage. This same fear contributed to the opposition expressed towards the proposed 1981 census question on ethnic origin.

On the whole, the biases involved in the use of surrogates for ethnic origin have been taken into account in estimating the size of the black population. Errors due to underenumeration, however, have been largely ignored. In 1951, there were 256,000 people enumerated in Great Britain who were born in the NCWP. By 1961, this figure had increased to about 0.5 million, with a further 0.1 million people of NCWP origin who were born in the UK. The size of the black NCWP born population in England and Wales was estimated as 103,000 in 1951 and 415,000 in 1961 (Eversley and Sukdeo, 1969, p.9). By 1966, the black population of England and Wales was estimated as 742,500, whilst for Great Britain, the population of NCWP ethnic origin was estimated as 886,000 or 1.7 per cent of the total population. The 1971 Census enumerated 1,151,000 people in Great Britain who were born in the NCWP. With the exclusion of those estimated to be white, and the inclusion of those estimated to be black and born in the UK, the population of NCWP ethnic origin was estimated at 1,360,000 or 2.5 per cent of the total population (OPCS, 1977). The proportion of the black population who were born in the UK was 35 per cent. The 1981 Census enumerated 2,207,000 people in Great Britain living in households with a NCWP born head. Adjustment for black omissions and white inclusions results in an estimated black population of 2.1 million or 4.0 per cent of the total population.[3] Almost half of the black population in 1981 were born in the UK.[4]

Estimates of the size of the black population for the years between censuses are made on an annual basis and are shown in Table 2. These estimates are based on census counts, adjusted to take account of annual net migration and natural increase. The relative contribution of net migration to the growth of the population is seen to be decreasing over time, and by the early 1980s it was as low as one third. This is obviously due to the decline in migration to Britain (see above, Chapter 3) but it also reflects the fact that population gains through natural increase are presently increasing each year. The size of natural increase is determined on the one hand by fertility and mortality rates, and on the other by the structure of the population. These are discussed below.

Table 2 also shows the annual growth rate of the population and its proportion of the total population of Great Britain. The growth rate is seen to be declining although fluctuations occur, due mainly to migration. Thus for example, growth temporarily increased in 1967–68 when the Kenyan Asians entered Britain, and again in 1972–73 when the Ugandan Asians arrived. The decline in the growth rate has been rapid, responding to the restrictive measures on immigration counterbalanced to some extent by increases in numbers of births. As a proportion of the total population, the black population has increased steadily, but by the early 1980s had reached only 4 per cent.

Table 2: **Estimated size and growth of population of New Commonwealth and Pakistani ethnic origin, Great Britain**

Mid-year to mid-year	Population at begin of year (thousands)	Growth over year (thousands)	% due to natural increase	% due to net migration	Growth per thousand	% of GB population at begin of year
1966–67	886	+87	–	–	98	1.7
1967–68	973	+114	–	–	111	1.8
1968–69	1087	+103	–	–	95	2.0
1969–70	1190	+91	–	–	76	2.2
1970–71	1281	+90	–	–	70	2.4
1971–72	1371	+82	55	45	60	2.5
1972–73	1453	+94	45	55	65	2.7
1973–74	1547	+68	57	43	44	2.8
1974–75	1615	+76	51	49	47	3.0
1975–76	1691	+80	50	50	47	3.1
1976–77	1771	+75	56	44	42	3.3
1977–78	1846	+74	59	41	40	3.4
1978–79	1920	+93	54	46	48	3.5
1979–80	2013	+91	59	41	45	3.7
1980–81	2104	+80	67	33	38	3.9

Source: OPCS Immigrant Statistics Unit (1966–1971 figures); OPCS Monitor PPI 81/6, Mid-1980 estimates of the population of New Commonwealth and Pakistani ethnic origin; OPCS Monitor PPI 83/2, Mid-1980 estimates of the population of New Commonwealth and Pakistani ethnic origin.

Ethnic origin: classification and distribution

The classification of people by ethnicity has been the subject of much discussion especially since 1978 when the issue was first raised publicly for inclusion in the census (White Paper, 1978). This discussion has concerned not only the criteria by which classification is or should be done, but also the amount of data that is involved. The theoretical arguments concerning the criteria for ethnic classification will not be rehearsed here since they are well-covered elsewhere (for example: Saunders, 1978; White, 1979; Killian, 1983).

Various levels of detail have been employed in the different sources of data on ethnic origin produced to date. Where broad groupings have been used, these have been criticised as giving no recognition to the differences between ethnic groups, especially in the case of the 'Asian' category. This is particularly important where the data are to be used for purposes where cultural factors may be important. Indeed, many who would be included in the Asian category would prefer that data on religion were also produced, and this was in fact recommended for the next census for 'Southern Asian' groups only (Home Affairs Committee, 1983, vol.I). On the other hand, the attention paid to ethnic classification can be counter-productive in that not only does it divert attention from the real issues of racism but it also serves to divide the black community, outcomes which are seen as intentional by and useful to government authorities. Following this argument, there should therefore be no classification of ethnicity, except that black or disadvantaged populations should be identified as such as distinct from the majority white population. These two arguments are complementary rather than diametrical: the main requirement is that data should serve the purpose for which they are intended, so that the level of detail should meet but not exceed that purpose (Booth, 1985a).

The actual development of questions identifying ethnic origin in official data production exercises has been piecemeal and more responsive to technical and statistical criteria than to theoretical considerations or the opinions of the black community (Booth,1985c, 1988). The early classifications used country of birth, involving in the census at least no new questions, and the introduction of the question on parent's country of birth was an easy extension of this. These early methods of classification were objective and technically simple, even though they involved a certain amount of error arising from people being born in a country other than that of their forebears.

When research into a census question on ethnic origin began in 1974, it was for a list of categories that 'would be generally understood and produce accurate answers' (Sillitoe, 1978b, p.2). Tests showed that the term 'Black' or 'Black British' was preferred by many West Indians, and that the term 'White' was understood much better by the indigenous population than terms such as 'European' (Sillitoe, 1981, p.33). Though they would have elicited more accurate data, these preferences were never to have been incorporated into a 1981 census question because the use of colour was proscribed as a policy decision (ibid., p.34). In fact, the 1981

34

Census did not carry a question on ethnic origin, ostensibly because of its opposition by the black community (OPCS, 1980a, 1980b).

Other data production exercises partially drew upon the experience gained from the census question tests, and various questions have been developed (Booth, 1985c, 1988). These do not usually use the term 'Black', though the use of 'White' is virtually universal. The emphasis is still on eliciting responses in the required form as accurately as possible, paying scant regard to, for example, the above stated preference for the term 'Black'. This concern with accuracy was indeed of paramount importance for the Home Affairs Committee (1983) in their report into racial and ethnic questions in the census, and though their recommended question includes the use of colour this is more of a palliative than a real category of classification (Booth, 1985c).

In practice, the two most common terms used to categorise the black population are 'West Indian' and 'Asian'. The West Indian category is rarely broken down by country, except sometimes in earlier statistics to identify the largest group, those of Jamaican origin. The Asian category is often divided into Indians (usually including Sri Lankans), Pakistanis and Bangladeshis, and a further group comprising those expelled from Kenya and Uganda may also be identified. For historical reasons, these classifications are not without problems of interpretation, especially over time, not only because of the creation of Pakistan and later Bangladesh, but also because many East African Asians were born in India. Such problems of interpretation of data by birthplace are, of course, additional to the errors arising from the fact that birthplace is not necessarily indicative of ethnic origin as in the case of the 'white Indians and Pakistanis'.

Of course, the population of NCWP ethnic origin includes a minority of people who are neither West Indian nor Asian. This includes black Africans, people of Chinese ethnicity from Hong Kong, and those from the Mediterranean, who are mostly Greek Cypriots, but also include people from Malta and Gibraltar.

The sizes of the populations of different ethnic origins in 1971 and 1976 are shown in Figure 9 (Appendix Table A11). This distinguishes between those who were born in the UK and those who were born in the NCWP. Because of the classifications used, the West Indian population is the largest, followed by that of Indian origin and then by the Pakistani and Bangladeshi groups combined. The earlier arrival in the UK of the majority of the West Indian population is evident in the large proportion of this group who were born in the UK. Between 1971 and 1976, most populations grew by both migration (the number born in the NCWP) and natural increase (the number born in the UK). The Mediterranean and West Indian groups are exceptions to this in that they did not increase as a result of migration. The Mediterranean group born in the NCWP remained fairly constant over the five year period, whilst the West Indian group actually decreased, a result of the return migration mentioned above and of the fact that this older population will have experienced a significant number of deaths. In most cases, the increase over the five year period due to natural increase is greater than that due to migration, a reflection of the fact that for these populations migration had already become secondary to growth within the UK in their demographic development. The main exception to this situation is the African Asian group, the reason being that this group was augmented as a result of the expulsion of Asians from Uganda in 1972, and by the continued flow from Kenya.

It is not possible to make a direct comparison of these 1971 and 1976 data with 1981 data because of the different methods of estimation. However, two sources are available for 1980 and these are shown in Figure 10 (Appendix Tables A12 and A13).[5] Despite their different bases, these sets of data from the 1981 Census and the 1981 Labour Force Survey (LFS) indicate roughly similar sizes for the West Indian, Indian, Pakistani and Bangladeshi populations. By 1981, the population of Indian origin is shown in Figure 10 to have increased sufficiently to be the largest group. Part of the increase is apparent rather than real, however. The census data overestimate the number of people of Indian origin who were born abroad because of the inclusion of white people in this definition. It is likely that this group includes more than the 15 per cent average of white people because from earlier censuses it is known that the proportion of white overseas born people born in India is relatively high. The data from the LFS on ethnic origin also give a false impression of rapid growth because they include people from East Africa who are of Indian origin and probably some people of Asian ethnic origin from the West Indies. Taking these factors into account, it is still probable that the 1980 population of Indian origin, as defined in the 1971 and 1976 data, has reached or even exceeded the West Indian population in size. This is due to both migration and natural increase, both of which are greater in the Indian, and indeed Bangladeshi and Pakistani, populations than in the West Indian population because of the latter's earlier stage in the migration process. Because of the administrative delays in allowing people (with the right) to come to the UK from these Asian countries, many of the dependants of the migrant workers who came here prior to the cessation of primary immigration have only recently arrived. From 1976 to 1980, about 19,000 such people arrived from India (see Table A7). This includes wives who have been waiting to join husbands in the UK, many of whom begin or resume childbearing after their protracted separation. Table A7 shows that about 7,000 wives entered Britain from India in 1976–80. On addition to these entrants, a further 26,000 Indians arrived during the same period, 10,000 of whom were fiancées (see Table A8).

Other groups are to greater or lesser extents incomparable over time. The 1981 Census data underestimate the size of the population component born in the UK by 10 per cent on average, but by far more than this for the West Indian population because of their earlier arrival in the UK and therefore greater proportion of UK born household heads. Difficulties also arise from the fact that different groups are used, both over time and between the 1980 Census and LFS. Indeed, the LFS data are additionally problematic because of the large numbers classified as of mixed ethnic origin and with ethnic origin not stated. Those of mixed ethnic origin involving a white parent would, in 1970, have been classified as the ethnic origin of their NCWP born parent. In these LFS data it is impossible without special tabulations to know which ethnic origins are involved, so that allocation to a main group is precluded.[6] The large group of origin not stated renders these data even less reliable. This group is,in fact,larger than the West Indian group and second only to the Indian group, though it should be noted that it includes all non-responses including those by the white indigenous population. Nevertheless,the level of non-response to this question on ethnic origin is high (1.13 per cent), and is in fact higher than the non-response rate in the 1979 LFS, despite its improved wording (Booth, 1985c). It is not improbable that this increased non-response reflects an increasing awareness on the part of the black population of the issues surrounding the production of data on ethnic origin.

Settlement in Britain

The small black community who resided in Britain prior to 1950 dwelt mostly in the ports of Liverpool, Bristol, Cardiff, Glasgow and London. These were seamen or their descendants, and people who had come to Britain to help in the war effort. In 1935, there were estimated to be 3,000 non-European seamen in Cardiff, mostly of African origin, and in 1948 Liverpool had a black population of 8,000 (Fryer, 1984). When post-war migrants arrived in Britain, they did not settle in these areas of early settlement. It was government policy at the time to discourage new settlement in the ports, partly for reasons related to employment opportunities, but mindful no doubt of their earlier racial violence (Joshua and Wallace, 1983; ibid.).

The areas of settlement of the black population were largely determined in the 1950s and 1960s according to the employment opportunities that were then available to the new black workforce. This is not to say that black people settled in areas with the highest demand for labour. Rather, in many cases they settled in areas which, though in need of labour, could not attract white labour, thus providing employment opportunities for black labour. These areas were also losing white labour to the more attractive regions, so that the black population was very often a replacement population (Peach, 1968, ch.6). Thus, London and the South East and the East and West Ridings of Yorkshire, where labour was in demand but where labour out-migration occurred, were areas that attracted relatively large black populations. So too did the Midlands and the North Midlands, regions with a demand for labour that was only partially met by white labour, especially in the metal manufacturing industries of the Midlands.[7] By 1961, approximately half of the West Indian, Indian, Pakistani and Bangladeshi population was living in London and the South East, where they comprised 1.1 per cent of the total regional population. Among the other regions, only the Midlands approached this proportion, with 0.9 per cent of the population (Peach, 1968, pp.66–67).

Within those regions, it was the conurbations that were able to provide the majority of black employment: these were the areas of both labour demand and white out-migration. In 1961, 71 per cent of West Indians, Indians, Pakistanis and Bangladeshis lived in the six major conurbations, again with London and the West Midlands predominant.[8] West Indians were more likely to live in the conurbations than Indians, Pakistanis and Bangladeshis: 80 per cent of West Indians lived in the six conurbations in 1961 compared to only 59 per cent of Indians, Pakistanis and Bangladeshis.

In general, this early pattern of settlement has determined the geographical distribution of the black population today. By 1966, the distribution had not changed significantly despite the arrival of new black labour during the sixties. The proportion of West Indians, Indians, Pakistanis and Bangladeshis living in the six conurbations was virtually the same at 72 per cent, and their distribution between regions was also similar. This was especially true of West Indians who maintained their concentration in the conurbations, but was less so for Indians, Pakistanis and Bangladeshis. Indians, for example, settled in the conurbations of the West Midlands and West Yorkshire from 1961 to 1966 in greater proportions than had previously been the case (ibid).

When ethnicity is considered in conjunction with geographical location, it is found that migrants of one ethnic group have not usually settled in the same regions, towns or wards as those of another. To take two West Yorkshire cities as an example, Bradford has more people of Pakistani origin than of any other NCWP origin, whereas Leeds has more of West Indian origin. Furthermore, within the West Yorkshire population of West Indian origin, those in Bradford are largely of Dominican origin, those in Huddersfield are largely Grenadians, and St. Lucians are concentrated in Leeds. Such distributions are the result of contacts between early migrants and their home communities: on being sent word of employment opportunities in an area, migrants would make their way to the area after arrival in Britain. Their compatriots helped them to find work and housing and to settle into their new environment.

Figure 11 (Appendix Table A10) shows the distribution of the black population in 1971 and 1981,[9] both in absolute terms and in relation to the total populations of these regions.[10] These more recent data show that, as in 1961, about half lived in the South East (including London) which also had the highest regional proportion of black people in its population, with almost as great a degree of concentration in the West Midlands. Other regions have maintained a similar relative distribution over time, especially over the later decade. Such stability in the distribution of the black population is not surprising. Given its fairly static nature in the sixties when labour immigration was occurring, even greater stability would be expected of the 1971 and 1981 distributions, since immigration during the seventies has been composed mainly of dependants. It is also possible that black people are less likely to move from region to region than are white people: such long distance moves are often associated with changes in employment of the higher social classes,in which few black people are found.

Though the relative distribution has remained stable, there are differences in the regional rates of growth from 1971 to 1981. In general, the greatest absolute increases have occurred in those regions with the greatest black populations in 1971, as would be expected. In relative terms, however, both the South East and the West Midlands have lower increases than the other regions with the highest proportionate increases occurring in regions with the smallest black populations, such as Scotland. A similar pattern is found in the changes over time in the black proportions of the total regional populations (see Appendix Table A10).

Within these regions, the black population is found in certain towns and cities, again due to early employment opportunities. Table 3 shows the provincial districts and London boroughs with the highest black populations relative to total populations in 1981. These are mainly the same places that have the largest black populations in absolute terms, but exceptions such as Blackburn occur.

The boundary changes that occurred in 1974 make comparison of provincial towns and cities between 1971 and 1981 meaningless.[11] Nevertheless, some indication of growth can be obtained from data on the population born in the NCWP, which are available for the provincial districts (as newly defined in 1974) for both 1971 and 1981. It is seen from these data in Table 3 that growth of both the size of the NCWP born population and its proportion of the total has been uneven. Whilst the NCWP born population has increased on average by 36 per cent in these eight cities, growth in individual cities ranges from 5 per cent in Wolverhampton to 80 per cent in Blackburn.

These increases in the populations born in the NCWP are, of course, due to migration and indicate roughly the pattern of new settlement. The very small net increase in Wolverhampton suggests that either any new arrivals born in the NCWP are largely offset by departures who are also NCWP born, or that the level of arrivals is very low. Whilst it is impossible to assess the extent of internal migration, it is worth noting that many of the foundries that employed much of Wolverhampton's black labour no longer operated in 1981. In addition, it is generally to be expected that areas with predominantly West Indian populations would experience a smaller inflow of new arrivals from the NCWP than would areas with Asian populations, because of current immigration patterns. This factor has probably contributed to the large relative increases in Leicester and Blackburn and in the London borough of Newham, all of which have larger Asian than West Indian populations.

Of course, migrants born in the NCWP make up only part of the black population, and growth due to natural increase is also a factor determining relative size. In addition, where proportions black are concerned, the growth of the white population is also relevant. Thus, though Blackburn ranks sixth in relative size, this city is well down the list in absolute size, coming not only after those districts in Table 3, but also after other districts including Coventry, Derby, Nottingham, Kirklees and Leeds.[12]

Table 3: The location of the black population, 1971 and 1981

District or borough	% of total population			black population (000s)		
	1981a	1981b	1971	1981a	1981b	1971
Leicester	21.3	15.3	8.2	59	42	23
Slough	20.9	13.5	8.8	20	13	9
Wolverhampton	15.4	8.2	7.5	39	21	20
Birmingham	15.0	8.7	6.3	149	87	69
Luton	13.9	8.8	5.2	23	14	8
Blackburn	11.4	6.7	3.8	16	9	5
Sandwell	11.4	6.3	4.7	35	19	16
Bradford	11.1	6.7	4.9	50	30	23
Inner London	18.8	12.3	8.8	456	298	266
Haringey	29.4	18.7	14.4	60	38	35
Hackney	27.5	16.5	11.6	49	30	25
Newham	26.5	17.1	8.5	55	36	20
Lambeth	23.0	14.0	10.9	56	34	33
Outer London	11.7	8.0	4.8	489	333	210
Brent	33.0	22.5	14.0	83	57	39
Ealing	25.0	17.0	11.1	70	47	33
Greater London	14.3	9.5	6.4	945	631	476
England & Wales	4.5	3.0	2.3	2,161	1,474	1,121
Great Britain	4.2	2.5	2.1	2,207	1,513	1,151

Source: OPCS and General Register Office Scotland (1974) Census 1971: Country of Birth Tables (Great Britain), HMSO, London; OPCS (occasional) Census 1981 County Reports, HMSO, London

Notes: Table includes only provincial districts with more than 10 per cent and London boroughs with more than 20 per cent of usually resident population living in households with a NCWP born head in 1981.
1981a: population living in households with NCWP born head.
1981b: population born in NCWP.
1971: population born in NCWP, provincial districts as in 1981. London boroughs did not change from 1971 to 1981.

Not surprisingly it is the capital city that has attracted the largest black population in absolute terms, with proportions of more than 20 per cent in several boroughs in 1981. Comparable data for 1971 are not available, but in 1966 Brent, Hackney, Lambeth, Haringey, Islington and Hammersmith were the six London boroughs with more than 5 per cent of their population comprised of West Indians, Indians, Pakistanis and Bangladeshis.[13] Thus Ealing and Newham have replaced Islington and Hammersmith among the six boroughs with the highest proportions.

Within the boroughs, as indeed within the provincial districts, the black population is unevenly distributed between wards. Again, the wards in which black people live were largely determined twenty to thirty years ago, when the replacement black population moved into the poorer quality housing vacated by the white population. Such housing was the only type that was generally available to the poorly paid black worker: it was cheap and not barred from them by discriminatory practices. The distribution of the black population by ward for the London boroughs shows that the highest concentrations by ward are not necessarily found in the boroughs with the highest overall concentrations. In fact, the Inner London ward with the greatest proportion of black people in its population in 1981 was Spitalfields ward in the borough of Tower Hamlets, with 63 per cent. Tower Hamlets has an overall proportion of 19.8 per cent. Among the Outer London boroughs, there are fewer wards with high concentrations, but two wards in Ealing exceed the Spitalfields level with 71 per cent in Glebe ward and 85 per cent in Northcote ward. Such high concentrations illustrate the clustered distribution of the black population.

Demographic structure

Changes in the demographic structure of a migrant population are an inevitable part of the migration process. As that process progresses, the population structure is transformed from one of irregularity to one which is balanced in demographic terms. The means by which this occurs have already been discussed in Chapter 1, and it suffices to mention here that they include the migration of the family members of primary migrants, and the natural spread of births over time due to the 35-year biological span of childbearing.

Age and sex structure

This process of change in the demographic structure is at an early stage for the black population in Britain. Though there are now roughly as many females as males, and though migration has virtually ceased, there is still a marked absence of elderly people in comparison to the total population, as well as relatively few adults aged 45 to retirement. This is seen in Figure 12 (Appendix Table A14) which shows the age and sex structure of the population living in households with a NCWP born head and of the total population. Indeed, comparison of these two age distributions shows that the black population has a very young age structure, a consequence of the youthfulness of past immigrants. Even by 1981, less than 4 per cent of the black population were of retirement age, compared to almost 18 per cent of the total population. The difference in these two age distributions is, in fact, greater than these data suggest because of the approximations involved in using household head to identify the black population: though the 15 per cent white people included in the population living in households with a NCWP born head will be distributed over almost all age groups, the 10 per cent of the black population not covered will by definition of their exclusion be concentrated in the young adult and younger age groups.

The structure of the total black population conceals considerable differences between those of different ethnic origins. This is clearly seen in Figure 13 (Appendix Table A15). Again, however, these data are somewhat distorted by the fact that they omit people living in households with a UK-born black head. Since the majority of these are of West Indian origin, the West Indian age/sex pyramid in Figure 13 should in reality be augmented by increased proportions born in the UK at ages 20-30 and 0-5 in particular.[14] Even with these adjustments, however, the West Indian population is generally older than those of Asian origin. This is confirmed by Labour Force Survey data in Appendix Table A16. It arises from a combination of several factors including the early start to West Indian migration, the fact that migration from the West Indies decreased to very low levels at an early stage, and the lower levels of and rapid decline in West Indian fertility (see below). This latter factor has contributed to the small cohorts at younger ages.

It is interesting to note that the Indian population also has relatively large proportions at older ages. Indeed, the proportions of elderly males and those aged 45-64 are greater than for the West Indian population. This is offset, however, by the fact that there are fewer Indian females at these ages. Again, this age structure reflects the history of the population. Migration from India began in the 1940's at a level that exceeded that from the West Indies until 1952, as Figure 1 has shown. In addition, Figure 6 shows that a large proportion of these early migrants were female. As wives, these females would be somewhat younger than the male migrants, leading to an imbalance by age in the sex ratios, as already noted for the elderly. The early arrival of these females, however, has led to a more balanced age structure overall since families were established at an early stage in the migration process. These effects on the age structure of the Indian population are supplemented by the fact that Indian fertility has fallen by about a third since 1971, resulting in smaller proportions at young ages.

The Pakistani and Bangladeshi population structures are less well-balanced than that of the Indian population. Their population pyramids have a much wider base and the adult populations are small relative to the child populations. More than 40 per cent of these populations are aged less than 16 years. The reason for this lies both in the late start to migration and in the relatively high level of fertility of the Pakistani and Bangladeshi populations. It is seen in Figure 6 that migration from Pakistan and Bangladesh did not occur in significant proportions until the late 1950's, and that of these early migrants almost all were male. It is the relatively late arrival of females from Pakistan and Bangladesh that has shaped the structure of these populations. Indeed, the differences between the two structures reflect the fact that women and children from Pakistan have on the whole arrived some years earlier than their counterparts from Bangladesh. Appendix Table A7 shows that dependent Pakistani women and children arrived in increasing numbers during the late 1970's with decreasing numbers since then, but that Bangladeshi dependants only began to increase in numbers in 1980.

For the Pakistani population, the migration of dependants had by 1981 resulted in roughly equal numbers of females and males, an indication that most dependants have now come to the UK. The age distribution of the population is by no means balanced, however, the most notable irregularity being the marked shortage of 16–19 year olds. This is largely due to the indirect effects of migration. The fact that there were very few Pakistani women in Britain during the early 1960's meant that there were few births at that time with correspondingly few UK–born Pakistanis aged 16–19 in 1981. In addition, the early 1960's was the period when male migration was relatively high (see Figure 6) leading to the separation of significant numbers of families and a corresponding reduction in births in Pakistan to dependant wives. For those children that were born in Pakistan at that time, the difficulties encountered in gaining entry clearance for older children will have contributed to their shortage in Britain. The fact that female migration increased in the mid–1960's has resulted in the relatively large proportion of children aged 5–15 born in the UK, and the more recent entry of dependants will have augmented the adult and younger child age groups. The high proportion of children aged 0–4 is in fact due to births occurring in the UK, again an indirect effect of migration. The increased numbers of women who arrived in the late 1970's and the women who arrive as fiancées (see Appendix Table A8) have contributed to births in 1977–81: after having had to wait some time for entry clearance to the UK, women waste no more time in starting or adding to their families.

For the Bangladeshi population, the migration process is even less well advanced than for the Pakistani population. The entry of dependants has not yet occurred to sufficient an extent to bring about a balance between the sexes, as is clearly seen in Figure 13, indicative of the fact that many dependants remain in Bangladesh awaiting entry clearance to the UK.[15] As in the Pakistani population, the late arrival of women has resulted in very few UK born children aged 16–19, and the separation of spouses has resulted in reduced numbers of children aged not only 16–19 but also 5–15, though these age groups will be augmented to some extent by the continued arrival of dependants. Indeed, it is clear from Figure 13 that the proportions of males aged 16–19 and 5–15 are not particularly low, indicating that it is mostly female children who are waiting with their mothers to come to the UK.[16]

It is clear that the demographic structure of the black population is a result of migration patterns over time and of the demographic characteristics of migrants. Given that primary migration has ceased, many aspects of the present structures reflect the degree to which the minority populations in Britain face difficulties in family reunification, difficulties which result from immigration rules and procedures even though by law family members have the right to come to Britain.

Knowledge of the demographic structure of the black population has other applications besides indicating the extent to which family reunification has not taken place. For local authorities, in particular, it indicates the size of the population for whom services are to be provided. Thus data on the ethnic composition of children are important in pre-school provision, primary and secondary education; and in the areas of health, housing, youth and the elderly, relevant data are necessary to plan or make a case for any special provision.

Dependency ratios

The structure of the population determines the dependency ratio[17] indicating the relative 'burden' of the non-economic child and elderly age groups on the economic age groups. Figure 14 (Appendix Table A17) shows dependency ratios for various minority populations.[18] It is seen that the elderly dependency ratio for all minority populations is very low, whilst for the white population it accounts for almost half of the total dependency ratio. For most minority populations, this low elderly dependency ratio more than compensates for their relatively high child dependency ratios giving an overall ratio that is less than that of the white population. Only the Pakistani and Bangladeshi populations have overall dependency ratios higher than those of the white population.

Dependency ratios are, of course, a function of the demographic structure of the minority populations, and their variation is thus a result of migration patterns. The West Indian population has a relatively low dependency ratio, a result not only of the small proportion of elderly people but also of the fact that falling fertility amongst this population has resulted in a relatively small proportion of children. The Indian (like the Chinese) population has a slightly higher overall dependency ratio, due partly to higher fertility but also to the larger elderly dependency ratio arising from early migration. The high child dependency ratios for the Pakistani and Bangladeshi populations result from their higher fertility and recent migration.[19] The low ratio for the population of African origin stems partly from moderate rates of fertility and partly from a high proportion of young adults in the population, probably including many students.

Sex ratios

The balance between females and males in the various minority populations is seen by reference to sex ratios (Appendix Table A18).[20] The West Indian population has slightly more females than males, as does the total population of Great Britain. Again, this better balance arises mainly from the earlier and more complete migration of West Indians, in that the population is composed mostly of complete families often with three generations in Britain. Apart from the direct balancing effect of migration, the older age structure of the population indirectly affects the sex ratio. Generally speaking, females tend to live longer than males. Thus, since the sex ratio at birth is on average 105 males per 100 females, it is not until older ages (depending on the rates of mortality for females and males) that there are more females than males. In older populations, therefore, the sex ratio is lower. This factor accounts for the low sex ratio in the total population, as is clearly illustrated in the large excess of females aged 60+ in Figure 12b, and it contributes, but to a lesser extent, to the low sex ratio of the West Indian population as seen in Figure 13.

The early migration of females from India has contributed substantially to the relatively balanced sex ratio of the Indian population, though as noted above there is a relative absence of older Indian women due mainly to the differential in age at marriage. The Pakistani and Bangladeshi[21] populations have much higher sex ratios reflecting their earlier stage in the migration process. Given that the sex ratio for the total population is less than 100, it can conservatively be concluded that the Pakistani female population is 20 per cent too small, and probably more so for Bangladeshis, indicating that many females are still waiting to join their husbands or fathers in Britain. This, of course, takes no account of male children waiting to join their fathers.

Among the remaining minority populations, it is interesting to note that the lowest sex ratios are for the mixed population (LSF data) and for those from East Africa and the Mediterranean (census data). In the case of the mixed population, a low sex ratio is expected because it is composed largely of children born in the UK, of whom there would be slightly more males than females because of the prevalence of males amongst births. For the East African population, a balanced population would be expected because of the fact that whole families migrated to avoid political and economic hardship in Uganda and Kenya. The same would be true of the Mediterranean population, most of whom are from Cyprus.

In general, sex ratios fall as migration continues, so that those populations that are still characterised by an excess of males will become more balanced as female dependant migration continues. For example, in 1971 the sex ratio of the population of Pakistani and Bangladeshi ethnic origins was greater than 200, but this had fallen to 127 by 1981 as a result of the concentration of women among Pakistani and Bangladeshi migrants in the intervening years.[22] In addition, even in the absence of continued migration, sex ratios will continue to fall to levels similar to that for the total population because of the differential in mortality between the sexes. This factor will, given current trends in migration, become the main determinant of the sex ratio.

Marital status

The extent to which wives are still separated from their husbands by immigration laws and procedures can be seen by examination of data on marital status. Here too, migration brings about an imbalance between married females and males which is only redressed after families have been reunited. Figure 15 (Appendix Table A19) shows that of those married members (including those in consensual unions) of minority populations who were born in their respective countries, the majority were male in 1981.[23] In line with the degree of balance by age and between the sexes, it is the Pakistan-born and Bangladesh-born populations that have the greatest imbalance with respect to the married population. This excess of males has been considerably reduced by the migration of dependant females in recent years. For the population born in Pakistan and Bangladesh the ratio of married men to married women in 1971 was 2.5 to 1, whilst by 1981 it had fallen to 1.2 to 1 for Pakistan and 1.9 to 1 for Bangladesh. Again, it is clear that the Bangladeshi population is at a much earlier stage in the migration process, and that by 1981 only just over a half of married males had been able to bring their wives to Britain.

Among the widowed and divorced populations shown in Figure 15, it is seen that there are more females than males, especially for the populations born in the West Indies and India. This is a reflection of the earlier and more complete migration of these two populations in that they are generally older and most dependants have come to Britain. The older average age of those born in the West Indies and India (see Figure 13) has resulted in relatively more deaths in comparison to the populations born in Pakistan and Bangladesh and hence in greater proportions widowed and divorced for both females and males. The excess of females in this category arises partly from the older average age of males who would therefore be expected to die before their wives and partly from the fact that male mortality is higher than female mortality. In addition, in the case of the population born in Bangladesh and to a lesser extent those born in Pakistan, the fact that not all wives have joined their husbands reduces the possibility of women living as widows in Britain: a wife who is waiting to gain entry clearance to Britain and whose husband dies is highly unlikely to be allowed to enter even if all or some of her children are already in the country.

A similar factor is also likely to reduce the number of divorced women in Britain who were born in Pakistan or Bangladesh and to a lesser extent India because of the recency of migration for many women. When marriages, especially recent marriages, end in divorce, there is a growing tendency to issue a deportation order on the divorced woman on the grounds that the marriage is suspected as having been one of convenience. This, of course, is also true for males who have recently entered as fiancés or husbands but there are now very few such entrants (see Chapter 2).

The proportions single in Figure 15 represent a mixture of adult migrants who have not yet married and children born abroad. For the population born in the West Indies, there are slightly more single females than males, a feature which is unusual. There are several possible explanations for this, including that it is not in fact true, and that young West Indian males have been underenumerated.[24] This is probably a partial explanation at least, but it is possible that other factors have also contributed to the large proportion of single females. These include the possibility that some of the single West Indian women who migrated to Britain in search of work have remained single; and the lower sex ratio at birth for West Indians (Visaria, 1967) than for the white population which would affect the composition of families whether born in the West Indies or in the UK. In addition, there is a substantial outward flow of West Indians from Britain, possibly comprising many single males (OPCS, MN Series).

For the populations born in India, Pakistan and Bangladesh there are more single males than single females. This is again a reflection of migration patterns. Many males migrated before marriage, and whilst most married in the UK or on return visits to their native countries, some have remained single. In addition, there is a tendency to bring male children to the UK prior to female children, and this in conjunction with the later stage in the migration process has resulted in the much larger sex differential for the Pakistani and Bangladeshi populations. This effect is increased by the fact that there are in general more male than female children because of the predominance of males amongst births. A further factor affecting these populations more than the West Indian and total populations is the sex differential in age at marriage: since females marry at younger ages than males (Jones, 1984), there are fewer single females.

Interethnic marriage

The extent to which members of a migrant population intermarry with members of the non-migrant population is a significant factor in the migration process. Generally, the greater the degree of intermarriage, the smaller the flow of dependant migrants who migrate for marriage purposes and the shorter the period of such migration. In addition, interethnic marriage clearly affects the demographic development of the migrant population. Not only are demographic characteristics such as fertility potentially subject to more rapid change, but the population in question becomes less easy to define. The existence of a new ethnically mixed generation raises the question of to which population they 'belong'. In Britain, as already discussed, people with one parent born in the NCWP were included in the black population as far as the 1971 Census is concerned. More recently, self-identification has been used.

The incidence of marriage within and between ethnic groups is not well-documented, principally because ethnicity or its proxy is not recorded at marriage registration, except in Scotland. Even if more comprehensive information were available from registration sources, such data would by their nature exclude consensual unions. Whilst this would be a negligible source of bias for Asian groups, for whom formal marriage is very important and hence virtually universal, it would be quite considerable for West Indians, many of whom are not formally married but cohabiting in stable consensual unions.

In the absence of registration data, several other sources have been used to estimate rates of interethnic marriage. These sources show that interethnic marriage is more common between black men and white women than the converse. Again, this is partly the result of migration patterns and the ensuing demographic imbalances. It has been estimated that among married Asians in 1974, 2 per cent of women and 5 per cent of men were married to a white person, whilst for West Indians equivalent proportions were one per cent of women and 8 per cent of men (Smith, 1976). If consensual unions are included, 8 per cent of black women and 14 per cent of black men had white partners in 1973-75.[25] More recent research has shown that among Asians, certain groups are more likely than others to marry white people (Robinson, 1982).

The existence of data on births of mixed race has been used to give an indication of the frequency of interethnic marriage.[26] For births in 1969-70, among parents born in India, Bangladesh and Pakistan, 9 per cent of women and 16 per cent of men were married to white (defined as British or other European born) partners, whilst among parents born in the West Indies, 4 per cent of women and 17 per cent of men had a white spouse (Bagley, 1972).[27] More recent estimates have been based directly on ethnic origin of spouses, rather than on birthplace of parents of births, and have shown that birthplace data overestimate the extent of interethnic marriage (Jones, 1984). Table 4 shows the extent of interethnic marriage as estimated from two large-scale surveys carried out in 1977-79 and in 1981. These estimates confirm both the sex and ethnic differentials of the earlier findings, namely that in the majority of cases interethnic marriages take place between black men and white women rather than the converse, and that such marriages are more common amongst West Indians than Asians. Table 4 also shows rates for people of African origin which indicate a similar pattern to West Indians. Where marriages between partners of different origins within the NCWP are concerned, Table 4 shows that the rates are generally lower, especially for West Indians. However, African and Pakistani women appear to be more likely to marry a man of another NCWP ethnic origin than a white man.

Indications are that interethnic marriage is increasing, despite the fact that many early male migrants had little choice but to marry a white woman. In 1977-79, 10 per cent of marriages with both spouses aged 45+ involved partners of different ethnic origins (either black/white or black/other black), whilst for marriages with both spouses aged less than 30 the equivalent percentage was 16 (ibid.).

Table 4: Estimates of interethnic marriage rates, percentages

Ethnic Origin	With white spouse		With other NCWP spouse	
	Women	Men	Women	Men
		1977–79		
West Indian	5	15	1	0
African	5	15	7	8
Indian	3	5	1	1
Pakistani	0	7	2	1
Bangladeshi	1	9	0	1
		1981		
West Indian	10	22	2	8
African	11	27	17	19
Indian	4	8	2	3
Pakistani	2	7	7	3
Bangladeshi	–	11	–	3

Source: P.R. Jones 'Ethnic intermarriage in Britain: a further assessment', Ethnic and Racial Studies, 1984, Vol.7, no.3 pp.398–405.

Note: 1977–79 data are from the National Dwelling and Housing Survey and refer to England (see Department of the Environment, 1978, 1980); 1981 data are from the Labour Force Survey and refer to Great Britain (see OPCS, 1982c).

Fertility trends

As the migration process progresses, immigration itself becomes a less significant factor in the development of the population, being replaced by births to migrant women. For the population of NCWP ethnic origin, the annual contribution of births to the development of the population has generally exceeded that of migration since at least 1970.[28] Clearly, with the early reduction in migration from the West Indies, births would have become the major factor well before 1970 for the West Indian population, whilst for the Indian, Bangladeshi and Pakistani populations combined births did not exceed immigration until 1979.

The annual number of births in a population is dependent on two factors: the age and sex structure of the population and fertility rates. It has already been seen that the age and sex structure of the black population in Britain is considerably affected by past migration patterns. Thus, in the early stages of the migration process, there were very few births because most migrants were male . Only as wives and fiancées have joined these males, has the number of births increased, and the number of births remains high in relation to the size of the population because of the fact that there is a high proportion of young adults in the population.

In addition to this structural factor, the fertility rates of NCWP migrants to the UK have tended to be higher than those of the indigenous population. This basic differential has been, and to some extent continues to be, exaggerated by the experience of migration. Wives and fiancées have generally had to wait some time before coming to the UK, and the fact that they resume or commence childbearing soon after migration in order to make up for lost time means that their post-migration fertility rates are artificially inflated. Neither this artificial nor the basic differential in fertility rates has been maintained, however, and in the case of West Indian born women, fertility rates have decreased to virtually the same level as for UK born women.

Data on births to ethnic minority women are classified according to country of birth of parent rather than by ethnic origin (OPCS, FM1 Series). This method of classification has by now become of very limited use because it identifies only those births occurring to actual migrants, whilst those occurring to black parents who were themselves born in Britain are indistinguishable from births to white parents. In 1971, this statistical bias was not significant because only 2.9 per cent of the black population had been born in the UK and were of childbearing age.[29] By the mid-1970s, an estimated 2–3,000 births per year occurred to black people who were born in the UK and because of the earlier West Indian migration patterns most of these births were of West Indian ethnic origin (OPCS, 1978a). By 1981, more than half of females aged 16–19 living in households with a NCWP born head were born in the UK (see Figure 12a), indicating that there is by now significant proportion of black births omitted from these data.[30] This omission clearly leads to an underestimation of the number of ethnic minority births.

In addition to these problems, the use of parent's birthplace to categorise births leads to further inaccuracies because births to white parents born in the NCWP during the period of British colonial rule are included. This factor, which leads to overestimation and hence counterbalances to some extent the effect of the omission of births to black UK born women, varies in significance by country of birth and by year. In 1971, 24 per cent of the NCWP born population were white, about half of whom were female.[31] For women of childbearing age born in the NCWP, about 7 per cent were white. For those born in India, African and Pakistan this proportion was 9, 13 and 2 per cent respectively. These proportions change over time due to the differing age structures between white and black women and between countries of birth. For women who would be aged 15 to 44 in 1981 (that is those who were 5 to 34 in 1971) the proportions white were 6, 20 and 2 per cent for women born in India, Africa and Pakistan respectively.[32]

These biases make interpretation of the data on births by birthplace of mother difficult, and they are poor estimates of black births. (The data appear in Appendix Table A20). The current number of West Indian births is underestimated by these data because of the considerable bias involved in the omission of births to UK born women. For births to Indian women, this bias is small but by now increasing, but is offset by the continued inclusion of births to white women born in the NCWP. The data on births to women born in Bangladesh and Pakistan are least affected by these biases: they are however inflated to the extent that newly arrived Bangladeshi and Pakistani women are making up for lost time in childbearing.

To gain a more accurate impression of the fertility patterns of the ethnic minority population, it is necessary to examine rates rather than numbers of births. An increase in the number of births is to be expected in a population that has been increasing by both immigration and natural increase. In relation to population size, however, rates have decreased. Total fertility rates by birthplace of women are shown in Figure 16 (Appendix Table A21). These rates represent the average number of births per woman if fertility were to continue as at present.[33] However, fertility is changing in a downward direction, as Figure 16 shows, and to the extent that this trend continues, these current rates overestimate the average number of children that women will have in their lifetime. This overestimation is clearly greater for those groups with the larger and very recent declines in fertility, such as women born in Bangladesh and Pakistan.

Figure 16 clearly shows that fertility has been decreasing for all groups of women, and that the differentials in fertility have been reduced over the last 10 years or so. A reduction in fertility after migration is not uncommon, and part of the reason for the lower levels of fertility amongst women born in the West Indies and India can be attributed to their earlier migration. Indeed, it seems likely from the pattern of decline that some reduction in fertility took place before 1970 for these groups of women at least. In contrast, the fertility rates of women born in Bangladesh and Pakistan are high, due in part to the relative recency of their migration allowing little time for any change in fertility to occur. Furthermore, the recency of migration of these groups suggests that their fertility rates are inflated, since they are likely either to be still in the period of 'catching up' on lost time in childbearing during the separation of wives from husbands already in the UK, or in the case of women migrating for marriage to have begun childbearing without delay.[34] This inflation factor is quite significant, and accounts for part of the rapid reduction in fertility between 1981 and 1983 for women born in Pakistan, since the immigration of women from Pakistan declined after 1977 (see Appendix Tables A7 and A8). Thus, the fact that the fertility of women born in Bangladesh declined over the period 1981–83 despite continued increases in the immigration of wives and fianceés from Bangladesh during the late 1970s and early 1980s (see Appendix Tables A7 and A8), suggests that there has been a significant decrease in 'real' fertility which is partially masked by the inflation factor.

The rates presented in Figure 16 refer to women by place of birth, and thus omit UK born black women from the minority populations (including them in the England and Wales and UK populations). They do not therefore accurately represent minority fertility, and are biased to the extent that UK born black women differ with respect to fertility from their NCWP born counterparts.[35] Data on the fertility of UK born black women is virtually non-existent, but it has been tentatively suggested that among West Indian women there is no 'major difference' in recent years in fertility rates between women born in the UK and the West Indies (Thompson, 1982). This is not surprising since any such difference would not be expected to be large given the fact that the fertility of women born in the West Indies is already very close to the overall average, towards which the rates for UK born West Indian women might be expected to tend. Since there is much more room for variation where other minorities are concerned, it cannot be assumed that the fertility of UK born women of other minorities is similar to that of their NCWP born counterparts. Given current trends in fertility, and in some cases the inflation factor due to recent migration, any difference is likely to be due to further reductions in fertility on the part of UK born women.

Two further factors affect the rates shown in Figure 1 in such a way as to exaggerate differentials in fertility. The first of these is social class. Since most of the black population are in the lower social classes whose fertility is higher than that of the middle and upper social classes (Cartwright, 1978), some of the difference in fertility must be attributed to this factor. Indeed, this factor probably more than explains the remaining differential in the fertility of West Indian born women. It should be noted that, as for UK born women, the fertility of women born in the West Indies is below replacement level.[36] It is possible that West Indian women (including those born in the UK since there is no major difference in fertility with respect to birthplace) are limiting their family size in order to improve their social class in the same way as people in social class IIIN (lower white collar workers) have traditionally done. The need to reduce fertility in order to achieve a higher social class, if not for oneself then for one's children, may be a factor influencing the decline in fertility amongst the black population.

The second factor that serves to inflate differentials in fertility is marriage. Both age at marriage and the proportions finally marrying affect fertility rates: a younger average age at marriage leads to higher fertility rates, as does a greater proportion eventually marrying. In comparison to UK born women, those born in India, Bangladesh and Pakistan not only marry earlier on average, but also marry in greater proportions, accounting for a small part of the fertility differential. It is difficult to assess the effect of this factor on the fertility of women born in the West Indies because of the frequency of consensual unions, but one source of data suggests that the frequency of marriage, including consensual union, among West Indian women is below the average for Great Britain (Thompson, 1982).

Mortality differentials

Perhaps the only aspect of the demography of the black population that has not received popular attention at some time or other is mortality. It would be easy to dismiss this as a lack of popular concern for the difficulties that blacks people face, but it must be recognised that the demographic structure of the population results in few deaths relative to the size of population. This lack of popular interest in mortality has undoubtedly contributed to the paucity of information available until relatively recently on the mortality of ethnic groups in Britain, and the relatively small numbers involved has limited analysis. Recent studies have, in fact, shown that in some cases black people are less likely to die than white people of the same age and social class,

The identification of deaths by proxy ethnic group began in April 1969 with the introduction of birthplace of deceased as an item of information obtained at death registration (OPCS, DH1 Series). These birthplace data (shown in Appendix Table A22) suffer from the same limitations already discussed in the case of data on the birthplace of mothers of registered births: all UK born black people are excluded, and those white people born in the NCWP are included. As time progresses and the proportion of the black population born in the UK increases, the first of these limiting factors increases in importance. Thus, this factor is of greater significance in the estimation of the mortality of the West Indian population than of the other minority populations, because of the higher proportion of West Indians born in the UK (see Figure 13 above), in turn due to their earlier migration and later stage in the migration process. In addition, it is of course data for the younger age groups that are most deficient in representing the mortality situation of the young black population. The second limiting factor of birthplace data, the inclusion of white people born in the NCWP, also affects different groups to different extents. The majority of white NCWP born people are not only in the older age groups, but were also mostly born in India as discussed above.

Relatively speaking, few deaths occur among the black population, largely due to the young demographic structure of the population in comparison to the total population. Since the black population is characterised by a near absence of elderly people, whilst the total population has a high proportion of elderly people (see Figure 12), and since most deaths occur in old age, the incidence of death among the total population is much higher than among the black population. In crude terms, the death rate[37] for people born in the NCWP is about 5 per 1,000, compared to about 12 per 1,000 for England and Wales as a whole,[38] and if the even younger UK born black population were included, the death rate would undoubtedly be significantly lower than 5 per 1,000. This age structure effect is very strong on the death rate, rendering it useless as an index for comparing real mortality rates.

In order to make valid comparisons of mortality between ethnic groups, indices that have been adjusted to take account of the effects of the age structure are used. Table 5 shows that standardisation for age reveals that

53

in 1970-72 in England and Wales, males aged 15-64 born in the West Indies had a standardised mortality ratio (SMR)[39] of 90, compared to 101 for those born in the African New Commonwealth, and 100 for all birthplaces (Benjamin, 1982). Standardisation for age and social class, also shown in Table 5, reveals that in 1970-72 males aged 15-64 born either in the West Indies or in India, Pakistan and Bangladesh had lower mortality than those born in England and Wales (OPCS, 1978b).

Table 5: Mortality by country of birth, standardised for (a) age and (b) age and social class, males 15-64, England and Wales, 1970-72

Country of birth	SMR(a)	SMR(b)
India, Pakistan and Bangladesh	101	98
West Indies	90	84
African New Commonwealth	108	121
Rest of New Commonwealth	98	102
England and Wales	99	100
All birthplaces	100	100

Source: OPCS, Occupational Mortality, 1970-72, Decennial Supplement, Series DS, no. 1 (London: HMSO, 1978b).

Table 6: Mortality by country of birth, standardised for age, for each social class, males 15-64, England and Wales, 1970-72, SMRs

Country of birth	Social Class						
	I	II	IIIN	IIIM	IV	V	All
India, Pakistan and Bangladesh	122	127	114	105	93	73	98
West Indies	267	163	135	87	71	75	84
African New Commonwealth	177	147	116	93	101	170	121
Rest of New Commonwealth	133	108	113	94	111	79	99
England and Wales	97	99	99	99	100	101	100
All birthplaces	100	100	100	100	100	100	100

Source: OPCS, Occupational Mortality 1970-72, Decennial Supplement, Series DS, no. 1 (London:HMSO, 1978b).

Mortality differentials by country of birth within social class are shown in Table 6, again for males aged 15-64. Though these SMRs are based on small numbers of deaths, and in fact the differences in SMRs in the higher social classes (I and II) are not statistically significant (Benjamin, 1982, p.60), their general pattern can be taken as indicative of mortality differentials. It is seen that whereas the mortality of NCWP born people is higher than that of the total population in the higher social classes, the reverse is true in the lower social classes. Differentials between social classes are shown in Table 7. It is seen that the clear social gradient in mortality for all birthplaces is not so easily discernible for the NCWP born groups. This is partly due to the small numbers involved, but it would also appear that other factors are involved.

Table 7: Mortality by social class, standardised for age, for each country of birth, males 15–64, England and Wales, 1970–72, SMRs

Country of birth	Social Class						
	I	II	IIIN	IIIM	IV	V	All
India, Pakistan and Bangladesh	96	105	105	113	108	102	100
West Indies	245	157	160	110	96	123	100
African New Commonwealth	112	98	95	82	95	193	100
Rest of New Commonwealth	102	85	110	98	125	106	100
England and Wales	75	80	98	105	114	138	100
All birthplaces	77	81	99	106	114	137	100

Source: B. Benjamin, 'Variation of mortality in the United Kingdom with special reference to immigrants and minority groups', in D.A. Coleman (Ed.), Demography of Immigrants and Minority Groups in The United Kingdom (London: Academic Press, 1982).

It has been suggested that migrants are healthy probably because of a self–selection process, and that they are employed in Britain in less skilled jobs than those of which they are capable (OPCS, 1978b; ibid.). There is evidence that both of these factors are true. In addition to the commonly found process of self–selection according to health, official criteria of selection were also imposed as already noted in Chapter 2. Not only did the Indian Government require all emigrants to pass a medical examination (*The Times*, 12.9.58) but X–ray checks for tuberculosis were introduced at ports of entry to the UK. In addition, the financial guarantees (for repatriation costs) required by both the Indian and Pakistani Governments, and the language and employment criteria by Pakistan, served to restrict emigration to the better educated and more prosperous higher classes. In contrast, the Jamaican and West Indian Governments' refusal to impose voluntary restrictions on emigration, except in the case of Jamaica to allow only those aged 18 to 50 to migrate for work, left migration open to all those who could afford the journey. Once in Britain, discrimination and racist practices ensured that these fit and able migrants took less skilled and lower paid employment than whites of equal ability. No such selection according to health or social class took place in the case of the expelled Asian migrants from East Africa, and the high SMR for the African New Commonwealth in Table 6 probably partly arises from this fact.

It is clear that a process of selection, whether formal or entirely informal, took place in determining who would migrate. Not only were the early migrants young adults and male, but they were also healthy, as indeed were later migrants. If male NCWP migrants are healthier than their UK born counterparts, female migrants from the NCWP do not appear to enjoy such an advantage. Table 8 compares the mortality of NCWP born females aged 20+ and of all females aged 20+ in England and Wales. Though the equivalent differential in male mortality (also shown) is in favour of NCWP born males (as in Table 6), for females this situation is reversed with females born in the NCWP suffering higher mortality rates than the average for England and Wales. This situation is probably partly due to the lack of self-selection according to health on the part of women, because the majority of women migrants are dependants rather than the primary migrant. Other factors, related to cause of death, are probably also involved (Marmot et al., 1983; OPCS, 1983c).

Perinatal and infant mortality

It has already been noted that a major deficiency of the available data on mortality is the fact that UK born black people are excluded. This is a particularly important omission in the case of children, since it prevents the identification of possible areas where medical services might be improved. Data on the deaths of very young children have, however, recently become available. Prior to this, information was sparse but included a 1970 survey which found perinatal mortality rates[40] of 31.7 and 23.1 for single births to mothers born in India, Pakistan and Bangladesh and in the West Indies respectively (Chamberlain et al., 1975). This compared with a rate of 21.3 for UK born mothers.

Table 8: Mortality by country of birth, standardised for age, for each sex, population aged 20+, England and Wales, 1970–72, SMRs

Country of birth	Females	Males
India, Pakistan and Bangladesh	106	99
West Indies	117	94
African New Commonwealth	124	129
All birthplaces	100	100

Source: M. Marmot, A. Adelstein and L. Bulusu, 'Immigrant Mortality in England and Wales', Population Trends, 1983, no. 33.

The more recent data are derived by linking births by birthplace of mother and infant deaths, and allow for greater detail in their analysis (Adelstein, 1980; OPCS, annual). Figure 17 (Appendix Table A23) shows infant mortality rates[41] by country of birth of mother from 1975 to 1984. The general trend is one of decline and of reduced differentials between each of the various minorities and the total population of England and Wales. The same is true of perinatal mortality rates, also shown in Appendix Table A23.

Various factors contribute to the higher perinatal and infant mortality rates of babies born to NCWP born women, including their lower average social class and generally poorer housing. Another contributory factor is the higher incidence of low birth weight amongst babies of women born in India, Pakistan and Bangladesh or Africa, and to a lesser extent the West Indies, than amongst babies born to UK born women (Macfarlane and Mugford, 1983). Genuine low birth weight is, of course, a matter for concern, but it seems that caucasian standards are being rigidly applied to pregnant women of small stature from India, Pakistan and Bangladesh with the risk of inappropriate obstetric intervention (ibid.).

It is not clear, however, why infant and perinatal mortality levels among babies with mothers born in Pakistan should be consistently higher than rates for other groups. The often held argument that higher fertility leads to higher infant mortality because of shorter birth intervals does not seem to apply: the highest fertility rates are among women born in Bangladesh for whom infant and perinatal mortality rates in 1984 were 8.1 and 14.1 respectively, compared to 15.4 and 16.9 respectively for births to women born in Pakistan (OPCS, 1986). It is possible, because of the clustered distribution of minority populations, that this differential reflects variation in the quality of health services in different areas, but further research is necessary before any conclusions can be drawn.

Notes

1. Not all ethnic groups were identifiable in this way: the exercise concentrated on people with parents born in India, Bangladesh and Pakistan.

2. For a summary and critique of this report, see Booth (1983a), and Booth (1983b). For a discussion of the question format proposed, see Booth (1985c). See also Booth (1988).

3. This is based on the 98.5 per cent of the population who live in private households.

4. The 2.2 million living in households with a NCWP born head can be divided into those born in the UK (896,000) and those born outside the UK, but not necessarily in the NCWP (1,312,000). To those born in the UK should be added the estimated 10 per cent of the population of NCWP ethnic origin who do not live in a household headed by a NCWP born person (i.e. 208,000). The proportion of the population of NCWP ethnic origin is thus estimated as 46 per cent. This calculation takes no account of the 15 per cent who are white, who because of their smaller family sizes would tend to bias this estimate in a downward direction. Data from the

1981 Labour Force Survey are in close agreement with this estimate, with 47 per cent of the black population born in the UK. See OPCS (1983a).

5. Neither of these sources is directly comparable with the 1971 Census data, nor are they comparable with each other. On the one hand, the 1981 Census data cover only 90 per cent of the black population and include 15 per cent white people. On the other hand, the 1981 Labour Force Survey data have a separate category for the population of all mixed ethnic origins, while East African Asians are not identified separately but included in their category of self-classification, mostly Indian. In addition, the populations differ between the three sets of data; the census data refer to the NCWP only while the LFS data cover all ethnic groups; and in reference to the non-UK born population the 1971 Census data refer to the NCWP born population while both 1981 sources refer to all those born outside the UK.

6. The census data omit the 10 per cent of the black population in households headed by a UK born black person many of whom are likely to be of West Indian origin because of the earlier migration of this group. Of the LFS data classified as mixed, it is estimated that 75,000 are of West Indian/White or African/White ethnic origin and UK born; most of these are likely to be of West Indian/White ethnic origin.

7. Duffield (1988) shows that black labour did not replace white labour per se, but that black labour took the unskilled jobs created by mechanisation in those industries without a strong trade union organisation to oppose black labour.

8. Greater London conurbation (47 per cent), West Midlands conurbation (14 per cent), South East Lancashire conurbation (3 per cent), Merseyside conurbation (1 per cent), Tyneside conurbation (1 per cent), West Yorkshire conurbation (5 per cent). See Rose et al. (1969, pp.100-101).

9. The 1971 and 1981 data refer to different definitions of the black population. These are fully discussed in Chapter 4.

10. These data refer to the newly defined regions which came into use in 1974, and are not directly comparable with data for previous years.

11. Bradford, for example, was a borough of less than 300,000 people in 1971, but became a district in 1974 which included Keighley and Ilkley and which in 1981 had a population of over 450,000.

12. 1981 Census data on the size of the black population and its proportion of the total population are: Coventry 29,000, 9.5%; Derby 18,000, 8.4%; Nottingham 21,000, 7.9%; Kirklees 30,000, 8.2%; Leeds 28,000, 4.0%.

13. Ranging from 7.4% in Brent to 5.4% in Islington and Hammersmith. Children born in the UK are not included. See Rose et al. (1969, p.102).

14. Note that by increasing these proportions, the proportions at other ages would decrease to compensate.

15. But see below, and note 21.

16. The age distribution of the Bangladeshi population in Figures 13 and 14 do not exactly tally, especially at ages 30-45 and 45-R. This is probably due to sampling error in the Labour Force Survey data.

17. The dependency ratio is defined here as the number of children aged 0-15 and elderly of retirement age divided by the adult population aged 16 to retirement (and multiplied by 1000).

18. Census data are not shown because of the significant effect on the dependency ratio of the biases introduced by the exclusion of 10 per cent of the black population and inclusion of 15 per cent white people.

19. Due to the continued separation of families, these child dependency ratios may in fact be downwardly biased.

20. The sex ratio is defined as the number of males per 100 females.

21. Appendix Table A18 gives sex ratios for both the 1981 Census and the 1981 Labour Force Survey. These are in rough agreement except for the Bangladeshi population. Examination of the census data shows that for the small Bangladeshi population, the bias involved in the omission of those not living in households with a Bangladeshi-born head is substantial. Since it is the younger population, which is more balanced between the sexes, that is omitted the census data are biased towards extreme values. It is probable that the Labour Force Survey has resulted in a more accurate estimate of the sex ratio of the Bangladeshi population. The 1983 Labour Force Survey supports the 1981 ratio. See OPCS (1984).

22. This figure is from the 1981 Census data. The corresponding figure for the 1981 LFS data is 122.

23. There are obvious problems with this comparison: the data by country of birth exclude all black people who were born in the UK. Because of sex differentials in age at marriage, this group probably includes more married females than married males.

24. Evidence of underenumeration in earlier censuses has been discussed above.

25. This is based on data from the General Household Survey, 1973–75, for marriages or unions where the male was aged less than 45 and on interviewer's assessment of colour. See OPCS (1978a).

26. The use of such data involves several errors. First, these data omit childless marriages, and are biased towards marriages with larger family sizes. Secondly they often omit information about the father of illegitimate children so that many consensual unions are excluded. Thirdly, they use birthplace as a proxy for ethnic origin, the inaccuracies of which are considerable (see below).

27. Bagley omits all illegitimate births from his calculations.

28. Data on births were not available prior to April 1969. There are exceptions to this, namely 1972 when the Ugandan Asians came to Britain and 1975–76 when immigration data show a temporary increase as discussed in Chapter 3.

29. Since there were more males than women in the population, the proportion of women born in the UK would be less than 2.9 per cent.

30. In addition, the 10 per cent omitted from the data in Figure 12a will include many young UK born women.

31. The 1971 Census enumerated 1,151,090 people who were born in the NCWP: 518,480 females and 632,610 males. The OPCS estimated that 877,800 black people were born in the NCWP: 385,000 females and 492,800 males. Hence 273,290 of those born in the NCWP were white (i.e. 24 per cent) and 133,480 (49 per cent) of these were female. See OPCS and General Register Office Scotland (1974) and OPCS (1977). Sex distribution data from OPCS.

32. These proportions are derived from estimates of the black and white NCWP born populations in Lomas (1973). They are internally comparable but are not comparable with the total proportion of 24 per cent because of the more limited criteria used by Lomas to identify white people. In addition, comparison between 1971 and 1982 proportions takes no account of mortality and migration in the intervening years. On the whole, the proportion of white women will have decreased because of black immmigration.

33. The total fertility rate takes into account the age structure of the female population of childbearing age, and represents the average completed family size in the hypothetical situation where current fertility rates apply over the whole span of the childbearing ages. This is not equal to actual completed family size because fertility rates are continually changing. The rates presented here relate births by birthplace of mother to women by birthplace, so that the bias arising from the inclusion in the data of white births to white NCWP born mothers is reduced considerably and consists only of that due to differential fertility between black and white women born in the NCWP.

34. Some evidence in support of this argument is provided by Thompson (1982).

35. This factor is potentially more important for the fertility rates of West Indian women, since possibly half of all births to West Indian women are to UK born West Indian women, than for those of women of other minorities most of whom were born outside the UK.

36. Replacement level is the level of total fertility at which the population replaces itself. If a woman has two children, she and her partner are replaced. In practice, the replacement level is about 2.1 children per woman, to allow for the death of female children prior to reaching childbearing age.

37. The death rate is defined as deaths per 1,000 people. It takes no account of the age structure of the population.

38. These rates are for 1981. The denominators are taken from the 1981 Census, and thus refer to April rather than to a yearly average or mid-year value. The error involved in this is negligible.

39. The standardised mortality ratio compares observed deaths with the number expected if overall mortality rates by age and other factors applied.

40. The perinatal mortality rate is defined as losses in the period from 28 weeks after conception to one week after birth per 1,000 births.

41. The infant mortality rate is the number of deaths at ages under 1 year per 1,000 live births.

5 Conclusions and expectations

In demographic terms, it is clear that the black population in Britain is still very much determined by migration. This is not to say that migration itself is currently an important determinant of the growth and structure of the population, but rather that the effects of migration are still strongly felt. The population is still undergoing the migration process: the demographic structure of the population is still unbalanced and subject to the various indirect effects of migration including changes in the basic demographic processes of birth and death. These imbalances and indirect effects have been documented and discussed above.

Though the initial reasons for migration were largely economic, political factors soon came to determine the nature of the flow. Successive legislation has not only reduced the number of migrants but it has also changed the character of migration. Primary migration for employment, which was mainly male, was soon subjected to immigration control, so that the majority of migrants comprised women and children. This is still the case, though the size of the current migrant flow is virtually zero despite the fact that there are still people waiting to come to Britain, both as dependents of those already here and under the voucher system for UK passport holders from East Africa.

It is largely through the legislative control of migration that political factors have also influenced the demographic structure of the black population. Demographic imbalances persist, most notably in populations such as the Bangladeshi and Pakistani population, which have been subject to the longest delays in terms of the migration of dependants. Less formal means of control of migration for political reasons have also had their effect on the demographic characteristics and hence structure of the population. The requisite medical examinations prior to migration, for example, have contributed to the lower mortality levels of migrants in comparison to the total population.

Looking to the future, it can be said with a considerable degree of certainty that the growth rate of the black population will continue to decline as it has for more than a decade. This is based on expected trends in the three contributory factors to growth: net migration, births and deaths.

Present trends in migration from the NCWP are set to continue by current legislation which becomes more and more restrictive with each minor change in the Immigration Rules. Even without these changes, the 1971 Immigration Act was written with a view to terminating migration from the NCWP altogether. The changes to the Rules merely speed up this process by tying up 'loop-holes' in the legislation through which some migrants have quite legally gained entry to Britain. In considering the growth of a population, however, emigration must also be taken into account. The emigration of black people to the NCWP occurs at a modest level and is unlikely to decrease in view of the fact that emigration to the West Indies is increasing. In terms of net migration with the NCWP, therefore, levels are low and are generally declining. In the absence of unpredictable changes in migration from the NCWP, the contribution of migration to the growth rate is thus likely to continue to decrease.

Further reductions in the growth rate are expected to occur due to a reduced rate of natural increase. Of the three factors which determine the rate of natural increase, namely mortality rates, fertility rates and the structure of the population, all are expected to result in reductions. Mortality rates can be expected to approach those for the total population because of the importance of environmental and health facilities in determining mortality levels. For males, the differential due to both self and imposed selection according to health will clearly disappear as these primary migrants become a smaller proportion of the population and eventually die. For females, mortality can be expected to improve slightly since levels are currently higher than those among the total population. For both sexes, however, mortality levels may in fact stabilise at a slightly higher level than the average for the total population because of the hazards involved in many of the working environments in which black people are employed and because of the generally inferior quality of the housing that is available to them. On balance, therefore, mortality levels for the entire black population can be expected to increase.

Fertility rates in the black population have been falling at least since 1970, when data became available, and are likely to continue this trend. Migrant groups adjust their fertility according to the conditions which they find in their new country of residence, and it is thus reasonable to expect that the more recently migrated groups will undergo a similar fertility transition to those groups which are further advanced in the migration process. In Britain, West Indian born women have reduced their fertility considerably, followed by a marked reduction in the fertility of Indian born women. The more recent women migrants, from Pakistan and Bangladesh, currently have high fertility levels, but reductions are already apparent especially amongst the Pakistani born women. It is expected that these two groups will follow much the same pattern of fertility decline as has already been seen amongst West Indian born and Indian born women. This is not to say that Pakistani and Bangladeshi born women are likely to reduce their fertility to the same low levels as West Indian born women in the next decade or so, but that a similar reduction in relative terms can be expected. Regarding the UK born black women, it is unlikely that their fertility levels will be significantly higher than their mothers', and may indeed be lower if these women further adjust their fertility to the prevailing conditions. It is however, probable that some fertility differentials will remain for some time between the black and total populations because of the importance of cultural factors in determining fertility levels, especially where religious factors are involved. In overall terms, then, the fertility of the black population is likely to continue to decline.

The third factor which determines the rate of natural increase in a population is its demographic structure. This is important because it defines the number of people to which mortality and fertility rates apply. The fact that the black population is aging, with an increasing proportion of people entering the older age groups, will result in a larger number of deaths even when mortality rates are constant. For births, it is the proportion of the population that is female and of child bearing age that is important. In the two largest groups, West Indian and Indian, this proportion is bound to be reduced in the near future because of the smaller numbers of children already born resulting from past reductions in fertility. Even at constant fertility levels, therefore, the number of births will fall.

Of the three factors, the age structure is the most predictable since most of the population of the near future are already born. This factor is also very important especially in a population with considerable demographic imbalances. The effects of the age structure on the rate of natural increase of the black population are such that even if fertility and mortality rates were to change in the opposite direction from that expected, the overall effect could still be to reduce the rate of natural increase. In other words, even if fertility rates were to increase, the birth rate would in the short term decrease due to the smaller numbers of women in the childbearing ages. Similarly, even if mortality rates were to decrease, the death rate would undoubtedly increase during the next decade or so because of the larger number of people in the elderly age groups. The expected increase in mortality and decrease in fertility levels would thus reinforce and quicken the decline in the rate of natural increase.

The 1980–81 growth rate of the black population was 3.8 per cent per annum, two-thirds of which was attributable to natural increase and one-third to net migration. To illustrate what a certain level of growth means in terms of future population size, growth rates can be converted into the length of time required for the population to double. If the 1980–81 growth rate of 3.8 per cent were to continue, the black population would reach double its 1981 size of 2.1 million by the year 1999. This is very unlikely to occur, however, because the growth rate will, in all probability, continue to decrease as it has done, with relatively minor fluctuations, since the late 1960s (see Table 2 above). It has already been seen that the net migration of NCWP citizens is decreasing, and that natural increase will be considerably reduced. If the growth rate were a constant 2.5 per cent, the 1981 black population would double by the year 2009; if the rate were even lower at 1.5 per cent, the black population would reach 2.8

63

million by the turn of the century, and would double by the year 2027. These projected population sizes are crude and are provided merely by way of illustration. The growth rate is not constant but changing, necessitating more complex methods of projecting population size.

Several population projections have been prepared for the black population in recent years. In 1977, it was estimated that there would be about 3.3 million people of NCWP ethnic origin living in Great Britain by the year 2001 (Brass, 1977). This projection was based on the following assumptions: mortality rates were assumed to be constant at the same level as for the total population; fertility was assumed to decline steadily to a total fertility rate of 2.0 by the end of the century; and net migration was assumed to be zero by 1990. With hindsight it can be said that assumed mortality was probably too high, that assumed fertility too low and assumed net migration too low. The margins involved are small, however, and the projected population size of 2.0 million in the year 1981 is only slightly less than the 2.1 million estimated from the 1981 census. Intermediate projected population sizes are shown in Table 9.

Table 9: Projected population sizes, 1971–2001

Year	Year projection made		
	1977	1979 low	1979 high
1971 (base)	1.28	1.28	1.28
1976	1.64	1.64	1.64
1981	2.00	1.96	2.03
1991	2.70	2.47	2.94
2001	3.30	–	–

Source: W. Brass, 'Welcome and Keep Out ...the two Signs on Britain's door', The Listener, 15 September 1977; OPCS, 'Population of New Commonwealth and Pakistani ethnic origin: new projections', Population Trends, 1979, no.16.

The projected population size of 3.3 million by the year 2001 was not the official figure. Also in 1977, the Franks Report suggested that the population of NCWP ethnic origin would be at least 3.8 million by the end of the century. Two years later, in 1979, new official population projections were published, giving a high and a low variant (OPCS, 1979). These projections, which are also shown in Table 9 were only taken to 1991. The assumptions on which they are based are: mortality rates equal to those for the total population and constant; total fertility of NCWP born women declining to 3.2 in 1981 and 2.7 in 1991, in the high variant, or to 2.8 in 1981 and 2.1 in 1991 in the low variant, with levels for UK born women half-way between these and replacement level; and net migration of a constant 40,000 per year in the high variant, or a steady decline to 15,000 by the year 1982 and constant thereafter in the low variant. It is seen from Table 9 that the two variants, high and low, produced by these assumptions span the 1977 projected population sizes. Since the 1981 population was estimated at 2.1 million, it seems that the 1977 projection is the more realistic.

These projections provide information on the size of the black population rather than on its structure.[1] Whilst size is indeed the result of the various political factors that have shaped migration and the migration process, it is not an important aspect of the demographic development of the black population. Changes in the structure of the population and in its vital rates are of much greater significance. It has been seen how the direct and indirect effects of migration have shaped the current population, providing an understanding of the structural imbalances that exist which in turn give rise to inevitable changes in the character of the population. Some of these changes are large and rapid enough to be of significance in the provision of local or special services, such as the reduced number of births and numbers of school children, whilst others are more gradual, such as the increasing number of elderly people. An awareness of the underlying causes and nature of such changes is important in the planning of services and in the anticipation and identification of any special needs.

Whilst the effects of the migration process and its political determinants will be felt demographically for several generations, their strength will inevitably be reduced with time. It cannot be assumed, however, that the black population will become demographically indistinguishable from the total by the next century.[2] Cultural factors may maintain some degree of fertility differential for certain groups, and the possibility of differentials due to racial discrimination cannot be dismissed. Whilst there is insufficient evidence to be decisive, the very low levels of West Indian fertility and the recent net emigration amongst this group may be the early signs of the demographic consequences of the political situation in which they find themselves. Whether or not this proves to be so, it is clear that the demographic structure and character of the black population has been determined by the political factors affecting migration and the migration process, and that these factors will continue to influence the population for many years to come.

Notes

1. The OPCS projections provide minimal information on age structure, and discuss the populations of 'wholly NCWP ethnic origin' and of 'partly NCWP ethnic origin' separately (OPCS, 1979).

2. For example, on fertility, Overton (1980) suggests that 'the vast majority of families with parents of NCWP ethnic origin (will) be the same size as those of other British families of the same social class' by the next century; and the OPCS projections are based on a 'process of convergence towards national average fertility'.

Appendix to part I

Abbreviations

OC	Old Commonwealth
NCWP	New Commonwealth and Pakistan
UKPH	UK passport holders
UKBG	UK born grandparent
F	females
M	males
T	total
..	insignificant number
n.s.a.	not separately available
n.a.	not available
–	not applicable

Notes

- Pakistan left the Commonwealth in 1973, but is included in the NCWP throughout these data unless otherwise stated; similarly, Pakistan is excluded from data on aliens unless otherwise stated.
- Totals may not equal the sum of separate parts due to rounding.
- Tables A7 to A9 contain the abbreviation .. (insignificant number) as well as 0's and very small numbers. This arises from the system of data presentation employed by the Home Office in publishing immigration data. The use here of .. to signify an insignificant but unknown and possibly zero number is retained to avoid confusion to readers making use of these tables. In other tables, .. means a small, but positive number.

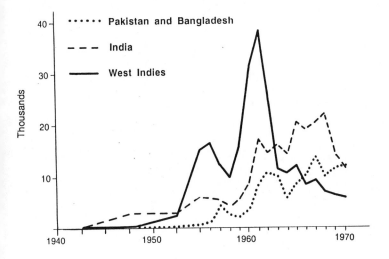

Figure 1: **Population with one or both parents born in NCWP by birthplace by year of entry to UK, 1971, Great Britain**

Source: G.B. Lomas, Census 1971: The Coloured Population of Great Britain (London: The Runnymede Trust, 1973).

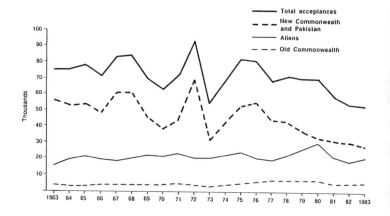

Figure 2:   **Acceptances for settlement in the United Kingdom, 1963–1983**

Source: Home Office, <u>Control of Immigration Statistics</u> (London: HMSO, annual).

Notes: Figures for the Old Commonwealth underestimate the actual level of Immigration because many Old Commonwealth citizens are patrial and hence free from immigration control. Total acceptances are underestimates of immigration for this reason and because the Irish are also excluded from immigration control.

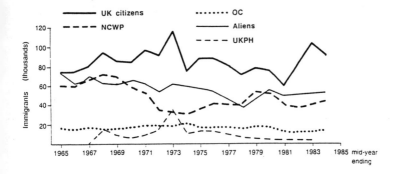

Figure 3: **Immigration to the UK by citizenship, 1964/5 to 1983/4**

Source: OPCS, International Migration, Series MN (London: HMSO).

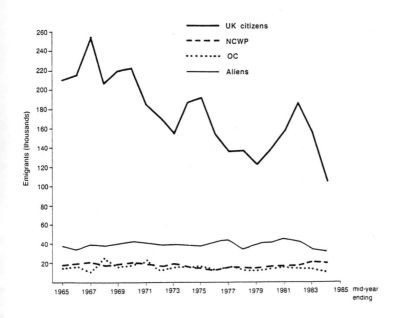

Figure 4: **Emigration from the UK by citizenship, 1964/5 to 1983/4**

Source: OPCS, International Migration, Series MN (London: HMSO).

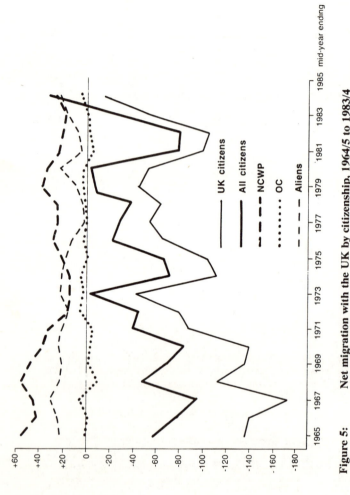

Figure 5: Net migration with the UK by citizenship, 1964/5 to 1983/4
Source: OPCS, International Migration, Series MN (London: HMSO)

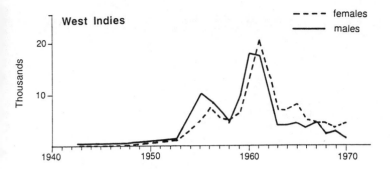

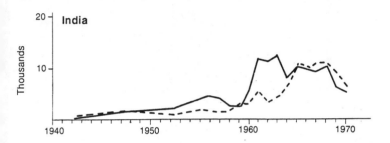

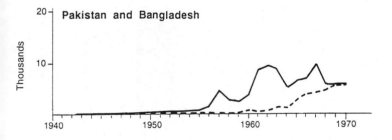

Figure 6: **Population with one or both parents born in NCWP born in West Indies, India, and Pakistan and Bangladesh by year of entry to UK by sex, 1971, Great Britain**

Source: G.B. Lomas, <u>Census 1971: The Coloured Population of Great Britain</u> (London: Runnymede Trust, 1973)

73

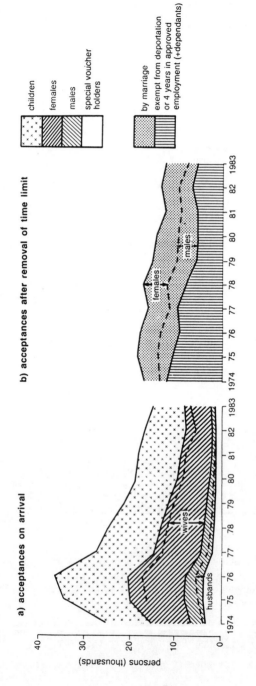

Figure 7: **Acceptances for settlement in the UK of citizens of the New Commonwealth and Pakistan, 1974–1983**

Source: Home Office, <u>Control of Immmigration Statistics</u> (London: HMSO, annual).

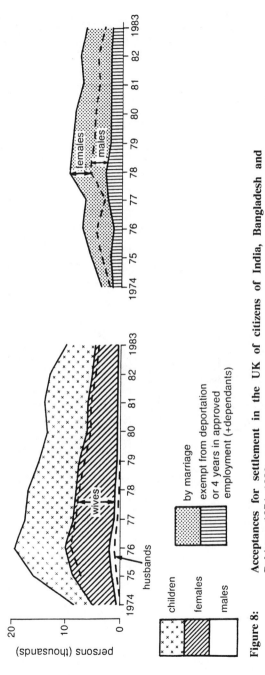

a) acceptances on arrival

b) acceptances on removal of time limit

Figure 8: Acceptances for settlement in the UK of citizens of India, Bangladesh and Pakistan, 1974–1983

Source: Home Office, <u>Control of Immigration Statistics</u> (London: HMSO, annual).

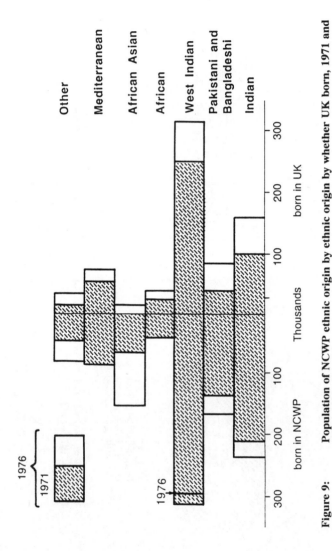

Figure 9: Population of NCWP ethnic origin by ethnic origin by whether UK born, 1971 and 1976, Great Britain

Source: OPCS, Immigrant Statistics Unit

76

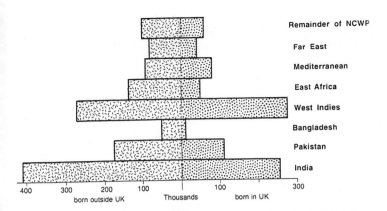

Figure 10: **a) Population living in households with NCWP born head by birthplace of head of household by whether born in UK, 1981, Great Britain**

Source: OPCS, Census 1981: Country of Birth: Great Britain (London: HMSO, 1983)

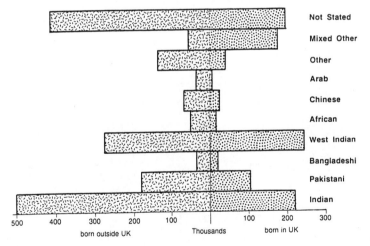

Figure 10: **b) Population by ethnic origin by whether born in UK, 1981, Great Britain**

Source: OPCS Monitor LFS 82/1, Labour Force Survey: country of birth and ethnic origin (London: HMSO, 22 February 1983)

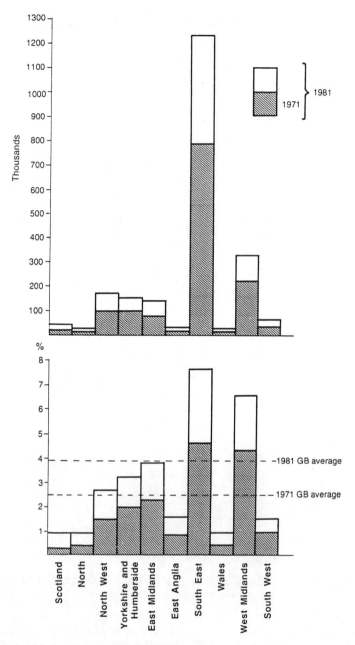

Figure 11: Regional distribution of the black population, 1971 and 1981, Great Britain

Source: 1971 Census, 1981 Census

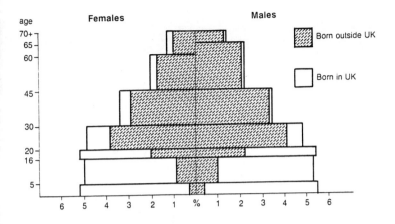

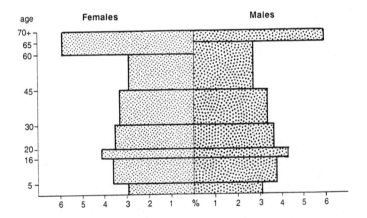

Figure 12:   a) Population living in households with NCWP born head by age and sex by whether born in UK, 1981, Great Britain

b) Total usually resident population, 1981, Great Britain

Source: OPCS, <u>Census 1981: country of birth: Great Britain</u> (London: HMSO, 1983)

79

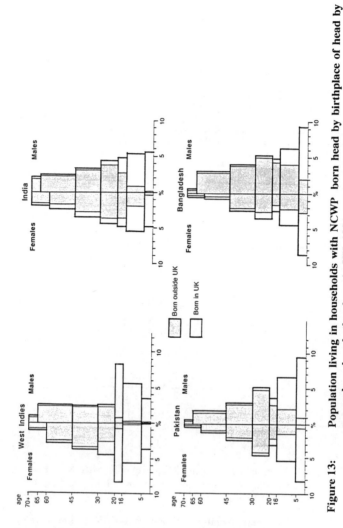

Figure 13: Population living in households with NCWP born head by birthplace of head by age and sex by whether born in UK, 1981, Great Britain

Source: OPCS, Census 1981: Country of birth: Great Britain (London: HMSO, 1983)

80

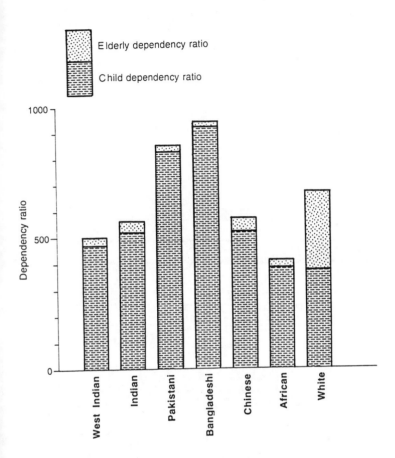

Figure 14: **Dependency ratios by ethnic group, 1981, Great Britain**

Source: OPCS Monitor LFS 83.1, <u>Labour Force Survey 1981:</u>
             <u>country of birth and ethnic origin</u> (London: HMSO, 22
             February 1983)

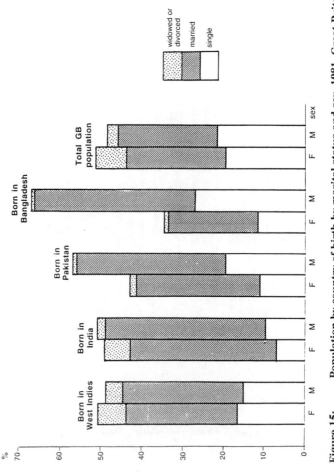

Figure 15: Population by country of birth by marital status and sex, 1981, Great Britain

Source: OPCS, Census 1981: country of birth: Great Britain (London: HMSO, 1983)

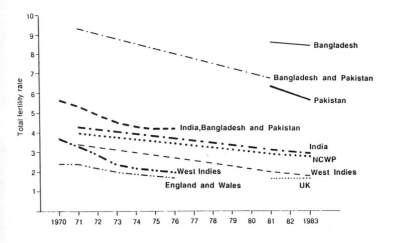

Figure 16:   **Estimated total fertility rates by birthplace of mother, England and Wales, 1970–1983**

Source: L. Iliffe, 'Estimated fertility rates of Asian and West Indian immigrant women in Britain, 1969–1974', Journal of Biosocial Science, 1978, 10, 189–197; OPCS Monitor FM1 84/9, Births by birthplace of parents, 1983 (London: HMSO, 11 December 1984)

Note: Iliffe's estimates are updated to 1976 by the author (solid line); OPCS estimates are not necessarily representative of actual trend between 1971 and 1982 (dotted line)

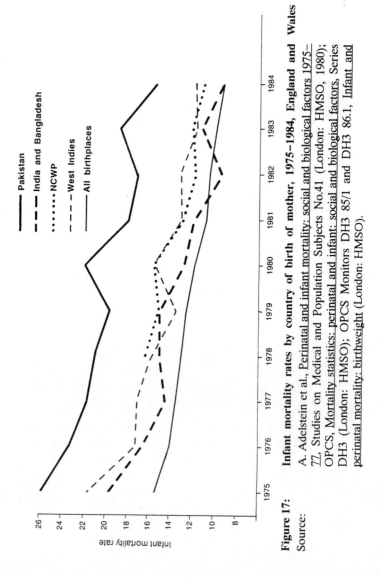

Figure 17: Infant mortality rates by country of birth of mother, 1975–1984, England and Wales

Source: A. Adelstein et al, Perinatal and infant mortality: social and biological factors 1975–77, Studies on Medical and Population Subjects No.41 (London: HMSO, 1980); OPCS, Mortality statistics: perinatal and infant: social and biological factors, Series DH3 (London: HMSO); OPCS Monitors DH3 85/1 and DH3 86.1, Infant and perinatal mortality: birthweight (London: HMSO).

Table A1 Population with one or both parents born in the New Commonwealth and Pakistan by birthplace by sex by reported year of entry into the UK, 1971, Great Britain, thousands

Birthplace

Year of entry	West Indies F	West Indies M	West Indies T	India F	India M	India T	Pakistan and Bangladesh F	Pakistan and Bangladesh M	Pakistan and Bangladesh T
1940-44	0.4	1.5	1.9	1.4	0.2	1.6	0.1	0.4	0.5
1945-49	1.2	1.4	2.6	8.2	7.2	15.4	0.3	0.1	0.4
1950-54	5.0	8.6	13.6	4.2	11.2	15.4	0.4	2.2	2.6
1955	4.9	10.3	15.2	1.8	4.2	6.0	0.2	0.6	0.8
1956	7.6	9.0	16.6	1.3	4.5	5.8	..	1.2	1.2
1957	5.4	6.8	12.2	1.7	4.0	5.7	..	4.4	4.4
1958	4.9	4.7	9.6	1.7	2.4	4.1	0.1	2.3	2.4
1959	6.7	9.4	16.1	3.0	2.7	5.7	..	2.1	2.1
1960	13.0	18.2	31.2	3.0	5.3	8.3	0.5	3.3	3.8
1961	20.6	17.6	38.2	5.7	11.4	17.1	0.2	9.6	9.8
1962	14.4	11.0	25.4	3.3	11.0	14.3	0.4	10.3	10.7
1963	7.1	4.1	11.2	4.4	11.8	16.2	1.2	8.9	10.1
1964	6.9	3.8	10.7	6.5	7.9	14.4	1.0	5.0	6.0
1965	7.8	4.4	12.2	10.4	10.1	20.5	2.4	6.5	8.9
1966	5.1	3.6	8.7	9.8	9.6	19.4	3.8	6.6	10.4
1967	4.7	4.7	9.4	11.0	9.2	20.2	4.0	9.9	13.9
1968	4.6	2.4	7.0	11.1	10.0	22.1	4.4	5.7	10.1
1969	3.6	2.7	6.3	8.8	5.9	14.7	5.6	5.6	11.2
1970	4.4	1.7	6.1	6.6	4.9	11.5	5.8	5.9	11.7

Source: G.B.G. Lomas, Census 1971: The Coloured Population of Great Britain (London: The Runnymede Trust, 1973).

Note: These data include only those people resident in Great Britain and enumerated in the 1971 Census. They thus exclude people who came to Britain but who left prior to 1971. Year of entry is as reported, and is not necessarily accurate. 1970 data obtained by adjusting Lomas's data for the fifteen months from January 1970 to Census day 1971.

Table A2 Acceptances for settlement in the UK by citizenship, 1962-1983

Year	OC	NCWP	Aliens	Total
1962*	2,361*	16,453*	15,606	34,420*
1963	3,735	56,071	15,354	75,160
1964	3,060	52,840	19,210	75,110
1965	3,454	53,887	20,629	77,970
1966	4,214	48,104	18,952	71,270
1967	4,335	60,633	18,346	83,314
1968	3,761	60,620	20,093	84,474
1969	3,581	44,503	21,862	69,946
1970	4,497	37,893	20,917	63,307
1971	4,577	44,261	23,467	72,305
1972	3,989	68,519	19,681	92,189
1973	3,099	32,247	19,816	55,162
1974	3,948	42,531	22,491	68,970
1975	5,387	53,265	23,877	82,529
1976	5,967	55,013	19,927	80,907
1977	6,572	44,155	18,807	69,534
1978	7,453	42,939	22,199	72,591
1979	6,972	37,047	25,874	69,893
1980	6,900	33,700	29,320	69,920
1981	5,350	31,380	21,790	58,520
1982	5,150	30,410	18,320	53,880
1983	5,800	27,550	20,120	53,460

Source: Home Office. (London: HMSO. Annual):-

1962-67. Commonwealth Immigrants Act 1962. Statistics

1968-72. Commonwealth Immigrants Acts 1962 and 1968. Statistics

1973-74. Immigration Statistics

1975-83. Control of Immigration Statistics

Note: Commonwealth Immigrants Act 1962 came into force on 1 July 1962: data marked * refer to July-December only. NCWP includes UK passport holders from 1 March 1968. NCWP from 1973 includes those with a grandparent born in the UK. most of whom are white: the numbers involved are small: see Table A6. OC includes only those OC citizens who are subject to immigration control (ie non-patrials). The Irish are excluded from these data since they are free of immigration control.

Table A3 Immigration to the UK by citizenship, 1964/5 to 1983/4, thousands

Mid-year to mid-year	OC	NCWP	Aliens	UK: UKPH	UK: Other	UK: All	Total
1964/5	16.0	73.5	60.0	--	73.7	73.7	223.2
1965/6	14.7	61.6	59.5	--	73.8	73.8	209.5
1966/7	17.4	66.4	69.5	--	78.8	78.8	232.0
1967/8	15.2	71.0	61.6	15.0	78.0	93.0	241.3
1968/9	14.7	68.0	61.0	8.0	75.9	84.0	227.3
1969/70	16.1	58.0	66.1	6.0	77.3	83.0	223.9
1970/1	17.9	52.0	60.6	9.0	87.5	96.0	226.6
1971/2	19.1	34.0	53.4	16.0	74.1	90.0	196.2
1972/3	18.3	32.2	61.2	33.6	79.6	113.2	224.9
1973/4	20.8	29.6	58.1	10.2	64.1	74.3	182.7
1974/5	16.1	35.0	55.6	12.7	74.8	87.5	194.1
1975/6	15.7	40.9	52.5	12.4	75.0	87.4	196.6
1976/7	15.6	39.4	45.4	8.8	71.6	80.4	180.8
1977/8	14.8	39.3	37.3	5.6	64.7	70.3	161.7
1978/9	16.6	52.1	48.3	4.3	72.4	76.7	193.7
1979/80	15.9	49.6	63.5	3.4	72.6	76.0	205.1
1980/1	10.7	39.0	48.2	2.8	55.1	57.9	155.8
1981/2	11.0	36.1	49.0	3.0	78.0	81.0	177.0
1982/3	11.0	38.0*	50.0*	3.0*	99.0*	102.0	200.0
1983/4	13.0	43.0*	53.0*	n.a.	n.a.	90.0	199.0

Source: OPCS, International Migration, Series MN (London: HMSO).

* Author's estimate

Table A4 Emigration from the UK by citizenship, 1964/5 to 1983/4, thousands

Mid-year to mid-year	OC	NCWP	Aliens	UK	Total
1964/5	15.3	18.1	37.5	210.0	281.0
1965/6	16.6	19.3	35.2	214.9	286.1
1966/7	12.0	21.4	39.2	253.7	326.3
1967/8	24.9	16.9	38.2	206.0	286.0
1968/9	16.7	19.1	40.0	219.9	295.6
1969/70	19.4	21.2	41.9	223.1	305.6
1970/1	22.8	18.5	39.7	185.0	265.9
1971/2	13.2	17.4	38.5	171.3	240.4
1972/3	15.7	19.0	39.5	155.4	229.5
1973/4	14.9	15.9	37.5	186.4	254.7
1974/5	16.5	15.4	38.1	191.0	261.0
1975/6	12.6	12.1	41.0	154.1	219.8
1976/7	15.6	15.0	43.3	134.6	208.5
1977/8	13.4	14.6	34.2	135.6	197.9
1978/9	12.4	13.7	39.5	121.8	187.4
1979/80	13.2	16.0	40.2	139.4	208.8
1980/1	16.0	16.4	44.3	157.9	234.5
1981/2	14.0	16.1	42.0	186.0	257.0
1982/3	13.0	20.0*	33.0*	156.0	222.0
1983/4	9.0	18.0*	31.0*	105.0	167.0

Source: OPCS, International Migration, Series MN (London: HMSO).

*Author's estimate.

Note: Emigration of UKPHs is negligible.

Table A5 Net migration with the UK by citizenship, 1964/5 to 1983/4, thousands

Mid-year to mid-year	OC	NCWP	Aliens	UK: UKPH	UK: Other	UK: All	Total
1964/5	1.0	55.0	22.0	-	-136.0	-136.0	-57.8
1965/6	-2.0	42.0	24.0	-	-141.0	-141.0	-76.5
1966/7	5.0	45.0	30.0	-	-175.0	-175.0	-94.3
1967/8	-10.0	55.0	23.0	15.0	-128.0	-113.0	-44.7
1968/9	-2.0	48.0	21.0	8.0	-144.0	-136.0	-68.3
1969/70	-3.0	37.0	24.0	6.0	-146.0	-140.0	-81.7
1970/1	-5.0	33.0	21.0	9.0	-98.0	-89.0	-39.4
1971/2	6.0	16.0	15.0	16.0	-97.0	-81.0	-44.2
1972/3	2.6	13.2	21.8	33.6	-75.8	-42.2	-4.6
1973/4	5.8	13.7	20.6	10.2	-122.3	-112.1	-72.0
1974/5	-0.4	19.6	17.5	12.7	-116.3	-103.6	-66.9
1975/6	3.1	28.8	11.6	12.4	-79.1	-66.7	-23.3
1976/7	0.0	24.4	2.1	8.8	-63.0	-54.2	-27.7
1977/8	1.4	24.6	3.1	5.6	-70.9	-65.3	-36.2
1978/9	4.2	38.3	8.9	4.3	-49.4	-45.1	6.3
1979/80	2.7	33.6	23.3	3.4	-66.7	-63.3	-3.7
1980/1	-5.2	22.7	3.9	2.8	-102.8	-100.0	-78.7
1981/2	-2.0	20.1	7.0	3.0	-108.0	-105.0	-80.0
1982/3	-2.0	18.0	17.0	3.0*	-57.0	-54.0	-21.0
1983/4	4.0	25.0	22.0	n.a.	n.a	-15.0	32.0

Source: OPCS, International Migration. Series MN (London: HMSO).

* Author's estimate

Table A6 Acceptances for settlement of citizens of NCWP by reason for entry (a) on arrival and (b) on removal of time limit, 1973-1983

(a) on arrival

Year	children	women: wives	women: others	men: husbands	men: others	special voucher	total	UKBG
1973	11,477	11,172			5,057	1,994	32,167	80
1974	9,987	9,031		517	2,342	3,379	25,257	49
1975	14,337	8,592	3,638	1,445	2,611	3,789	34,412	98
1976	16,088	9,972	3,041	1,832	2,051	3,708	36,692	125
1977	13,012	8,670	1,675	853	1,332	2,032	27,574	168
1978	11,744	8,198	1,560	539	1,288	1,752	25,081	192
1979	9,873	7,307	1,264	520	903	1,604	21,471	165
1980	9,420	5,890	1,230	280	750	1,390	18,960	130
1981	9,610	5,780	870	110	680	1,360	18,410	100
1982	8,860	4,770	1,150	20	720	1,290	16,810	70
1983	7,080	4,650	1,020	20	670	1,540	14,980	130

(b) on removal of time limit

Year	employ.	marriage: women	marriage: men	exempt deport.	other: children	other: women	other: men	total	UKBG
1973	45	2,302	120	n.s.a		n.s.a	7,196*	n.s.a	n.s.a
1974	87	3,498	1,515	7,390	725	4,161*	1,090	17,182	43
1975	191	4,151	3,598	7,843	883	973	720	18,729	26
1976	259	4,532	4,496	6,555	825	772	569	18,159	37
1977	758	4,930	1,615	6,953	754	781	679	16,360	53
1978	1,877	5,456	4,254	3,366	784	1,182	612	17,598	68
1979	2,282	5,389	4,372	684	905	1,110	880	15,354	65
1980	2,110	4,950	4,350	n.s.a.	960	1,330	760	14,580	60
1981	2,260	4,110	3,130	n.s.a.	1,110	1,430	1,160	12,810	60
1982	2,260	4,160	2,960	n.s.a.	1,000	1,930	840	13,470	60
1983	2,240	4,970	2,170	n.s.a.	1,050	1,120		12,390	50

Source: Home Office. Control of Immigration Statistics (London: HMSO, annual).

Note: 1973 totals are not available for (a) and (b) separately. UK born grandparents data include Pakistan until 31 August 1973 only. 1974 exemptions from deportation are also included in other (women and men, marked*). From 1980, people exempted from deportation are included in others (women and men).

Table A7 Acceptances for settlement on arrival of citizens of India, Bangladesh and Pakistan by reason for entry, 1973-1983

Year	children	women: wives	women: others	men: husbands	men: others	total	UKBG
India							
1973	1,883		2,927		485	6,217	23
1974	1,479		2,248	110	320	4,157	19
1975	2,596	2,220	721	535	406	6,478	59
1976	2,632	2,162	684	718	336	6,532	50
1977	1,415	1,379	358	299	200	3,651	54
1978	1,289	1,439	380	112	216	3,436	78
1979	1,031	1,396	314	112	152	3,005	70
1980	810	1,070	180	60	100	2,230	60
1981	660	920	180	30	90	1,870	20
1982	450	600	190	..	70	1,320	20
1983	450	880	190	..	90	1,620	60
Bangladesh							
1973	1,014		596		119	1,727	2
1974	445	55	220	3	40	763	0
1975	1,801	867	167	13	129	2,977	1
1976	2,208	1,174	136	25	137	3,680	0
1977	1,872	920	34	19	134	2,979	1
1978	2,461	1,344	54	8	167	4,034	5
1979	2,170	1,289	59	23	147	3,688	4
1980	3,140	1,520	140	10	180	5,000	..
1981	3,600	1,660	110	20	230	5,620	..
1982	4,480	1,810	280	..	240	6,820	0
1983	2,980	1,400	180	..	120	4,670	0

Table A7 (Continued)

Year	children	women: wives	women: others	men: husbands	men: others	total	UKBG
Pakistan							
1973	1,562	1,684	273	3,632	6	3,561	–
1974	1,566	477	1,322	11	185	6,183	–
1975	2,912	2,516	407	94	254	9,503	–
1976	4,681	3,846	412	232	332	10,947	–
1977	5,807	4,533	256	65	286	9,483	–
1978	5,052	3,820	301	46	264	8,166	–
1979	4,389	3,277	280	45	175	6,360	–
1980	3,580	2,140	460	30	160	6,520	–
1981	3,880	2,220	240	20	170	4,690	–
1982	2,680	1,520	310	..	180	3,830	–
1983	2,210	1,260	240	..	110		–
India, Bangladesh and Pakistan							
1973	4,459	5,207			877	11,576	31
1974	3,490	4,322		124		8,481	19
1975	7,609	5,603	1,295	642	545	15,938	60
1976	9,521	7,182	1,232	975	789	19,715	50
1977	9,094	6,832	648	383	805	17,577	55
1978	8,802	6,603	769	166	620	17,036	83
1979	7,590	5,962	653	180	696	14,859	74
1980	7,530	4,730	780	100	474	13,580	60
1981	8,140	4,800	530	70	440	14,030	20
1982	7,630	3,930	780	0	490	12,830	20
1983	5,630	3,540	610	10	330	10,120	60

Source: Home Office, Control of Immigration Statistics (London: HMSO, annual).

Note: 1973 data not available separately for acceptances on arrival and on removal of time limit (Table A8): total shown here.

UK born grandparent data for Pakistan until 31 August 1973 only.

Table A8 Acceptances for settlement on removal of time limit of citizens of India, Bangladesh and Pakistan by reason for entry, 1973-1983

Year	4 years employ.	marriage: women	marriage: men	exempt from deport.	other: children	other: women	other: men	total	UKBG
India									
1973	13	906	3	n.s.a.	n.s.a.	n.s.a.	n.s.a.	n.s.a.	n.s.a
1974	18	1,249	261	n.s.a.	49	146	749	2,472	6
1975	28	1,104	1,450	750	88	137	96	3,653	5
1976	61	1,638	1,977	444	89	132	93	4,434	5
1977	265	1,777	628	532	90	207	115	3,614	20
1978	846	2,110	2,377	295	184	398	141	6,351	21
1979	838	2,194	2,378	82	239	340	116	6,187	6
1980	720	2,030	2,030	n.s.a.	270	470	160	5,670	10
1981	710	1,520	1,530	n.s.a.	340	480	120	4,700	20
1982	590	1,270	1,240	n.s.a.	270	560	130	4,060	10
1983	570	1,710	690	n.s.a.	320	280	110	3,690	10
Bangladesh									
1973	7	15	0	n.s.a.	n.s.a.	n.s.a.	n.s.a.	n.s.a.	n.s.a.
1974	7	46	14	n.s.a.	4	24	162	257	2
1975	4	86	34	153	8	4	9	298	0
1976	10	55	73	117	15	11	13	294	1
1977	48	60	20	163	20	7	7	325	1
1978	71	80	49	99	28	11	8	346	0
1979	49	44	67	12	15	15	21	223	0
1980	30	30	80	n.s.a.	20	10	30	210	0
1981	20	30	40	n.s.a.	40	20	40	190	0
1982	20	30	60	n.s.a.	30	20	30	200	:
1983	30	40	50	n.s.a.	30	20	30	200	0

Table A8 (continued)

Pakistan

Year	4 years employ.	marriage: women	marriage: men	exempt from deport.	other: children	other: women	other: men	total	UKBG
1973	6	103	4	n.s.a.	57	n.s.a.	414	n.s.a.	n.s.a.
1974	27	155	102	n.s.a.	54	85	28	840	–
1975	27	366	515	512	58	39	57	1,541	–
1976	54	798	685	474	58	70	75	2,196	–
1977	78	1,121	315	548	86	98	65	2,384	–
1978	138	1,642	579	291	86	141	36	2,942	–
1979	138	1,735	577	93	80	114	90	2,779	–
1980	70	1,600	740	45	80	105	90	2,730	–
1981	90	1,420	570	20	130	120	90	2,450	–
1982	120	1,740	800	10	170	130	90	3,060	–
1983	80	1,650	630	n.s.a.	90	90	80	2,610	–

India, Bangladesh and Pakistan

Year	4 years employ.	marriage: women	marriage: men	exempt from deport.	other: children	other: women	other: men	total	UKBG
1973	26	1,024	7	n.s.a.	110	n.s.a.	1,325	n.s.a.	n.s.a.
1974	52	1,450	377	n.s.a.	150	255	133	3,569	8
1975	59	1,902	1,653	1,415	162	180	163	5,492	5
1976	125	2,491	2,735	1,035	168	213	197	6,924	6
1977	391	3,049	963	1,243	298	312	214	6,323	21
1978	1,055	3,832	3,005	685	340	550	173	9,639	21
1979	1,025	3,973	3,022	187	370	469	280	9,189	6
1980	820	3,660	2,850	n.s.a.	510	585	260	8,620	10
1981	820	2,970	2,140	n.s.a.	470	620	250	7,330	20
1982	730	3,040	2,100	n.s.a.	440	710	220	7,310	10
1983	680	3,390	1,370	n.s.a.		390		6,500	10

Source: Home Office. Control of Immigration Statistics (London HMSO, annual).

Note: 1973 data not available separately for acceptances on arrival (Table A7) and on the removal of time limit: total shown in Table A7.

UK born grandparent data for Pakistan until 31 August 1973 only.

1974 and 1980-1983 exemptions from deportation are included in others (women and men).

Table A9 Acceptances for settlement of citizens of the West Indies by reason for entry (a) on arrival and (b) on removal of time limit, 1973-1983

(a) on arrival

Year	children	women: wives	women: others	men: husbands	men: others	total	UKBG
1973	1,537	633	255	206	110	2,680	5
1974	1,110	60	175	43	110	1,578	5
1975	1,093	190	139	106	85	1,674	6
1976	831	211	130	122	63	1,388	30
1977	568	194	98	88	71	1,043	22
1978	510	175	96	66	51	943	23
1979	325	149	80	64	40	685	18
1980	290	140	50	30	20	860	10
1981	230	70	30	..	..	380	..
1982	150	50	20	..	10	250	..
1983	120	70	..	..	..	240	..

(b) on removal of time limit

Year	4 years employ.	marriage: women	marriage: men	exempt from deport.	other: children	other: women	other: men	total	UKBG
1973	4	289	4	n.s.a.	n.s.a.	n.s.a	n.s.a.	n.s.a	n.s.a.
1974	3	448	115	n.s.a.	44	1,210	328	2,148	9
1975	10	405	199	1,221	62	79	49	2,016	2
1976	6	284	151	711	42	54	25	1,273	6
1977	31	287	61	656	31	72	30	1,168	4
1978	70	229	124	260	29	65	29	806	4
1979	66	159	171	46	32	75	28	578	2
1980	130	160	170	n.s.a.	30	100	50	650	..
1981	120	120	130	n.s.a.	50	130	70	600	..
1982	110	70	80	n.s.a.	50	120	50	510	..
1983	90	160	80	n.s.a.	40	90	40	510	0

Source: Home office. Control of Immigration Statistics (London: HMSO, annual).

Note: 1973 not available for (a) and (b) separately.
1974 and 1980-1983 exemptions from deportation included in others (women and men).

Table A10 Regional distribution of the black population, 1971 and 1981, Great Britain

Region	1971 population thousands	1971 % of total	1981 population thousands	1981 % of total	% increase in population	% increase in %
Scotland	18	0.3	46	0.9	156	300
North	14	0.4	26	0.9	86	125
North West	98	1.5	169	2.7	72	80
Yorks & Humberside	97	2.0	154	3.2	59	60
East Midlands	78	2.3	141	3.8	81	65
East Anglia	14	0.8	28	1.6	100	100
South East	786	4.6	1,228	7.6	56	65
Wales	12	0.4	24	0.9	100	125
West Midlands	222	4.3	327	6.5	47	51
South West	33	0.9	64	1.5	94	67
Great Britain	1,371	2.5	2,207	4.2	61	68

Source: OPCS, Immigrant Statistics Unit (1976; 1977: see notes below); OPCS (occasional) Census 1981 County Reports. HMSO. London.

Notes: 1971 data refer to the population of NCWP ethnic origin. The regional distribution of this population is given in OPCS Immigrant Statistics Unit. 'Country of birth and colour 1971-4'. Population Trends, 1975, no. 2. and these have been revised by a factor of 1.371/1.486 according to new estimates given in OPCS Immigrant Statistics Unit. 'New Commonwealth and Pakistani Population Estimates'. Population Trends, 1977, no. 9. The 1981 data refer to the population living in households headed by a NCWP born head. These two sets of data are not strictly comparable. The 1981 data for Great Britain are unadjusted for known biases in order that the GB figure should be comparable with the regional data. After adjustment, the 1981 GB population is 2.1 million or 3.9 per cent of the total population.

Table A11 Population of NCWP ethnic origin by ethnic origin by whether born in the UK or NCWP, 1971 and 1976, Great Britain, thousands

Ethnic origin	mid-1971 born in NCWP	mid-1971 born in UK	mid-1976 born in NCWP	mid-1976 born in UK
Indian	209.1	98.0	230.6	159.7
Pakistani & Bangladeshi	131.5	39.5	162.9	83.0
West Indian	303.6	249.6	291.0	313.6
African	46.3	23.3	58.0	39.0
African Asian	62.7	5.2	145.8	14.2
Mediterranean	83.5	56.1	84.9	74.5
Other	46.4	16.7	87.2	33.2
NCWP	883.1	488.5	1054.6	717.2

Source: OPCS, Immigrant Statistics Unit, unpublished table.

Table A12 Population living in households with a NCWP born head by birthplace of head of household by whether born in UK or outside UK, 1981, Great Britain

Birthplace of household head	Born outside UK	Born in UK
India	412,498	261,206
Pakistan	177,209	118,252
Bangladesh	47,622	16,939
West Indies	272,186	273,558
East Africa	132,648	48,673
Mediterranean	90,763	79,315
Far East	80,381	39,742
Remainder of NCWP	98,346	57,907
NCWP	1,311,653	895,592

Source: OPCS, Census 1981: Country of birth: Great Britain (London: HMSO, 1983d)

Table A13 Population by ethnic origin by whether born in UK, 1981, Great Britain, thousands

Ethnic origin	Born outside UK	Born in UK
Indian	499	220
Pakistani	180	103
Bangladeshi	33	19
West Indian	275	244
African	48	17
Chinese	67	24
Arab	33	3
Other	136	41
Mixed	57	177
Not Stated	412	196

Source: OPCS Monitor LFS 83/1. Labour Force Survey: Country of birth and ethnic origin (London: HMSO. 22 February 1983a)

Table A14 Population living in households with a NCWP born head by age and sex by whether born in UK compared to total usually resident population by age and sex, 1981, Great Britain, percentages

Age	Living with NCWP born head				Total usually resident population	
	Females		Males			
	Born outside UK	Born in UK	Born outside UK	Born in UK	Females	Males
0- 4	0.3	4.9	0.4	5.1	2.9	3.1
5-15	1.9	9.1	2.3	9.4	8.0	8.4
16-19	1.6	2.6	1.8	2.6	3.3	3.4
20-29	7.7	2.1	8.3	1.4	7.0	7.1
30-44	8.6	1.6	9.8	0.2	9.8	9.9
45-R	5.0	0.9	8.5	0.1	8.8	11.0
R+	2.0	0.5	1.3	0.1	11.5	5.8
All	27.2	21.7	32.3	18.9	51.3	48.7

Source: OPCS. Census 1981: country of birth: Great Britain (London: HMSO. 1983d)
Note: R = retirement age (60 for women. 65 for men)

Table A15 Population living in households with NCWP born head by birthplace of head by age and sex by whether born in UK, 1981, Great Britain, percentages

	Females		Males		Females		Males	
	Born outside UK	Born in UK	Born outside UK	Born in UK	Born outside UK	Born In UK	Born outside UK	Born in UK
Age	Household head born in West Indies				Household head born in Indian			
0- 4	0.1	3.3	0.1	3.3	0.2	4.8	0.2	5.0
5-15	0.4	12.0	0.4	12.0	2.0	9.4	2.1	9.7
16-19	0.6	5.9	0.6	6.0	2.2	1.7	2.2	1.8
20-29	5.7	2.9	4.6	2.2	7.6	1.3	7.9	1.0
30-44	9.2	1.3	7.7	0.2	8.6	1.8	9.6	0.2
45-R	7.5	0.6	10.5	0.1	5.1	1.2	8.7	0.1
R+	1.7	0.2	1.0	..	2.9	0.8	2.0	0.1
All	25.1	26.3	24.7	23.9	28.5	20.9	32.7	17.9
	Household head born in Pakistan				Household head born in Bangladesh			
0- 4	0.9	8.1	1.0	8.5	1.8	6.8	2.1	7.1
5-15	3.2	9.0	4.7	9.9	5.2	4.6	8.8	4.9
16-19	1.7	0.8	2.2	0.8	1.7	0.4	3.4	0.4
20-29	8.6	0.7	9.7	0.4	6.7	0.5	9.9	0.3
30-44	6.8	0.8	8.7	0.1	7.0	0.5	11.8	0.1
45-R	3.3	0.5	7.7	0.1	2.1	0.3	12.3	0.1
R+	0.7	0.3	0.7	0.1	0.3.	0.1	0.6	..
All	25.3	20.1	34.7	19.9	24.8	13.3	49.0	12.9

Source: OPCS. Census 1981: Country of birth: Great Britain (London:HMSO. 1983d)

Note: R = retirement age (60 for women, 65 for men)

Table A16 Population by ethnic origin by age, 1981, Great Britain, percentages

Ethnic origin	0-15	16-29	Age 30-44	45-R	R+
West Indian	31	28	20	18	2
Indian	33	29	21	14	3
Pakistani	45	25	17	12	1
Bangladeshi	48	22	13	17	1
Chinese	33	32	22	9	3
African	27	35	28	8	2
Mixed	58	23	11	6	2
White	22	21	20	20	18

Source: OPCS Monitor LFS 83/1, Labour Force Survey, 1981:country of birth and ethnic origin (London: HMSO, 22 February 1983a)

Note: R = retirement age (60 for women, 65 for men)

Table A17 Dependency ratios by ethnic group, 1981, Great Britain

Ethnic origin	Dependency ratio		
	Child	Elderly	Overall
West Indian	470	30	500
Indian	516	47	563
Pakistani	833	19	852
Bangladeshi	923	19	942
Chinese	524	48	571
African	380	28	408
White	367	300	667

Source: OPCS Monitor LFS 83/1, Labour Force Survey 1981: country of birth and ethnic origin (London: HMSO, 22 February 1983a)

Note: child dependency ratio = 1000 x population aged 0-15/population aged 16-retirement
elderly dependency ratio = 1000 x population of retirement age/population aged 16-retirement
overall dependency ratio = child + elderly dependency ratios

Table A18 Sex ratios of the population living in households with a NCWP born head by birthplace of head of household, and sex ratios by ethnic origin, 1981, Great Britain

Birthplace of head of household	Sex ratio(1)	Ethnic origin	Sex ratio(2)
West Indies	95	West Indian	96
India	102	Indian	105
Pakistan	120	Pakistani	122
Bangladesh	163	Bangladeshi	119
Far East	112	Chinese	113
East Africa	103	African	111
Mediterranean	102	Mixed	102
All birthplaces	95	White	94

Source: 1. OPCS, Census 1981: country of birth: Great Britain (London: HMSO, 1983d)
2. OPCS Monitor LFS 83/1, Labour Force Survey 1981: country of birth and ethnic origin (London: HMSO, 22 February 1983a)

101

Table A19 Population by country of birth by marital status by sex, 1981, Great Britain, percentages

Birthplace	Single	Married	Widowed and divorced
Females			
West Indies	16.5	27.4	7.1
India	6.8	36.0	6.3
Pakistan	10.8	30.7	1.7
Bangladesh	11.3	21.1	0.9
All birthplaces	19.4	24.5	7.5
Males			
West Indies	15.1	29.7	4.1
India	9.4	39.5	2.0
Pakistan	19.4	36.5	0.8
Bangladesh	27.0	39.3	0.5
All birthplaces	21.7	24.4	2.5

Source: OPCS. Census 1981: country of birth: Great Britain (London: HMSO, 1983d)

Table A20 Live births by birthplace of mother, 1970-1984, England and Wales, thousands

Birthplace of mother

Year	UK	NCWP	West Indies	India	Bangladesh	Pakistan	Total
1970	684.5	46.0	14.1	13.5		7.8	784.5
1971	689.7	45.2	12.5	13.4		8.2	783.2
1972	640.0	43.0	10.8	13.2		8.0	725.4
1973	596.9	41.0	9.1	12.7	0.9	6.8	676.0
1974	564.2	40.0	8.1	12.3	0.9	6.8	639.9
1975	530.5	40.0	7.7	12.0	1.0	7.0	603.4
1976	511.2	42.0	7.2	12.0	1.4	8.2	584.3
1977	494.5	44.3	6.9	12.3	1.6	9.5	569.3
1978	517.8	48.0	7.1	12.4	1.8	11.2	596.4
1979	554.2	52.2	7.3	13.1	2.2	12.5	638.0
1980	569.1	55.5	7.1	13.5	2.7	13.8	656.2
1981	551.4	53.2	6.2	12.4	3.1	13.3	634.5
1982	544.4	53.4	5.9	12.2	3.4	13.4	625.9
1983	549.4	52.0	5.3	11.5	3.9	13.4	629.1
1984	556.5	52.4	5.3	11.1	4.1	13.4	636.8

Source: OPCS. Births Statistics 1977. Series FM1. No.4 (London: HMSO. 1978): OPCS Monitor FM1 84/9. Births by birthplace of parent 1983 (London: HMSO. 11 December 1984); OPCS Monitor FM1 85/4. Births by birthplace of parent, 1984 (London: HMSO. 12 September 1985).

Table A21 Estimated total fertility rates by birthplace of mother, 1970-1983, England and Wales

Birthplace of mother	1970	1971	1972	1973	1974	1975	1976	1981	1983
India, Bangladesh & Pakistan[1]	5.6	5.3	4.9	4.5	4.3	4.2	4.2		
West Indies[1]	3.7	3.3	2.9	2.4	2.2	n.a	2.0		
England & Wales[1]	2.4	2.4	2.2	2.0	1.9	1.8	1.7		
India[2]		4.3						3.1	2.9
Pakistan & Bangladesh[2]		9.3						6.7	n.a
Pakistan[2]		n.a						6.3	5.6
Bangladesh[2]		n.a						8.6	8.4
West Indies[2]		3.4						2.0	1.8
NCWP[2]		4.0						2.9	2.8
UK[2]		2.3						1.7	1.7

Source: 1. L. Iliffe. 'Estimated fertility rates of Asian and West Indian immigrant women in Britain, 1969-1974'. Journal of Biosocial Science. 1978. 10. 189-197. Updated to 1976 by the author.

2. OPCS Monitor FM1 84/9. Births by birthplace of parent, 1983 (London: HMSO, 11 December 1984).

Table A22 Deaths by birthplace of deceased, 1970-84, England and Wales, thousands

Year	UK	NCWP	West Indies	India	Bangla-desh	Pakistan	Total
1970	522.6	4.2	0.8	–	2.4	–	575.2
1971	524.7	4.6	0.9	2.2	..	0.3	567.3
1972	552.2	4.9	1.0	–	2.7	–	591.9
1973	550.1	5.1	1.0	2.6		0.3	587.5
1974	549.6	5.4	1.0	2.7		0.3	585.3
1975	547.7	5.7	1.1	2.9		0.3	582.9
1976	563.0	6.0	1.1	3.0		0.3	578.5
1977	542.3	5.9	1.1	2.9	0.1	0.3	575.9
1978	551.5	6.3	1.2	3.0	0.1	0.4	585.9
1979	558.7	6.6	1.2	3.2	0.1	0.4	593.0
1980	547.7	6.8	1.3	3.3	0.1	0.4	581.4
1981	544.6	6.9	1.3	3.3	0.1	0.4	577.9
1982	548.1	7.0	1.3	3.3	0.2	0.5	581.9
1983	545.7	7.4	1.4	3.5	0.1	0.5	579.6
1984	532.7	7.6	1.5	3.5	0.2	0.6	566.9

Source: OPCS Monitor Series DH1. Deaths by birthplace of deceased (London: HMSO, annual).

Table A23 Infant and perinatal mortality rates by country of birth of mother, England and Wales, 1975-84

Country of birth of mother	1975	1976	1977	1978	1979	1980	1981	1982	1983	1984
Infant mortality rates										
India and Bangladesh	19.7	16.6	14.4	15.0	15.0	12.8	11.9	9.5	11.2	9.4
Pakistan	25.9	23.4	21.8	21.1	19.7	22.0	18.0	17.2	18.8	15.4
West Indies	21.6	17.2	17.1	15.7	13.5	15.4	13.0	13.1	11.7	11.8
NCWP	n.a.	n.a.	n.a.	16.3	15.1	15.6	12.9	11.8	12.1	11.1
All birthplaces	15.4	14.0	13.5	13.0	12.6	11.9	10.9	10.6	10.0	9.3
Perinatal mortality rates										
India and Bangladesh	25.6	24.4	22.0	21.3	20.2	15.7	15.3	13.7	13.3	13.7
Pakistan	28.9	26.0	25.2	24.9	21.4	26.3	18.5	20.1	20.2	16.9
West Indies	26.2	21.5	21.9	21.0	17.7	17.9	11.9	14.3	11.2	13.4
NCWP	n.a.	n.a.	n.a.	20.7	18.5	18.2	14.8	15.0	13.8	13.7
All birthplaces	19.2	17.7	16.9	15.5	14.6	13.3	11.8	11.2	10.4	10.1

Source: A.M. Adelstein et al., Perinatal and infant mortality: social and biological factors 1975-77. Studies on Medical and Population Subjects No. 41(London: HMSO, 1980); OPCS. Mortality statistics: perinatal and infant: social and biological factors. Series DH3. nos. 7, 9, 13 and 14 (London: HMSO, 1982, 1983, 1985a and 1985b respectively); OPCS Monitors DH3 85/1 and DH3 86/1. Infant and perinatal mortality: birthweight (London: HMSO, 1985c and 1986).

Part II
GUEST WORKERS OR IMMIGRANTS?
THE WEST GERMAN DILEMMA

6   The West German study

The current debate in West Germany about migrant workers has received the attention of politicians on the one hand, and of researchers, most notably sociologists and political scientists, on the other. The debate concerns the status of the migrant population within West Germany: is their status temporary as the Government maintains and as the popular term Gastarbeiter (guestworkers) suggests, or is it permanent, as immigrants, as is argued by many? These views essentially represent a dichotomy between the de jure status of migrants, as defined by their legal position, and their de facto status, as described and determined by their existence in West Germany.

It has been argued elsewhere that a demographic approach to the study of migration to, and migrants in, Western Europe would provide a major contribution to obtaining an objective answer to the question of permanency because it affords a means by which the de facto situation of migrants can be assessed (Booth, 1982). To date, the focus of attention of researchers has been economic, in that migrants are seen in terms of their role in the labour market rather than any other; and this continues throughout the more recent studies on the so-called second generation, whose education is designed with economic criteria in mind and who are subject to high levels of unemployment. Such an approach, however, does not adequately determine the present de facto status of migrants. This study aims to contribute a demographic dimension to the guestworker – immigrant debate by examining in detail the migration behaviour of migrants to, and the demographic structure of migrant populations within, West Germany.

Post–war migration to West Germany

At the end of the Second World War, West Germany was in a state of collapse. Though her economic recovery was soon underway, the early demand for labour was more than satisfied by the ten million expellees from former German territories in Poland and the Soviet Union and by the three million refugees from East Germany who had crossed the border by 1961. This influx of people was offset to some extent by emigration from West Germany, but unemployment continued throughout the fifties. In 1950 more than one million were unemployed, and by 1958 this had only fallen to 800,000. Heightened economic expansion during the next few years, the start of the 'economic wonder' in West Germany, increased the demand for labour and unemployment fell rapidly. In 1961, however, Germany's main labour supply quickly dried up with the erection of the Berlin Wall. This and other factors, including the low birth rate in West Germany and the increasing resistance on the part of West Germans to undertake certain forms of employment, led the West German government to seek other supplies of cheap and unskilled labour (Rist, 1979; Korte, 1980; O'Loughlin, 1980).

The obvious source of such labour lay in Southern Europe where unemployment, especially in rural areas, was high. Indeed, Italy had already provided agricultural and construction labour since the mid-fifties under a bilateral agreement made in 1955, though by 1959 only about ten per cent were agricultural. Germany now sought to procure similar agreements with several countries, and agreements were made with Spain in 1960, Greece in 1960 (renewed in 1962), Turkey in 1961 (the 1964 revision came into effect in 1968), Portugal in 1964, Italy in 1965 and Yugoslavia in 1968. As a member nation of the EEC, Italians enjoyed relative ease of entry to Germany, progressing to complete freedom by 1968. These six countries were the main source of labour throughout the sixties and early seventies when the migration of labour was at its greatest, and have remained so throughout the seventies and early eighties. Although official policy was to restrict foreign labour to Europeans, other countries also entered into labour agreements with Germany (Japan in 1956 for miners only, Morocco in 1963, Tunisia in 1965, and Korea in 1970 for miners only), but the numbers involved have been small (Castles and Kosack, 1973; Volker, 1975).

Under the bilateral agreements, the German government actively recruited labour through the nearly four hundred recruitment offices established in the countries concerned. These recruitment offices received requests for labour for specific vacancies in firms and organisations in West Germany. Would-be migrants were interviewed, screened for criminal and political records and medically examined: contracts were signed; papers were issued; and transport and accommodation were arranged. Of course, individuals could still migrate through the traditional channels whereby a visa and work permit are obtained from embassies and consulates on the definite offer of employment, but the majority chose the much simplified recruitment system organised centrally by the Federal Labour Office. Either way, the mechanism directly controlling the flow of labour was the demand for labour in West Germany since both channels linked workers with specific jobs.

The economic regulation of the movement of labour into West Germany continued throughout the sixties and early seventies. By 1966 the number of foreign workers employed in West Germany had grown steadily to 1.3 million but the ensuing recession resulted in a reduction to 1.0 million in 1968. With renewed economic growth the number again increased, rapidly

110

reaching 2.6 million in 1973 (see Table 58). But not only was the foreign workforce growing at a healthy pace: the resident foreign population was also expanding, due to the arrival of the spouses and children of the workforce, and had more than doubled in five years to reach almost 4.0 million by 1973 (see Table 72). By then, however it was becoming clear that the migration of foreign labour to West Germany was developing a momentum of its own, driven by the attraction of relative prosperity in the Federal Republic even in times of recession (Power 1979). With the reality of the so-called 'oil crisis' upon them,[1] the Federal Government issued the Auslanderstopp in late November 1973 thereby banning all further recruitment of workers from non-EEC countries despite existing bilateral agreements. Only in Italy did recruitment continue, but on a very limited scale, though freedom of movement was maintained under EEC regulations. The intention of the Auslanderstopp was to reduce the size of both the foreign workforce and resident population, and indeed a reduction in the workforce was achieved as Table 58 shows. But the effect on the size of the foreign resident population (see Table 72) was minimal: the departure of certain sections of the workforce was compensated for by the arrival of the dependants of those workers who had decided to stay, prompted by the knowledge that the possibility of return to the Federal Republic, once they had left, no longer existed. The effect of the Auslanderstopp was thus to increase the consolidation of the foreign population within West Germany.

Since 1973, further restrictive measures have been introduced to encourage migrants to leave West Germany. These include differential child benefit payments, restrictions on the employment of family members and progressively severe restrictions on family reunion (Castles, 1980; SOPEMI 1981), though their effect has not always been as intended (Castles, 1980). These restrictive measures are in accordance with the Federal Government's claim that Germany 'is not a country of immigration', as declared, for example, by the Bundesminister fur Arbeit und Sozialordnung (1977). There is thus a contradiction between the legal position of migrants, that is their de jure status, and their de facto status, a contradiction that is itself mirrored and perpetuated by the other side of government policy which claims to be one of integration for at least part of the existing migrant population.

It is this contradiction that is the subject of academic, political and public debate in West Germany. Often, however, the issue is discussed in terms of generalisations. Clearly, it would be absurd for anyone to deny that both temporary and permanent migrants exist side by side in that some may return to their country of origin tomorrow whilst others may live out their lives in West Germany. But the debate has nevertheless tended to polarise into these two extreme positions. Neither are differences of nationality taken into account. Instead, the foreign population is discussed as if it were one homogeneous group, except that Turks might be singled out by some as the large group posing the greatest problem. The guestworker-immigrant debate suffers from such generalisations and lack

111

of objectivity. This might be partially remedied by the contribution of a detailed demographic analysis of the kind presented below.

Data sources

The data on which this analysis is based are obtained from official sources.[2] The migration data are published by the Federal Statistical Office (Statistisches Bundesamt) and are derived from population registration.[3] Both departures from old residences and arrivals at new residences are required by law to be registered at local offices by every person involved irrespective of the duration of intended residence or absence.[4] Place of origin and destination are recorded so that international movements can be separated from internal movements. However, it is impossible to distinguish in these data both between short-term movement and more permanent changes in residence, and between first and subsequent arrivals or departures in the Federal Republic: the data are based on cases rather than on persons. These case statistics thus present an inflated indicator of 'real' migration, not least because of the practice prior to 1974 by some foreigners of de-registering on leaving for vacation in order to draw on their contributions[5] to the national insurance fund (Bundesinstitut fur Bevolkerungsforschung, 1974). On the other hand, out-migration is known to be underestimated because for those with no pension rights there is no advantage in de-registering on leaving the country. Hence, since these data include movements which are not long-term enough to qualify as immigration or emigration as usually defined in demographic and statistical research, they cannot be regarded as accurately measuring the volume of international migration.[6] Despite these problems, these data can be used to indicate trends and to assess the changes that have taken place over the last twenty or thirty years that are internal to these data series.

The migration data are available by sex for total persons and for persons in the labour force (Erwerbspersonen), though this latter categorisation is not a reliable source of labour statistics.[7] Again, however, the data can be used to detect trends over time. Finally, the data refer to all non-German citizens migrating to (or from) Germany from (or to) certain countries: whilst in some cases this may include some foreigners whose nationality is not the same as the country from (or to) which they have migrated, the number of such cases is very small. Tables 1 to 12, and 13 to 57 are derived from these data, and Tables 64 to 71 are partially derived from them.

In addition to these general migration data, other data are available concerning the number of foreign workers newly entering West Germany. These data are published by the Federal Labour Office (Bundesanstalt fur Arbeit) and are derived from the records of the local labour offices which are responsible for issuing work permits. They include only those workers who require a permit to work so that Italians are excluded because of their EEC membership. They also exclude newly entering family members of those nationalities that do require permits because they are barred from working immediately after entry.[8] Table 12A is derived from these data.

Data on foreign employees in West Germany are also published by the Federal Labour Office. Before 1961 the figures were produced for July only and referred to those who had permission to work. In 1961, the data began to appear five, and later four, times a year (the June figures are used here) and coverage was increased to those who needed permission to work whether they worked or not. In 1973 there was a further change which resulted in no data being available for that year. From June 1974 onwards the data have been obtained from the Social Insurance Employment Statistics on a quarterly basis. These data are officially estimated to cover about 90 per cent of foreign workers, but other estimates suggest much lower coverage (see Wilpert (1983) and discussion below). The remaining 10 per cent (or more) are comprised of those who are self-employed (a reliable estimate of which will not be available until the next census), civil servants (who are exempt from national insurance payments, but of whom very few are foreign), and those who work for less than 15 hours a week and earn less than a certain minimum income (at present DM 390 per month). It is this latter category that probably accounts for the discrepancy in the estimated coverage of these data. The data are available by sex and by nationality. Tables 58 to 63 are derived from these data, and Tables 64 to 71 are partially derived from them.

Data on the resident population in West Germany are also obtained from the population register, described above. These data are used in conjunction with information from the annual microcensus to adjust census data. The resulting estimates refer to the population on 30 September of the relevant year. They are published annually in a volume on foreigners (Statistisches Bundesamt, annual) and bi-annually in a special volume on the structure of the foreign population (Statistisches Bundesamt, bi-annual).

Terminology

Throughout this study the term migrant is used to refer to people who are non-German and who have moved to West Germany. The country of origin of a migrant may be referred to as the sending country. Migrant members of the labour force are termed migrant workers or migrant labour, and those who are not in the labour force are dependants of migrant labour. The labour force includes those at work and those seeking employment. The movement of people into West Germany is referred to as the in-migration of in-migrants; and the movement out as the out-migration of out-migrants. The term migrant is used to describe migrants who may be said to be permanently resident in West Germany.

Notes

1. The 'oil-crisis', with its attendant falling demand for labour, was the official justification for the Auslanderstopp. Other explanations suggest that the introduction of microprocessors and the trend towards the export of capital to sources of cheap labour in the Third World were more instrumental in bringing about the Auslanderstopp (Heimenz and Schatz, 1979; Castles, 1980; Froebel et al, 1980).

2. By their nature, therefore, they do not include illegal migrants. One estimate, described as very vague, suggests that there are 200,000 such people in West Germany.

3. Population registration began in West Germany on 1 January 1950 for administrative purposes. Migration statistics are a by-product of this system. For foreigners the information collected at registration is passed on to the local aliens departments and subsequently to the Central Register of Foreigners (Auslander-Zentral-Register) kept in Koln. This register is also an administrative tool and as such is checked for errors and omissions. Though there are no statistics published directly from this source, the register is used by the Federal Statistical Office in conjunction with the initial population registration system to produce migration data (Bundesinstitut fur Bevolkerungsforschung, 1974)

4. Tourists are not included in these data: according to the United Nations (1979) intended stays or absences of less than eight weeks are excluded.

5. Employees and employers contribute an equal amount to the national insurance fund. On leaving the country, employees receive only the proportion paid into the fund by themselves, the remaining half being left in the fund. Migrant workers who leave the country are thus penalised financially.

6. International recommendations stipulate that international migration should be defined as those movements across international boundaries which constitute a change of residence, and that for comparative purposes only those with intentions to stay or remain abroad for more than one year should be included. See United Nations (1979) and 'Draft recommendations on statistics of international migration: report of the Secretary-General' (United Nations, E/CN.3/483). Comparison with data from other countries illustrates the degree of variation possible in measuring the same flow. For example, there is a large discrepancy in the West German and Italian statistics on the flow of Italians in both directions between the two countries. In both cases, the German statistics indicate a much greater volume of migration (often more than double), despite the broad Italian definition of international migration which, for example, includes as an emigrant a person leaving the country temporarily. The levels of immigration and emigration for a country are, of course, related: a person not classified as an emigrant on leaving italy cannot later be classified as an immigrant on her or his return.

7. Personal communication from Elmar Honekopp, Institut fur Arbeitsmarkt – und Berufsforschung, Bundesanstalt fur Arbeit (17 August 1982). This is seen in the discrepancy between labour in-migration in Table 8 and the annual number of new work permits in Table 12A.

8. In 1976 the Stichtagsregelung decreed that those dependants of foreign workers who entered West Germany after the 'key data' of 30 November 1974 would not be issued with work permits. This key date was later (in June 1977) extended to 31

December 1976 for the children of foreign workers. From 1 April 1979 the Stichtagsregelung was abolished in favour of a waiting period: spouses cannot obtain a work permit until four years after entry (or in exceptional circumstances three years, reduced to two years by the legislation of 3 August 1981), and children until 2 years or as little as six months if a recognised course of training is pursued. Any further reductions in these restrictions are not likely in the near future. In all these cases a work permit is issued only if no German labour is available. (See Honekopp and Ullmann, 1980; SOPEMI, annual.)

7 Migration to and from West Germany

The study of migration and migrant populations is, from a demographic standpoint, rooted in the analysis of data on the flows of migrants from one country to another as much as in the analysis of the migrant population within its country of residence. Most studies of migration to Western Europe have failed to address this former aspect of the migration process, taking as their basic data the latter aspect, namely the resident population. This approach fails to take into account the full extent of movement or changeover within the population. In addition, because the resident population has grown over time rather than decreased, the approach tends to acknowledge the presence of in-migration only, whereas in fact there have been significant flows of migration out of the country.

Not only is it important to examine the extent of migration in both directions, and its net effect, but it is also important to determine the nature of that migration. A simple dichotomy into labour and non-labour or dependants helps to clarify the character of migration and the further division by sex provides added detail. Such an examination of migrant flows is presented below, not only for migrants to West Germany in total, but also for those from each of the six countries of particular interest which supply the bulk of the Federal Republic's current minority population and labour force. These migrant flows are also related to the stocks of employees of the relevant nationalities, so that the significance of migration for each population can be assessed.

Migrant flows

Table 1 shows the total number of in-migrants, and the number from each of six main sending countries. It is seen that the bilateral agreements and economic recession considerably affected the flow of in-migration until the Auslanderstopp in 1973. The early agreement with Italy is evident, as is the importance of the 1968 agreements with Turkey and Yugoslavia. Table 2 shows more clearly the relative size of the flow from each country. The proportion from the six countries combined decreased in the years of recession, demonstrating the fact that this section of the foreign

116

population and workforce (see Table 9) suffers disproportionately in times of recession. After the Auslanderstopp, this proportion remained fairly high at about 60 per cent because of the in-migration of family members, but has steadily decreased as this process is completed for more and more families. The rapid fall in 1981 is due almost entirely to the reduced flow from Turkey which has been brought about by the introduction of stricter controls concerning political asylum.

It should be firmly kept in mind that the data concerning flows of migrants to and from West Germany include both multiple entries and short-term as well as long-term movement. While the volume of in-migration shown in Table 1 exceeds 13 million, the volume of out-migration for the same period exceeds 9 million. Table 3 shows the pattern and volume of out-migration for the six countries and for all foreign countries. Though the outward flow exceeds the inward flow on only a few occasions, such as in 1967 as a result of the recession, the volume of out-migration is considerable. Until 1973, the proportion going to the six countries (Table 4) was very similar to that coming from these countries; after that date there are proportionately more out-migrants than in-migrants even when net migration is positive. Thus it may be said that in general migrants from these six countries were as likely as migrants from the rest of the world to move out of the Federal Republic once they had moved in, and that the effect of the Auslanderstopp was to accelerate the rate of out-migration to the six countries relative to that to other countries.

This general pattern conceals considerable differences between the six countries. Taking Tables 1 to 4 together with Table 5, showing net migration, different patterns begin to emerge depending largely on the dates of the bilateral labour agreements. Sizeable flows of migrants from Italy, Greece and Spain began to enter West Germany relatively early. The recession of 1966-7 severely checked this flow, the former volume of which was never resumed from Italy and Spain. Migration from Portugal, which has perhaps the most straightforward pattern, was also affected by the 1966-7 recession, but soon resumed a steady increase until 1973. Flows from Turkey and Yugoslavia gained strength rather later but were affected less severely by the recession, recovering afterwards to more than double their former volume. Out-migration prior to 1966 increased in volume for each country [1] due to the increased number of migrants per se. The recession brought a general acceleration of this flow but this was not as great as the reduction in in-migration: in combination these resulted in negative net migration. For Italy, Greece and Spain, the volume of out-migration, as of in-migration, continued until 1973 at below or only slightly above their pre-recession levels, but whereas in-migration tended to decrease prior to 1973 out-migration tended to increase resulting in the declining values of net migration seen in Table 5, which in the case of Greece became negative again in 1973. The flows to Portugal, Turkey and Yugoslavia continued after 1967 to reflect in-migration: those to Portugal and Turkey rose steadily, whilst that to Yugoslavia initially increased but then declined.

117

The migration of labour

To gain a fuller understanding of the migration patterns to and from West Germany, it is necessary to divide the population flows into those who are migrant labour and those who are dependant on this labour. The data already presented are classified along these lines from 1962 (see section on Data Sources). Tables 6 and 7 show that a very high proportion of early in-migrants and out-migrants were classified as migrant labour. For this reason the early pattern of labour migration is much the same as that of total migration. However, a divergence in these patterns occurs as the proportion of migrants that are labour diminishes with the increasing number of spouses and children who joined workers in the Federal Republic.

Tables 8 and 9 show the number and percentage of labour in-migrants. The bilateral labour agreements are clearly reflected in these tables, as is the curbing effect on labour of the 1966-7 recession. Indeed, the effect of the recession was greater on the movement of labour into West Germany than on dependants, as shown by the reduced percentages in Table 6 for the recession years. The effect was also greater on labour from the six countries than on other migrant labour as shown by the reduced proportion from the six countries in 1967 in Table 9. From this table it is also evident that flows from different countries were affected to greater or lesser degrees. The first year of the recession brought proportionately reduced flows from Spain, Greece and, to a lesser extent, Turkey. Indeed, flows from these three countries had already begun to decrease in 1965. In contrast, the flow of labour from Yugoslavia increased both in relative and in absolute terms. By the second year of the recession, all six countries suffered drastic decreases in their labour flows to the Federal Republic, with the greatest relative reductions from Spain, Greece and Italy (the longer-standing, more established flows).

After the recession, the volume of labour in-migration rapidly, but briefly, gained strength, followed by a general decline in the early seventies due partly to the success of measures taken from 1970 onwards by the West German Government and Federal Bank to check excessive economic activity (Bundesinstitut fur Bevolkerungsforschung, 1974), and partly to measures specifically designed to curb in-migration. In 1972, the Federal Government raised the fee paid by employers for the recruitment of labour through official channels, and in November of the same year migration by visa was restricted. In addition, the Yugoslav government sought to discourage the migration of skilled labour and in 1972 introduced legislation to restrict migration from Yugoslavia of the highly trained. Because of this restriction, the highest proportion of labour in-migration in 1973 came from Turkey (Volker, 1975), and it is likely that this trend would have continued if economic criteria had prevailed.

Labour out-migration is shown in Tables 10 and 11. During the early sixties, its volume increased with the number of migrant workers employed in West Germany, reflecting the mobility of such labour and the extent to which visits were made to the sending countries where wives and children usually remained. The 1966–7 recession precipitated a temporary acceleration in the outward flow of labour, resulting in net out–migration as shown in Table 12. It appears from Table 7, however, that the proportion of labour out–migrants amongst all out–migrants fell from 1966 to 1968 indicating that those who were most affected by the recession in this way had dependants with them in West Germany. It seems, therefore, that workers with no dependants in West Germany found it easier to survive the recession. It is impossible to determine from the data, however, the extent to which workers left with their dependants and the extent to which dependants returned to their countries of origin with the workers remaining in West Germany.

As might be expected, the recession affected labour from the six countries more than other migrant labour (see Table 11). Again, the effect was uneven. Though in absolute terms the outward flow increased substantially for each country, in relative terms Italy received a smaller share of returnees. The reasons for this are unclear, but it seems that it is a continuation of the existing trend in which labour out–migration to Italy comprised a decreasing share of the total outward flow of labour, whilst that to the other five countries generally increased. The recession would be unlikely to reverse this trend because on average Italians would be expected to enjoy greater security of employment due to their longer history of migration to West Germany. Moreover, if this were the case, an acceleration of the trend would be expected in times of recession: Table 11 shows that this did indeed occur.

After the recession, the flow of labour out–migration decreased substantially, and though in all cases increases occurred after one or two years, for Italy, Greece and Spain their respective pre–recession levels were never attained. In contrast, flows to Portugal, Turkey and Yugoslavia increased considerably. The net effect of these movements during the six years after the recession and before the Auslanderstopp was an immediate return to a positive balance of labour migration. In 1971 and 1972, however, this net in–flow was substantially reduced, and in the case of Greece became a net out–flow. In 1973 Greece alone continued this trend, due to a further reduction in in–migration, whilst net flows from all other countries increased considerably due mainly to increased in–migration.

It was partly this increase in the flow of labour to West Germany that prompted the Federal Government to issue the Auslanderstopp in November 1973. This had an immediate effect on the in–migration of labour, as was intended, and a more subdued effect on labour out–migration. The data in Table 8 indicate the extent of the effect on the inflow of labour. In one year, the total flow was reduced to 40 per cent of its 1973 level, with a greater share of this reduction borne by the six countries than by other countries (see Table 9). In fact, the flow from Portugal was affected most being reduced to only 8 per cent of its 1973 volume, followed by flows from Spain, Turkey and Yugoslavia. Though Italy and Greece suffered more than fifty per cent reductions in their flows of labour to West Germany, these were less than average.

It may at first be surprising that non-EEC labour in-migration should appear to exist at all after 1973. The explanation for the continued inflow in Table 8 lies partly in the nature of the data and partly in certain exceptions to the Auslanderstopp. It has already been stressed that these data are based on cases of migration rather than on migrants and as such include workers who are re-entering West Germany after absences in their countries of origin. This includes a large, but unknown, number of young men who have been absent from West Germany in order to complete military service in their country of origin as required by virtue of their citizenship of that country.[2] There is also a very limited number of people who are exceptions to the Auslanderstopp: these include those in certain professions, such as dentistry; executives and specialists in foreign enterprises; and foreigners married to Germans. In addition, until June 1980 people seeking political asylum in the Federal Republic were entitled to (apply for) a work permit, a channel of entry used mainly by Turks.

The numbers of migrant workers who newly entered West Germany are shown in Table 12a. These data are in fact of newly-issued work permits. They do not include family members who are of working age and who are newly entering the Federal Republic because such people are by law barred from working until a specified period of time has passed. The increase in the number of Turks obtaining new work permits in 1979 marked the beginning of the increased use of political asylum as a means of entry to West Germany. People seeking asylum in West Germany have traditionally been allowed to work, and a series of three permits are issued until a decision is reached concerning their application for asylum. Since this process is lengthy, asylum seekers can hope to spend 2 or 3 years in West Germany even if their application is unsuccessful. In June 1980 in response to the increasing number of applications the Federal Government introduced a waiting period of one year, during which asylum seekers were forbidden to work. During this waiting period, asylum-seekers are provided for by the Federal Lands (see Kraus, 1983). This measure proved to be successful in that it reduced the number of Turkish asylum-seekers considerably: from 29,219 new issues of work permits in 1980 to 3,580 in 1981. Because of the time lag after June 1980, these 1981 permits would have been issued to 1980 asylum applicants. In addition, the federal government introduced compulsory visas for Turks in 1980. This was related more to Turkey's agreements for association with the EEC than to asylum, however, and in fact the same steps were taken by France and the Benelux countries (Weidacher, 1983). This reduction in entrants was not sufficient for the German authorities, however, and in October 1981 the waiting period was extended to 2 years.[3,4] In the first five months of 1982, only 231 Turkish asylum-seekers were granted a first work permit.

Since 1973, the volume of labour in-migration from the five non-EEC countries has fluctuated without a discernible pattern because of the absence of any dominating factors influencing this type of movement which by definition, with the exceptions just discussed, no longer contains 'real' migration in the sense of the entry of new labour. The data do show,

120

however, the clear differences in the relative volumes of movement from different countries (see Table 9). Flows from Portugal, Spain and Greece are exceedingly low, whilst those from Turkey and Yugoslavia remain somewhat higher. With the exception of flows from Turkey after 1977 and Greece in 1981, and despite fluctuations in the absolute levels of migration, often reflecting changes in the overall volume, there is a general decline in the proportion of movement over time. The recent increase in the proportion from Greece is related to her entry into the EEC, whilst the earlier proportionate increase from Turkey arises largely from the increased number of people seeking political asylum in West Germany.

Further indication of the effect of the Auslanderstopp on non-EEC labour in- migration is seen in Table 6. There was an immediate reduction in the proportion of labour migrants amongst all migrants, demonstrating the greater effect on the movement of labour than of dependants. The extent of this reduction, which depends on changes in the volume of dependant in-migration as much as on changed labour migration, is greatest for flows from Portugal, followed by those from Turkey, Spain, Greece and Yugoslavia. Hence, the lowest proportions of labour (less than a fifth) in 1974 came from Portugal, despite her highest proportion in 1973, and Turkey, whilst almost half of the total flow from Yugoslavia consisted of members of the labour force. After these initial reductions there has been a tendency for the proportion of labour to increase slightly.

The proportion of labour in the flow of migrants from Italy also declined, though by only 14 per cent, after the Auslanderstopp, indicating a similar but much smaller effect to that for non-EEC migratory flows. This lesser effect is also seen (in Table 9) in the increase in the proportion from Italy of total labour migration, and is of course due to free movement enjoyed by Italian citizens under EEC regulations since 1968. Nevertheless, the actual volume of labour migration from Italy was reduced by more than fifty per cent in 1974 (see Table 8). This can largely be attributed directly to the Auslanderstopp, demonstrating the significance of active recruitment even where free movement exists. In addition, 1974 and 1975 were years of recession during which lower migratory flows would be expected, as was the case in 1966-7.[5] As the economy began to recover in 1976 the flow of labour in-migration increased, declining again as the 1980's brought further recession. The post-1973 flow of labour from Italy is thus closely related to the West German economy, but at a new, reduced level determined no longer by recruitment but by the independent migration of individuals (that is in addition to the size of the existing Italian labour force where multiple entries are concerned). The continuing influence of the economy on the flow of labour is also evident from the proportion of the total migrant flow from Italy that is labour, seen in Table 6: in times of recession labour accounts for a slightly reduced proportion of the total inward flow indicating that in general labour is more adversely affected by recession than are dependants.

The effect of the Auslanderstopp on the outward flow of labour is seen in Tables 10 and 11. The overall flow increased slightly in 1974, but then decreased. Similar, but more marked, effects occurred to flows to the five non-EEC countries. However, unlike labour in-migration, the relative outward flows of labour from each country remained much the same as in 1973, and in overall terms the effect on the six countries was only marginally more than on other countries (see Table 11). In addition, Table 7 indicates that the effect of the Auslanderstopp on labour out-migration relative to its effect on dependant out-migration was not sufficient to make more than a slight delay in the already established trend towards smaller proportions of labour amongst all out-migrants, and was non-existent in the case of Italy.

Since 1973, there has been a continuation of this general reduction in the proportion of labour among all out-migrants accompanied by a steady reduction in the proportion of the outward labour flow to the six countries combined. With only minor exceptions, the proportion of labour out-migration to the non-EEC countries has decreased, and by 1981 flows to Greece, Spain and Portugal combined accounted for less than 7 per cent of the total, whilst those to Yugoslavia and Turkey were rather higher (see Table 11).

As already indicated, the Auslanderstopp appears to have had no effect at all on the outward flow of labour to Italy. Table 10 shows that there was no interruption in the declining volume of labour out-migration and Table 7 shows no interruption in the declining proportion of labour among all out-migrants. Because of the effect on other countries, however, the proportion of labour leaving West Germany for Italy began to increase in 1976 and continued until 1979. In 1980 the recession brought a temporary increase in the outward volume of labour, which is also detected in the proportion of labour among out-migrants, as the earlier recession had done in 1966. Despite this, the proportion of labour leaving for Italy fell, indicating the lesser effect of the recession on Italians in West Germany than on other migrants. Given this, it seems likely that part of the reduction in the proportion of labour leaving for Italy in 1974 and 1975 was due to the recession at that time.

The net effect of the Auslanderstopp is clearly seen in Table 12: the positive net flows of labour into West Germany were immediately reversed, and the existing net outflow to Greece was increased. In terms of the size of the net outflow, the effect has diminished over time, especially for Italy where net in-migration commenced again as early as 1977. This trend reflects the dominant influence on these net data of in-migration, which also accounts for the positive values for flows with Greece in 1981, with Turkey in 1979-80 and with Yugoslavia in 1980.

Dependant migration

The classification 'dependant' has been obtained by differencing total and labour migration. It therefore comprises all migrants who are not primary migrants, that is those who are not permitted to work or seek work in

West Germany: this includes children aged less than 16, spouses without work permits and elderly relatives, and after November 1974 all spouses and 16 and 17 year old children barred from working first by the Stichtagsregelung and later by its replacement legislation.

It has already been seen in Tables 6 and 7 that dependants have formed an increasing proportion of migrants over time, especially after the Auslanderstopp. Fluctuations in this proportion have been more the result of changes in the volume of labour migration than of dependant migration itself. It is seen in Tables 13 and 14 that the 1966-7 recession caused some reduction in the flow of dependants entering West Germany, but this was nowhere near as severe as the fall in labour in-migration, and presented only a temporary set-back in the increasing flow of dependants from all six countries. This trend was reversed in the early seventies for dependants first from Greece in 1971, and later from Spain in 1973, with a suggestion of a similar reversal manifest in the slight fluctuation in the flow from italy. Dependants from Portugal, Turkey and Yugoslavia, however, continued to enter West Germany in increasing numbers during this period.

The immediate overall effect of the Auslanderstopp on dependants was negligible. In the year after the Auslanderstopp, the total number of dependants entering West Germany was only very slightly less than in 1973, with the same proportion coming from the six countries. Examination of individual flows, however, reveals that, with the exception of that from Greece which was temporarily increased, all other flows either were reduced, as in the case of Yugoslavia, Italy and Spain, or increased at a reduced rate, as for Portugal and Turkey (see Tables 13 and 14). In the following year, large absolute reductions occurred in all flows, probably partly due to the recession in 1974-5, and this downward trend continued until 1981 for Spain and with only minor interruptions for Portugal and Yugoslavia. The flow of dependants from Greece also continued to decline steadily until 1979 after which its volume increased as did labour in-migration due to agreements concerning Greece's entry to the EEC. Of the five non-EEC countries under analysis, only Turkey resumed an increasing flow of dependants to West Germany after 1975, until the changed regulations concerning political asylum curbed this flow in June 1980. These patterns are also reflected in the relative proportions seen in Table 14.

The flow of dependants from Italy also increased after 1975, but became almost constant in the late 1970s and finally declined in 1981. This pattern is the same as that of labour migration from Italy, and is closely related to the West German economy, though as already noted dependants are less susceptible to changes in the economy than are labour. It would seem, then, that part of the reduction in the in-flow of dependants in 1974-5 was due to the recession and that the effect of the Auslanderstopp on dependants from Italy was less marked than it might at first appear from the data. This economic factor would affect dependants from Italy after 1973 more than non-EEC dependants because under free movement 'new' Italian labour could still enter West Germany with their dependants so that the economic factors regulating this primary flow would also determine this secondary flow. The economic regulation of the entry of the dependants of existing labour would be roughly equal for Italians and non-EEC migrants because the costs involved would be similar.

The pattern of dependant out-migration is shown in Table 15. The volume of migration increased steadily prior to 1966 as the population of dependants in West Germany grew. The 1966-7 recession brought a considerable increase in this flow both generally and to each of the six countries, and the increased proportions in Table 16 indicate the extent to which the recession disproportionately affected migrants from these countries in this respect. Following this inflated exodus of dependants from West Germany, the flow resumed a lower, but in all cases higher than pre-recession, level and after some initial hesitation in the form of reduced levels from Greece and Spain and Portugal, also resumed a steady increase, again reflecting the size of the resident foreign population. During this period the proportion of dependants leaving for the six countries combined increased steadily, as did the proportions going to Portugal, Turkey and Yugoslavia. Dependant out-migration continued to increase in volume until 1975 or 1976, after which the levels began to decline. The Auslanderstopp had no apparent effect on the volume or proportion of dependant out-migration, but it is possible that counter-balancing factors existed: the 1974-5 recession might be expected to result in an increase over and above the prevailing trend, and if this were the case it implies a reduction in the flow due to the Auslanderstopp. However, whilst the recession would be expected to lead to the increased out-migration of workers who found themselves unable to support their dependants, it would at the same time curtail the shorter-term movement of dependants for educational and other visits because of the costs involved. In addition, the Auslanderstopp may have caused some migrants, who had part of their families with them, to make a final decision to return to their countries of origin, since the option of working for short periods at a time in West Germany no longer remained open. These various factors cannot be quantified from the data. However, the fact that both the overall proportion from the six countries and the flows of dependant out- migration began to decrease in 1976 or 1977 suggests that the Auslanderstopp did have considerable effect, masked earlier either by the recession or by the countering effect of the Auslanderstopp itself. For dependants from Greece and Spain, this trend continued until 1981; whilst for those from Portugal, Turkey and Yugoslavia it turned upward again in 1980 or 1981, possibly due to the recession. As expected, Italian migrants were least affected by the Auslanderstopp, if indeed it had any effect given the effect of the recession in increasing the outflow of dependants, and in 1977 this flow resumed its pre- 1974 level and slightly increasing trend. Only in 1981 did the recession bring a significantly increased flow.

In terms of net migration, shown in Table 17, the early positive flow of dependants was reduced or reversed by the 1966-7 recession. This effect was less severe for the more recent flows from Portugal, Yugoslavia and

Turkey, and indeed had no discernible effect in the first year of the recession on flows from Portugal and Yugoslavia. The more established flows from Italy, Greece and Spain were more severely affected by the recession, resulting in negative flows. In the late sixties, flows from all countries increased substantially, but those from Italy, Greece and Spain began to diminish again in the early seventies. Since 1974, most flows of dependants have been negative, with the notable exception of that from Turkey. This pattern largely mirrors the pattern of net labour migration, except for Italy which has a positive flow of labour but a negative flow of dependants.

The information expressed in Tables 6 and 7 as proportions can also be expressed as ratios of dependants per unit of labour. This is done in Tables 18 and 19. For in- migrants, shown in Table 18, it is seen that the ratio of dependants to labour increased over time until the mid-1970s. This was due to the increasing number of dependants entering the country relative to the flow of labour. Thus, the ratios are high for 1966-7 because of the greater effect of the recession on labour than on dependant flows. In 1974, the ratios increased enormously, as a result of the Auslanderstopp and the continued entry of dependants, and has remained relatively high. Large differences exist between the individual flows, however, especially since 1973. The lowest ratios are found for italy because of the continued free entry of labour and relatively low ratios are also found for Spain and Yugoslavia, and for Greece in later years. Much higher ratios are found for Portugal and for Turkey. The lower ratio in 1979 and 1980 for Turkey is due to the fact that adult Turks were entering West Germany seeking political asylum during these years.

The ratio of dependant out-migrants to labour out-migrants is shown in Table 19. The greater effect of the 1966-7 recession on labour is seen in the low ratios compared to following years, but the Auslanderstopp and ensuing recession are barely evident in the increasing trend over time. These ratios are much less variable between countries than the in-migration ratios, but similarities exist in that the ratios for Italy are lower than those for other countries and those for Turkey are the highest.

Female and male migrants

Further insight into the post-war patterns of migration to West Germany can be obtained by looking at females and males separately. Data on sex are available since 1962.

Not surprisingly, given the nature of early migration, a large proportion of early in-migrants were male as shown in Table 20, though female labour was not uncommon. Over time, this proportion has generally decreased, with the greatest reductions occurring during the 1966-7 recession and after the Auslanderstopp. The proportion of males among out-migrants shown in Table 21 was also very high at first but has gradually declined with no apparent effect of either the recession or the Auslanderstopp. In general, males make up a higher proportion of out-migrants than of in-migrants, with post-1973 migrants from Greece and

Italy as the only exceptions. This indicates that, once there, female migrants are more likely to remain in West Germany than are male migrants, suggesting either the presence of males with families abroad or a higher short- term mobility of males.

As might be expected from the very high proportions of male entrants that are labour (see Table 22), male in-migration, shown in Table 23, followed much the same pattern, though at a lower level, as labour in-migration until 1973. This similarity continued after 1973 for males from Italy, but for the non-EEC countries the Auslanderstopp led to a divergence away from labour patterns. In addition, differences between the non-EEC countries developed, and these are discussed below under male labour and male dependant migration. Male out-migration, shown in Table 24, also followed the same pattern as labour, again due to the dominance of labour among male migrants (see Table 25). It follows therefore, that net male migration, shown in Table 26, is also roughly similar to net labour migration at least until 1973. Clearly, the overriding factor in male migration has been the demand for labour.

Female migration is shown in Tables 27 and 28. The general pattern of in- migration is similar to that of males, but at a much lower volume until 1973 after which the volumes are more equal for non-EEC countries. The flow of females from Italy has continued in the post-1973 period at a lower level than males because males dominate in the labour market, which under free movement remains the dominant determinant of italian migration patterns. The fact that female entry patterns are very similar to male, and therefore general labour, patterns is partly but not entirely due to the moderately high proportion of labour among female in-migrants, as shown in Table 29, and discussed in detail below. Female out-migration (Table 28) has differed both in volume and pattern from male out-flows, despite the fact that the proportion of labour among female out-migrants, shown in Table 30, is roughly similar to that for in-migrants. The pattern of out-migration is discussed in greater detail below under female labour and female dependant migration. Net female migration follows roughly the same pattern as for males. Table 31 in comparison with Table 26 shows, however, that females were less affected than males by the 1966-67 recession, especially those from Portugal, Turkey and Yugoslavia for which net in-flows were maintained. Similarly, the Auslanderstopp had a less severe effect on females in that their net out-flows after 1973 were much lower in comparison to previous net in-flows. In other words, though female net migration was much lower than male net migration prior to the Auslanderstopp, relatively few females left West Germany after 1973.

Sex differences in the flow of labour to West Germany can be seen by comparison of Tables 32 and 33, showing female flows, with the equivalent data for males shown in Tables 34 and 35. It is seen immediately that the volume of female labour in-migration has consistently been considerably lower than for males. In addition, female labour from the six countries consistently accounted for a lower proportion of total female labour in-migration than male labour from these countries comprised of the total male in-flow. This is also true for flows from Italy and Turkey, but the proportions from Greece, Spain, Portugal and Yugoslavia have all exceeded their respective male proportions. In particular, the flows of female labour from Spain until 1967 and from Greece and Yugoslavia until the early seventies were proportionately higher than the flows of male labour.

The same comparisons for labour out-migration can be made from Tables 36 and 37, showing females, and Tables 38 and 39, showing males. Again, the volume of female migration is much lower than male migration, and the overall proportion of female labour out-migrants from the six countries is also considerably lower than for males. Furthermore, the same countries that have relatively high in-flows of female labour compared to male labour also have relatively high out-flows. The flow to Greece has consistently been proportionately greater for females than for males throughout the entire twenty year period, and flows to Spain, Portugal and Yugoslavia have also exceeded their male counterparts.

Tables 40 and 41 show how small a proportion of total labour migration female labour comprises, indicating the extent to which male labour flows dominate the patterns of total labour migration (already described above). Because of this similarity of male and total migration patterns, there is little need to discuss male labour migration separately, and thus only female labour flows are examined in detail.

Female labour migration

It has already been implied that female labour from individual countries does not constitute the same proportions of total female labour migration as their male counterparts. This arises partly from the fact that women of some nationalities are more likely to enter the labour force than those of other nationalities, and in this respect, Turkish women, who are mostly of Muslim faith, might be expected to comprise the smallest proportion of labour in-migrants from any sending country. In addition, the relative proportions of female labour entering West Germany depend on time in that flows of migrants from individual countries are not at the same stage of development. Thus in the early sixties, those countries with the more established flows of labour to the Federal Republic might be expected to have higher proportions of female labour migrants, because in general males migrate first followed by female labour and dependants. Flows from Italy, Greece and Spain would contain relatively more females under this assumption. This implies, however, that the rate of growth of the female labour in-flow is greater than that of male labour in-migration, a condition which is not necessarily true. The flow of female labour may increase substantially but still remain small relative to an ever-increasing male flow.

Table 40 shows that the proportions of labour in-migrants that are female vary both between the six sending countries and over time. In the early to mid sixties, when migration from Portugal, Turkey and Yugoslavia was considerably less well established than that from Italy, Greece and

Spain (see Table 1) and when the flow of female labour was rapidly increasing (see Table 32), females made up a consistently larger than average proportion of labour from Greece, Spain and Yugoslavia. The proportion from Greece was particularly high, not only reflecting the more established nature of migration from Greece but also suggesting a higher propensity of Greek women to work. The higher than average proportion from Spain would seem more to reflect established migratory flows (given the lower rates in later years), whilst that from Yugoslavia probably reflects a higher propensity to work. In contrast to these, the proportions from Italy and Turkey were both lower than average, but for differing reasons. The proportion of females among labour in-migrants from Italy remained low despite the more established flow from Italy, and despite the fact that female labour from Italy comprised almost one third (an equal proportion to the flow from Greece) of female labour from the six countries (see Table 33). The reason for this lies in the then recent massive increase in in- migration, comprised mainly of male labour (see Tables 1 and 34) which greatly outnumbered female labour. The low proportion of females among labour in-migrants from Turkey arises partly from the early stage in migration but also confirms the lower propensity of Turkish women to work.

The 1966-7 recession did not produce as immediate an effect on female labour as on male labour. In 1966, the overall in-flow of female labour increased slightly, and increases also occurred in the flows from Yugoslavia (as for the male flow), Portugal and Italy. In addition, the reductions in flows that did occur, from Greece, Spain and Turkey, were less marked than for males (see Tables 32 and 34). On balance, however, the six countries accounted for a slightly smaller proportion of the total female labour in-flow in 1966 (Table 33), followed by a larger reduction in 1967. In fact, the flows from all six countries were considerably reduced in 1967, with the greatest relative reductions being from Greece and Spain. Even in 1967, however, the effect of the recession on female labour was not so great as on male labour, as can be seen from the inflated proportions in Table 40: despite the large absolute fall in female labour in-flows, it is seen that for flows from all but Greece and Turkey the female proportion of labour increased.

After the recession, the volume of female labour in-migration increased rapidly due to preferential recruitment policies concerning women (Abadan-Unat, 1977). Much of this increase was due to the increased flow from Yugoslavia, which in 1968 exceeded for the first time the previously dominating flow from Italy and continued to do so until 1972. The flow soon began to decline again, due to the same economic criteria affecting total (and male) labour migration (see above), and it is seen from the reduced overall proportions in Table 33 that these criteria disproportionately affected labour from the six countries. The proportion of females among labour in-migrants continued after the recession to generally vary inversely with their volume. In other words, the proportion of females tended to decrease when the volume increased, such as immediately after the recession and in 1973, and vice versa as in the early seventies (see Tables 32 and 40).

The Auslanderstopp reduced the overall flow of female labour to West Germany relatively less than the male flow. For labour from the six countries, however, females were slightly more adversely affected than males, with an immediate reduction of 72 per cent compared to 70 per cent for males. In fact, of the six individual countries only Greece, Turkey and Yugoslavia had greater reductions of female labour flows than of male, whilst females from Italy, Portugal and Spain were affected rather less than males. In addition, the 72 per cent overall reduction conceals considerable differences between countries: female labour in-flows from Portugal, Turkey and Spain were reduced by more than 80 per cent, from Yugoslavia by 73 per cent, from Greece by 61 per cent, and from Italy by 45 per cent.

This lesser effect on the flow from Italy is in line with expectation because of the free movement of Italian citizens within the EEC, and it is seen from Table 32 that the flow from Italy has remained high relative to flows from non-EEC countries. The effects of the 1974-5 recession, of the economic recovery towards the late seventies and of the recession of the early eighties can also be seen.

The proportion of females among labour out-migrants is shown in Table 41. Again, there is considerable variation between countries, reflecting the variation in the proportion of females among labour in-migrants. In the early years, the proportion of females among labour out-migrants was lower than among labour in-migrants, but this trend has been generally reversed. The 1966-7 recession caused increases in female and male labour out-migration to roughly the same degree. After the recession the volume of female labour out-migration (Table 36) decreased, and after some variation in the late sixties remained relatively stable, with the exception of an increasing but small flow to Portugal, until 1973. The Auslanderstopp and the 1974-5 recession resulted in an increased out-flow but the level has since decreased.

The net movement of female and male labour is shown in Tables 42 and 43 respectively. Whilst the male labour flow was negative for Italy, Greece and Spain in the first year of the recession, in no case was the female flow negative until 1967, and for two countries, Portugal and Yugoslavia the flow remained positive. Female labour flows were thus less adversely affected by the recession than male labour. This does not imply that female labour was more favourably disposed: unemployed wives could remain in the country with an employed husband, but an unemployed male breadwinner might find it preferable, or indeed necessary, to leave. After the Auslanderstopp, the flow of both female and male labour was negative though the male flow was much greater than the female flow, and apart from the flow from Italy has remained negative with only a few exceptions in recent years.

Country comparisons

In order to facilitate the examination of migration from and to each country, Tables 44 to 57 provide the basic measures for each individual country and for all countries of migration with West Germany. These tables show four measures: the proportion of migrants who are labour; the proportion of labour migrants who are male; and the proportion of male migrants who are labour; and the proportion of female migrants who are labour. The general pattern is shown in Tables 44 and 45. Labour has comprised a decreasing proportion of migrant flows over time, especially after the Auslanderstopp, because of the entry of dependant wives and children. Nevertheless, the proportion of males among labour migrants has not decreased appreciably. Male labour comprised more than three quarters of the flows of males until 1973, after which the proportion fell but has never been less than half. Even after the end of recruitment, more than half of the male migration between West Germany and other countries is of labour. In contrast, female labour represents only about a quarter of the total female flow.

Migration to and from Italy (Tables 46 and 47) differs from migration with other former recruitment countries because of the free movement of labour. Even before this distinction came about, however, the f lows to and f rom Italy were comprised of higher proportions of labour for both sexes and higher proportions of male labour. The Italian flow was thus predominantly comprised of male labour, and this has continued after recruitment ceased. Though the proportion of female labour amongst all female migrants has decreased, indicating the presence of a substantial proportion of dependant wives and female children, this proportion is high relative to other countries. Though Italians were the first nationality to migrate to West Germany on a large scale, they have not followed the pattern exhibited by other nationalities, such as Greece and Spain, whereby labour became less dominant in migrant flows as dependants joined the male breadwinner. This is not to say that some dependants from Italy did not enter West Germany, but that the security of the right to employment and residency in a sister EEC country gave Italians a much greater freedom to migrate at will both to and from West Germany.

The Greek pattern of migration, summarised in Tables 48 and 49, indicates that the migration process was at a later stage even before the Auslanderstopp brought the recruitment of labour to a halt. The rapidly decreasing proportion of labour among all migrants indicates the presence of a substantial proportion of dependants among the Greek population. Even among male in-migrants, only 50 per cent were labour in 1973. A contributory factor to this short time span of the migration process of Greeks is probably to be found in the early high proportion of female labour, both among labour generally and amongst females. From the beginning of migration to West Germany until the Auslanderstopp, the balance between the sexes has been much greater for Greeks than for any other nationality. This and the greater tendency for Greek women to work has led to the earlier entry of dependants such that by 1973 dependants formed more than half of all in-migrants and almost half of out-migrants.

The flow of migrants from Spain was also well-established by the early sixties. Here, however, the proportion of labour among migrants had not decreased substantially prior to the Auslanderstopp, as Tables 50 and 51 show. The process of migration has been more gradual with dependants featuring less in migrant flows than in the case of Greece.

The Portuguese flow has never been very significant compared to the flows from other countries. In the early sixties this flow was more balanced in terms of both gender and labour-dependant ratios than in later years, indicating the late start of male labour dominance. In the late sixties and early seventies, Portuguese migration remained in the early stages of the migration process with high proportions of male labour but relatively low proportions of labour amongst female migrants. After the Auslanderstopp, the proportion of labour among in-migrants has been very low, particularly among female migrants, as Table 52 shows. For out-migrants, these proportions are not so low relative to those for other countries (see Table 53). This would suggest that whilst some labour and dependants are leaving West Germany, those who are entering are mainly dependants who have been separated from the family breadwinner.

Tables 54 and 55 show the migration characteristics of Turks. Whilst the proportion of labour was comparatively high in the late sixties, it decreased considerably in the early seventies as dependants were brought into West Germany. Though migration from Turkey was established rather later than that from Italy, Greece and Spain, the high proportion of dependants amongst migrants in the early seventies suggests that for Turks the migration process was occurring relatively quickly. This has not been facilitated by the in-migration of females as labour, as it has for G reeks, since the proportion of females amongst labour migrants is low. Rather, the flow of male labour during this period remained relatively stable whilst the flow of dependant wives and children increased. A process of family reunification and consolidation was thus taking place prior to the Auslanderstopp. After the Auslanderstopp the movement of Turks consisted mainly of dependants, especially for in-migration. Female migrants in particular are virtually all dependants. Though the net migration of labour was negative until 1978, the net migration of dependants was positive. In 1979 and 1980 the net migration of labour was positive due to the increased use of political asylum as a means of entering West Germany, and males represented more than 90 per cent of the inflow of labour. With the introduction of the waiting period prior to employment for such people, however, the flow of labour is again negative and dependants comprise the bulk of the flow into the country.

Migration from Yugoslavia, shown in Tables 56 and 57, also began rather later. The proportion of labour has remained relatively high, not only for males but also for females. In the period 1968 to 1973, the proportion of male labour exceeded that from Italy, whilst at the same time the proportion of female labour exceeded that from Greece. This is partly due to the late start of Yugoslav migration, but in comparison to

Turkish migration the Yugoslav migration process shows little signs of moving towards dependent migration. Part of this difference may be explained by a smaller number of dependants amongst the Yugoslav population compared to the Turkish population but this factor cannot account for the entire difference.

In general, it should be noted that since 1974 for all countries the proportion of labour among out-migrants is higher than among in-migrants. This accords with the greater net outflow of labour than of dependants. With the exception of Italians in the more prosperous years and Turks under the asylum laws, labour has been leaving West Germany on a large scale. The net outflow of dependants is on a rather smaller scale, and for Turks and in some years for the Portuguese the flow is positive. Only in the case of Turkey, however, does the net inflow of dependants exceed the net outflow of labour. Thus for Greeks, Spanish, Portuguese and Yugoslavs, the recent trend is of the exit of labour with a smaller number of dependants, leading to more consolidated and demographically balanced populations within West Germany. For Turks, this process of consolidation is occurring at a faster pace because of the net inflow of dependants whilst some labour continues to leave. This is contrasted with the Italian situation in which dependants are leaving the country on balance, whilst labour continues to enter West Germany when economic conditions are favourable. Whilst the Italian population contains an element that might be termed immigrant it is clearly also composed of migrant labour in the temporary guestworker sense. For the other populations, however, this temporary mode of employment and residency is no longer available to them, and whilst many have chosen to leave West Germany on a permanent basis many others are bringing in their families with the intention of remaining in West Germany as immigrants for at least the foreseeable future.

Migration in relation to employment

The migration of labour has largely determined the size of the foreign labour force in West Germany but more recently the dependants of labour entrants have entered the labour market despite the restrictions of the Stichtagsregelung and its replacement legislation (see above). The numbers of employees per sending country are shown in Table 58, and in proportional terms in Table 59. It is seen that the 1966-7 recession did not adversely affect the employment of foreigners until 1967 and 1968, and that this represented a minor interruption in the growth of the number of foreign employees. After the Auslanderstopp, foreign employment decreased, though for Turks and probably for the Portuguese there was a years delay before the decline actually occurred. In terms of the proportional composition of foreign employees, the changes over time directly reflect the migration patterns already discussed. Italians comprised more than two-thirds of the labour from the six recruitment countries in 1960, but Greeks and Spaniards soon arrived in sufficient numbers to reduce the Italian proportion even though Italian employment continued to grow. By the early seventies Turks comprised almost a quarter of foreign employment (and 30 per cent of that from the six recruitment countries), followed closely by Yugoslavs. The relative growth of Turkish employees continued after the Auslanderstopp, whilst those from other non-EEC countries decreased and the Italian proportion has remained stable.

This pattern in foreign employment is the same for male employment, shown in Tables 60 and 61. It is not exactly, the same, however, for the smaller number of female employees, as Tables 62 and 63 show. Whilst Italians comprised the majority of female employees from the recruitment countries in 1959-60, Greek and Spanish women almost equalled the Italian proportion by 1962. The Greek and Italian proportions have remained roughly equal, except very recently when Greek women have left employment, but the share of Spanish women in employment began to decline with the 1966-7 recession and has continued so that by 1981 only 4 per cent of foreign female employees were Spanish. Portuguese women, like Portuguese men, have always been a relatively insignificant part of the labour force, and at no time has either sex exceeded 3.5 per cent of employees. The proportion of Turkish and Yugoslav women among employees has increased, such that Yugoslav women at first predominated overall, but the Turkish proportion roughly equalled the Yugoslav proportion after 1973 and had exceeded it by 1979. Turkish women comprised a quarter of all female foreign employment in 1981, that is one third of the employment of women from the six recruitment countries.

The relative contributions of foreign women to the number of employees reflect in part the relative sizes of the different foreign populations, shown in Table 72, and in particular, the female resident population shown in Table 73. The propensity of women to work differs between nationalities however. In 1981, the highest rate of participation in employment among women from the six recruitment countries was among Yugoslav women with 46 per cent. In the same year, Portuguese, Greek and Spanish women in employment comprised 38, 36 and 34 per cent of their respective populations, whilst 32 per cent of Italian women were in employment. Among Turkish women, these data show that only 24 per cent were in employment in 1981. These participation rates are low in comparison with those found in special studies, the discrepancy being particularly high for Turkish women, between 65 and 70 per cent of whom are in employment (Wilpert, 1983). The discrepancy in these levels of participation arises from the fact that official data on employees include only those people registered in the federal insurance system. Though this covers most of the foreign male employees, it is clear that many foreign women are not registered with this system. The official data on employed women thus gives only a partial picture of female employment.

The examination of migration in relation to the number of employees reveals further differences in the migration patterns of the various foreign populations in West Germany. Table 64 shows the number of employees per in-migrant for the six recruitment countries, and for all foreigners. The ratio has increased over time as foreign employment increased, and though after the Auslanderstopp foreign employment decreased or stabilised, the ratios continued in many cases to increase because of the reduction in in-migration. These ratios highlight the differences between the nationalities involved, especially after the Auslanderstopp. For Italy, where migration has remained high due to free movement, and for Turkey, where the entry of dependants and, for a brief period, of asylum-seekers has kept in-migration levels high, the ratios have remained relatively low. In contrast, the post-1973 ratios for Spain are particularly high, due mainly to low levels of in-migration. The high ratio for Greece in 1972-3 is a reflection of the reduced level of in-migration at that time, due to the change in the political situation within Greece.

Equivalent ratios per out-migrant are shown in Table 65. Here again the ratios have generally increased over time. Those for Italy are low because of free movement and roughly mirror the ratios in Table 64. For other countries, however, the pattern is rather different. Prior to the Auslanderstopp, out-migration was much less common than in-migration leading to higher ratios of employees per out-migrant. The ratios for Spain and Yugoslavia were rather lower than for Greece, Portugal and Turkey, reflecting a slightly higher propensity to return (either temporarily or permanently) to the country of origin. After the Auslanderstopp, the ratios declined as many migrants left West Germany, but these ratios have since increased due to the lower levels of out-migration in recent years.

The ratios shown in Tables 64 and 65 relate to all migrants whether they be labour or dependants. Given that the Auslanderstopp has already prevented the entry of labour as primary immigration, except as shown in Table 12a, dependant or secondary migration has became a focus of interest for the German authorities. Table 66 shows the ratio of the number of employees to the entry of dependants. Prior to the Auslanderstopp, these ratios were very high compared to the ratios for in-migration generally (Table 64). This demonstrates the low level of dependant migration and hence the minimal extent to which employees brought dependants into West Germany. Thus in 1965, only 1 in 16 Spanish employees brought in a single dependant. For most countries, this low dependant in-migration remained until 1973, but the Turkish higher rate of dependant in-migration is seen in the lower ratios. Even here, however, only one dependant per 5 or 6 employees entered the country per year. Prior to the Auslanderstopp, these dependant ratios do not include the spouses of employees who entered the country as labour with work permits. The ratios are thus rather higher than family reunification rates would suggest: in other words the ratios under-estimate the rate at which members of an employee's family join the employee, but this under-estimation is not great. After the Auslanderstopp, the ratio temporarily declined but for most countries soon rose as the entry of dependants declined. Again the high level of dependant in-migration for Turkey is seen in the low ratios. Those for Italy are not so low as for Turkey (compare Table 64) because of the continued entry of labour from Italy.

These ratios of employees per dependant in-migrant are divided into female and male employees in Tables 67 and 68. The lower ratios for female employees reflects their smaller numbers in these official data. If male employees are taken to represent family units the rates of family reunification can be seen in Table 68. After the Auslanderstopp, Turkish dependants entered West Germany at the rate of one per 3 or 4 family units per year, whilst Spanish dependants entered at the much slower rate of about one per 18 family units. Whilst the Spanish rate of family reunification is clearly very slow, and has never been among the fastest, this is more a reflection of the late stage in the process of migration than of delays in the entry of dependants. Spanish employees have on the whole either left West Germany or have brought in their families so that the consolidation of the Spanish population is more advanced than for other migrant populations. In contrast, the Turkish population is much less advanced in the migration process. Relatively speaking, few Turkish workers left West Germany after the Auslanderstopp, and the majority chose to remain in the country and bring in their families. This process of reunification continues, though the rate at which Turkish dependants enter West Germany is not particularly high. The entry of dependants is discouraged by the regulations concerning their entry; for example, adequate family accommodation in terms of floor space is a condition of entry. Such conditions operate to delay the entry of dependants for many years. It has been estimated that in about 1980 there were about one million children remaining in the sending countries who are eligible to enter the Federal Republic. Recent measures and recommendations have sought to limit this number by removing their right to entry.[6]

The movement of dependants out of West Germany is related to the number of total, female and male employees in Tables 69, 70 and 71 respectively. Prior to the Auslanderstopp, these ratios were very high, illustrating the low frequency with which dependants returned to their countries of origin either permanently or for short periods. The rate of dependant out-migration for the Portuguese is particularly low with as little as 1 dependant per 50 employees per year returning to Portugal. This is in contrast to the relatively low ratio of Portuguese dependant in-migrants (Table 66). Though all such ratios of dependant out-migration are greater than those of dependant in-migration, the differences differ between countries of origin. The Italian ratios differ the least, a reflection of the greater mobility of Italian dependants whose migration behaviour is influenced by the free movement of labour. The out-migration of dependant Greeks is the second most common, especially in the early 1970s when the difference between the two ratios was very small indeed. Whilst Spain and Turkey had roughly equal ratios of dependant out-migration, their in-migration ratios were quite dissimilar. Thus Turkey had a large difference between dependant in-migration and out-migration ratios whilst the difference for Spain was less marked. Like Greece, however, both countries had fewer out-migrants per employee prior to the Auslanderstopp than in previous years, due to increased out-migration rather than to any reduction in employee numbers.

The out-migration of dependants in relation to female and male employees are shown in Tables 70 and 71. These follow the same pattern as for total employees, but differences between countries vary between the sexes because of the different proportions of females among employees by nationality (see Tables 61 and 63). Regarding male employees as family units, it is seen that Italian and Greek families were the most likely to send or take a dependant abroad, followed by the Spanish, Turkish, Yugoslavs and Portuguese. After the Auslanderstopp, these ratios declined considerably, and instead of exceeding the in-migration ratios, in most cases for the first time were less than them. In other words dependant out-migration has occurred at a faster rate than dependant in-migration in recent years. The exceptions to this are Turkey, where dependants have continued to enter West Germany at a positive net rate, and Portugal where 1974-5 and 1978-9 were also years of net dependant in-migration (see Table 17). Though these countries have net in-migration of dependants, their ratios of employees to out-migrants are not always as high as those for other countries. Yugoslavs, for example, have higher ratios of employees per dependant out-migrant than Turks, but their negative net migration results also form a higher ratio of employees per dependant in-migrant. The striking difference between dependant in- and out-migration ratios occurs in the case of Spain. Out-migration is considerably more frequent an occurrence than in-migration, and though Spanish dependant out-migration is roughly on a par with other nationalities, in-migration is particularly rare. This is due to Spanish migrants being at a later stage in the migration process.

Summary

It is clear from this examination of the migration trends to and from West Germany that considerable differences of migration behaviour exist between the six main migrant groups. The migrant population is not one homogeneous group entering West Germany at a steady rate. Female migrants behave differently to males and labour migrants differ from dependants; and these relationships vary between nationalities. These different groups of migrants have responded in different ways to the opportunities and restrictions presented to and imposed upon them regarding employment and residence in West Germany. Their responses in terms of their migration behaviour have to a large extent shaped the various migrant populations that are currently resident in West Germany.

Notes

1. With the single exception of Italy in 1964.
2. Personal communication with Elmar Honekopp, Institut fur Arbeitsmarkt- und Berufsforschung, Bundesanstalt fur Arbeit (17 August 1982). Military service is obligatory in all six countries, but for Greeks, Yugoslavs and Italians living abroad exemptions usually apply. Spanish, Portuguese and Turkish citizens are obliged to do some military service regardless of residence abroad.

4.   The waiting period was maintained at 12 months for people from East European countries. This may explain the continued entry of Yugoslavs at a relatively steady level.

5.   The relative importance of these two factors is unknown. However, a crude comparison with the 1966-7 recession suggests that about half of the reduced flow in 1974 was directly due to the cessation of recruitment. It is seen in the table below that in the first year of the 1966-7 recession, the flow from Italy was reduced at almost the same rate as that from countries other than the six under study, but that it was considerably more reduced in the second year. Assuming the same relative situation in 1974-5, the flow from Italy in 1974 would be expected to be reduced to about 73 per cent of its 1973 level in the absence of the Auslanderstopp, and about 3 1 per cent in 1975. The Auslanderstopp is thus estimated to have resulted in about 24 of the 51 per cent reduction, or roughly half of the fall in the inward migratory flow from Italy.

Country of origin	% of 1965 level		% of 1973 level	
	1966	1967	1974	1975
Italy	85	35	49	27
Others*	88	64	75	59

*Countries other than Italy, Greece, Spain, Portugal, Turkey and Yugoslavia.

6.   The federal government seeks to 'persuade' migrants to go about family reunification in a 'socially responsible' way. Thus in December 1981, the government recommended (and many Lands implemented) that certain groups should no longer be eligible for entry. These included:

(i)   16 and 17 year old children of migrants.

(ii)   children of migrants who had only one parent living in West Germany (with exceptions for those with only one parent because of widowhood, divorce or illegitimacy).

(iii) family members of migrants who are in the Federal Republic for training or as contracted labour.

(iv)   spouses of the children of migrants, whether they (the children) were born in the FDR or not, unless they have an uninterrupted period of 8 years residence, have not yet reached the age of 18, and the marriage has existed for one year.

More recent recommendations (3 March 1983) call for the maximum age of entry for dependant children to be reduced to only 5 years, and for spouses to have to wait several years before gaining entry.

8 The resident population

Population size

The growth of the resident population of migrants in West Germany is shown in Table 72. It is seen that before any bi-lateral agreements were made concerning labour, Italians were the largest group followed closely by Yugoslavs. With the agreements of 1960 with Greece and Spain, these two populations began to grow but were nowhere near as large as the Italian population in 1961. By 1967, all countries except Yugoslavia had signed a bi-lateral agreement concerning the recruitment of labour and these populations had grown accordingly. The Yugoslav population was not unduly small, however, since the more highly skilled labour from this country had found employment in West Germany through channels other than official recruitment agencies. For the earlier established flows of migrants from Italy, Greece and Spain, the populations grew steadily until 1971. The beginnings of recession in that year caused these populations to fall slightly as unemployment forced some migrants to leave West Germany, but they increased again in 1973 not because of improved economic conditions but because of the impending controls on migration. Though these controls in fact applied to labour only, the fear of dependant control caused an increase in the net migration of dependants in 1973. For the more recently established migratory flows from Portugal, Turkey and Yugoslavia, the recession of the early 1970s did not have sufficient effect to reduce the population sizes, and these populations grew considerably in 1973, particularly the Portuguese population. In all cases therefore, there was a concerted effort on the part of migrants to get to Germany before controls were introduced. That this applies to dependants as well as labour is indicative of the fact that many migrants did not regard themselves as temporary guestworkers but as more permanent immigrants.

After the Auslanderstopp the populations of Italians, Greeks and Spanish fell and in the case of Spanish migrants has continued to decline until 1981 when it was only 62 per cent of the 1973 level and marginally smaller than in 1967. The Greek population also declined for some time, only gaining slightly in 1980 and 1981, when it was 73 per cent of the 1973 level. In contrast, the Italian population recovered numbers as soon as the mid–1970s recession was over and increased steadily almost reaching its 1973 level in 1981. For the Portuguese, the decline in their population did not begin until 1975 and has been very gradual with a brief increase in 1980. By 1981 the Portuguese population has only reduced by 2 per cent of its 1973 level. The Yugoslav population also began to decline in numbers in 1975, but in 1979 began to increase again, so that by 1981 it was 91 per cent of the 1973 level. Finally, the Turkish population has not decreased at all, and has grown to 170 per cent of its 1973 level, equivalent to an average annual growth rate of 6.6 per cent. The total foreign population in West Germany has increased since 1973 by 17 per cent, an average annual growth rate of 1.9 per cent.

In terms of its proportion of the total population of West Germany, the migrant population has increased steadily from 3.2 per cent in 1968 to 6.4 per cent in 1973 and 7.5 per cent in 1981. This proportional increase is not entirely due to the growth of the migrant population, however. It is also due to the decreasing size of the German population. In 1968, there were 58.4 million Germans resident in the Federal Republic; by 1973 there were 58. 1 million and by 1981 only 57.1 million. The average rate of growth since 1973 of the German population is thus – 0.2 per cent per annum. The concern expressed in West Germany about the presence of the migrant population is partly a result of these divergent rates of growth. That the greatest hostility centres on the Turkish population cannot be divorced from the fact that it is this group that has consistently increased in size when other migrant groups have decreased.

Population structure

Data concerning the demographic composition of the migrant population have been produced only relatively recently. The distribution of the various populations according to sex is shown in Tables 73 and 74 from 1974–1981. In all cases, the number of males exceeds the number of females, a result of the migration of males for labour prior to family reunification, and the presence of males who may intend to return to their country of origin rather than remain in West Germany indefinitely. The proportion of females is increasing over time, however: in 1974, 38 per cent of all foreign residents were female, increasing to 41 per cent in 1981. The highest proportion of females in 1974 was amongst the G reek population with 46 per cent female, and this proportion has remained the same in 1981. The 1974 proportions were 39 per cent for the Spanish and Portuguese, 38 per cent for Yugoslavs and 36 per cent for Italians and Turks. By 1981, these proportions had risen to 42, 46, 43, 38 and 41 per cent respectively. Thus the Greek and Portuguese populations are the closest to reaching equal proportions between the sexes, and the Italian population is furthest away from this goal due to the continued migration of unaccompanied males under the free movement of labour regulations.

When only adults are considered, the proportions of women are significantly lower than for the entire populations. Table 75 shows the proportions of females and males aged 16 and over, and the proportions of children aged 0 to 15. It is seen that the proportions of women are considerably lower than those of men in 1974, but that the difference between them diminishes with time. This is not due to any appreciable decrease in the proportion of men. This decrease in the male adult proportion of the population has occurred because of the concentration of women and especially children amongst post–Auslanderstopp migrants. Thus by 1981, only the Italian population comprised as much as 50 per cent men. This proportion and the proportions of Italian women and children have remained virtually unchanged since 1978 indicating that an equilibrium has been attained, though economic conditions, to which Italian labour is more responsive, may change this equilibrium temporarily.

The Greek and Spanish populations have also maintained almost constant proportions since 1978. The Greek population had a relatively low proportion of men and high proportions of children and especially of women in 1974, indicative of its earlier migration and more advanced stage in the migration process. The Spanish population has had more average proportions since 1974, and in comparison with the Greek has a low proportion of children with a correspondingly high proportion of men. Though the Spanish migratory flow was also established relatively early, the predominance of men has been maintained, indicating the greater tendency of Spaniards to migrate alone. Indeed, the lower proportion of Spanish children indicates that this occurs quite extensively, since the average family size in Spain is rather higher than that in Greece.[1]

The Portuguese, Turkish and Yugoslav populations all have continuing decreases in the proportion of men and continuing increases in the proportion of children. The Turkish population had by far the largest proportion of children in 1981, with 36 per cent. This represents a large increase since 1974, almost all of which has occurred at the expense of males, whose proportion is now the lowest among the six minority populations. Part of this high proportion of children amongst Turks arises from the relatively high fertility of the Turkish population.[2]

Table 76 shows the age structure of the foreign population in West Germany in 1974, 1978 and in 1981. Since the migrant population from the six sending countries comprised about 73 per cent of the total foreign population in 1981, these data can be taken as indicative of general trends for the six nationalities. The population in 1974 was heavily concentrated in the young adult age groups, 21 to 44, as a result of the predominance of labour amongst migrants. Even after some years of recruitment, the greatest proportion of migrants were aged 25–29. With the end of recruitment and the consolidation of the population, a dual process of redistribution occurred. On the one hand, the reunification of families increased the proportions of children; whilst on the other, the decision to remain in West Germany resulted in greater proportions of older age groups as the migrants grew older and in some cases also brought elderly dependant relatives to live with them. By 1981, the distribution of age, though still being concentrated in the early adult age groups, was considerably more even than in 1974.

Equivalent distributions for 1978 for each nationality, shown in Table 77, demonstrate the differences between the six minority populations. The modal age of Italians is younger than average, influenced by the fact that Italian labour is not barred from entry to West Germany. Indeed in the two younger groups, covering ages 18 to 24, there is a considerably higher than average proportion which is more similar to the 1974 average situation than that in 1978. There is a corresponding dearth of 30 to 44 year olds, again due to free movement in that Italians did not have to choose between remaining in West Germany or leaving permanently. Where family labour rotation is practiced, it is the younger adults who work abroad, and this could be a factor in explaining the Italian distribution. The Greek and Spanish populations have rather flatter, or move even, and later distributions than average, their proportions being relatively high and uniform at ages 25 to 49. As for all populations except Italy, they are typified by a lack of adolescents and young adults, the result of the concentration of migrant labour into the young adult age groups so that many migrant workers are not yet old enough to have adolescent and adult children. These slightly older Greek and Spanish populations do in fact have somewhat higher proportions of young adults. A further feature of these two earlier migrant populations is their bimodal (ignoring the initial age group) distribution. Both populations have modes at ages 30–34 and 40–44 with a trough at age 35–39. The reason for this is uncertain, but it could be due to the drastic cut-back in labour in-migration in the 1966–7 recession. If most in-migrants were aged about 23–28, the effect of the recession would have been to reduce the relative size of that cohort, resulting in low proportions aged 35–39 in 1978. This effect would not be seen for the other non-EEC countries because in-migration from these countries was not well established prior to the 1966–7 recession (see Tables 1 and 8). Indeed, in the cases of the Portuguese and Yugoslav populations the rather later start to migration is seen in their more peaked distributions: no sooner had migration from these countries become established than the Auslanderstopp reduced the flows resulting in the large differences in the proportions in the peak age group and the younger adjacent group. Why the Yugoslav population should peak at the rather young age 25–29 is unclear from the data, but it does suggest that Yugoslav labour was rather younger than that from the other recruitment countries. By the same reasoning, the Turkish labour appears to have been rather older than average, such that the mode of this distribution occurs at age 35–39.

The relative absence of adolescents and young adults in the migrant populations has already been mentioned. In general, there are more children aged 0 to 9 than there are in the age range 10–19. Again this is due to migration patterns, in that the young adults migrants were the parents of younger rather than older children in 1978. The data divide the first 10 years into two age groups of six and four years length, so that it is difficult to assess trends, but it seems from the Turkish and Yugoslav data at least that there is an increasing number of children. This is to be expected given the age structure of the adult population.

Dependency ratios

In comparison with the total population of West Germany, the migrant population is relatively young. This is seen in Table 78. The migrant population has greater proportions at ages up to 44, and smaller proportions thereafter. The concentration of the foreign population in the adult age group 15 to 44, is still highly advantageous to the West German economy, as indeed were the young, unaccompanied males who originally migrated to West Germany to prevent labour shortages during the most expansive phase of the West German economy (Castles et al, 1984). There are very few foreigners of pensionable age in West Germany, so that migrant workers are still subsidising the pensions of elderly Germans. This is seen in the dependency ratios in Table 79. When the adult population aged 15 to 44 is considered, the pensioner dependency ratio of the total population is of an order of magnitude greater than that for the foreign or migrant population. A lower dependency ratio of the migrant population is also true for children aged 5–14, and for children aged 0–4 the migrant ratio is marginally higher than that of the total population. In total, therefore, the dependency ratio of the migrant population is only 427 dependants per 1000 adults compared to the much larger 747 for the total population.

When the older, less productive working age population is included in the adult population, smaller dependency ratios are obtained especially for the total population because of the high proportion (about one third of those of working age) who are aged 45–64. The margin between the two populations is thus reduced, and in the case of children the migrant dependency ratio is higher than that for the total population. Overall, however, migrants still maintain a considerably lower dependency ratio than the total population, with only 348 dependants per 100 adults compared to 499 for the total population.

Table 79 also shows dependency ratios relating those in the labour force to those who do not work. For children, the migrant dependency ratios are higher than for the total population, but for the elderly the enormous disparity in the ratios is maintained. For both children and the elderly, the migrant ratio is considerably lower than that for the total population. The final figures in Table 79 take non–labour force adults into account, including these in the total number of dependants. This overall ratio is 979 for migrants and 1203 for the total population. These labour force dependency ratios for migrants are, in fact, probably too high because of the fact that female labour is to a large extent excluded from the data on employment. The disproportionate contribution of migrant labour to the social and other services of West Germany is thus likely to be greater than these ratios suggest.

Length of stay

Perhaps the most obvious indicator of whether a migrant population can be described as temporary or permanent is the average number of years spent in the receiving country. This information is presented for each of the six sending countries in Table 80. (Note that the groupings of years are not all of the same length). These data are obviously a reflection of past in-migration patterns but they also partly mirror the age distribution of the resident population since they include children. It is seen that the earlier established migrants have significantly higher proportions who have been resident in West Germany for 20 years or more. Given that the early bi-lateral agreements took place in 1960 with Greece and Spain, these proportions are to be expected. The high Italian proportion is also due to early migration, whilst Yugoslavs were entering West Germany in the 1950's and early 1960's long before recruitment began in that country. The relative proportions who have spent 15-19 years in West Germany follow this same pattern. These are the people who entered the country in 1962-66 before flows from Portugal, Turkey and Yugoslavia had been fully established (see Table 1). The proportion of Spaniards is particularly high, due to the fact that this period accounted for a relatively large proportion of Spanish in-migration because levels were never fully regained after the 1966-7 recession. The highest levels of in-migration from Spain were in fact in 1964 and 1965. For all nationalities, the proportion who have resided in West Germany for 10-14 years exceeds the proportion of 15-19 year residents by a considerable margin. This is most notable for the Portuguese, Turks and especially the Yugoslavs since migration from their respective countries began in earnest after the 1966-7 recession. These migrants with 10-14 years of residence migrated to West Germany in 1967-71, the years in which unprecedented levels of migration occurred, except from Spain and Italy. It is thus this length of residency that is the most common.

Those with 8-9 years residency in West Germany in 1981 migrated in 1972 or 1973, just before the Auslanderstopp. The proportion is relatively high because of the large numbers of people who entered just prior to the Auslanderstopp. This is particularly true of the Portuguese and Turkish populations (see Table 1). The lower proportions with shorter durations of residency in West Germany, are of course, the result of the Auslanderstopp. There are exceptions, however, such as the high proportion of Italians who migrated to West Germany in the more prosperous period before the current recession. In addition, the proportion of Turks with durations of stay of less than eight years is high, reflecting the continued entry of dependants. Indeed, the proportion with 1-3 years residency is almost equal to the proportion with 10-14 years residency, covering a longer period. These recent Turkish migrants are those people who entered seeking asylum, mainly in 1980.

Notes

1.   The total fertility rate in 1978 in Greece was 2.29 and in Spain 2.80. See Council of Europe (1980). Any deviation from these national total fertility levels for migrants is assumed to be roughly equal for both nationalities.

2.   Turkey's total fertility rate in 1975-9 was 4.5. See Council of Europe (1980).

9 Summary and conclusions

The migration of labour to West Germany was initially welcomed and encouraged by the federal government. Labour was needed to fuel the massive economic expansion that was occurring and there were enormous advantages in obtaining cheap, temporary labour from abroad who would perform the tasks that Germans had abandoned when better opportunities presented themselves. The recruitment system ensured that the best workers were selected so that profits would be maximised. The work permit and residence permit systems ensured that migrants were monitored and, given their limited duration, that employment and residence in West Germany could be temporary, even if in practice renewals were allowed.

This control of migration began to break down as migration began to develop its own momentum and as rights concerning the entry of dependants were granted. It was clear in the early 1970s that not only had dependant migration developed to such an extent that families were settling down to permanent residence but also that some sections of the migrant population were continuing to increase from new migration. With this in mind and with the impending economic crisis of the mid–seventies, the federal government took severe action in issuing the Auslanderstopp banning the further recruitment of foreign labour. The general move towards more permanent settlement in West Germany was accentuated by the Auslanderstopp, as both the migration patterns and structure of the resident population show.

Whilst these generalisations hold good for each of the migrant populations discussed, they do so to differing extents. The migration process of movement from one country and settlement in another has taken place at different times, at different paces and to different extents. There are large elements of the migrant populations that have never progressed to the settlement stage of the migration process, choosing instead to return to their country of origin, whilst other equally large elements have remained in West Germany for many years and intend to remain there for many more.

144

The free movement case: Italy

The Italian case is atypical of migration to West Germany. This is largely a result of the free movement of labour between the two countries which came into full effect in 1968. Even before then, however, Italians were entering West Germany in far larger numbers than any other group (Table 1). The whole process of migration began much earlier for Italians than for other nationalities, first with the 1955 bi-lateral agreement and encouraged later by the 1965 agreement and negotiations over EEC entry. The volume of in-migration both of labour and in total reached an early peak in 1965 (Tables 1 and 8). Despite the free movement of labour from 1968, the volume of migration actually declined, and never regained any thing approaching its 1965 level, which incidentally has not been reached by any other nationality. Though free movement had no apparent effect on the level of migration at that time, it has been of major significance in more recent years, principally because it allows labour migration to continue whilst other nationalities are barred from taking up employment in West Germany by the Auslanderstopp and supporting legislation. This is not to say that the Auslanderstopp had no effect on the migration of Italians: recruitment in Italy was severely limited and labour in-migration was reduced by roughly 50 per cent. Nevertheless the proportion of labour amongst all migrants (Tables 6 and 7) has remained relatively high, especially regarding in-migration, and in general Italian labour migration continues to be regulated by economic criteria.

It is clear from these high levels of labour migration that some Italians are working in West Germany on a temporary basis. This is confirmed by the high proportion (including children) who have been in the country for less than a year or 1 – 3 years whilst the population size has not grown commensurately (Tables 80 and 72), and by the young age structure of the adult population (Table 77). These temporary workers are mostly male: about two-thirds of recent in- and out-migrants are male (Tables 20 and 21) and about 80 per cent of male in-migrants are labour (Table 22). These proportions are high compared to those for other nationalities after 1973, and are only slightly less than the Italian pre-Auslanderstopp proportions. These unaccompanied male workers are also evident from the large excess of adult males in the population (Table 75).

Whilst temporary labour migration remains a feature of the Italian migration process, more settled elements also exist. These are evident from the relatively high proportion who had been in West Germany for twenty years or more by 1981 and in the high proportions of Italians aged 55 and over in 1978. The levels of migration of dependants are relatively high, however, especially in relation to female employees (Tables 66 to 71). This would suggest that some families or family members are living in West Germany on a temporary basis. This is to be expected under the free movement regulations since for Italians there is no necessity to make a permanent decision about living in West Germany or not. The Italian migrant population is thus comprised of three elements: those who have settled in West Germany as families; those who have part or all of their family with them and who maintain closer links with Italy in that they and their dependants migrate relatively frequently; and those who are unaccompanied, mostly male and in the main temporary. In addition, it is evident from the negative net migration of dependants since 1973 (Table 17) that many Italians have left West Germany on a long–term basis.

The older established migration: Greece and Spain

Migration from Greece and Spain was established later than that from Italy but was considerably earlier than that from Portugal, Turkey and the main flow from Yugoslavia (Table 1). Both Greece and Spain signed bi-lateral agreements for labour recruitment in 1960, the effect of which was to increase their share of foreign employment to about 15 per cent each by 1965 (Tables 58 and 59). The 1966–7 recession had a greater effect on Spanish employees than on Greek employees, however, and thereafter the two populations began to diverge, though still remaining closer to each other in character than to the other migrant populations.

The pattern of Greek migration is one of increase (apart from the recession of 1966–8) to 1970 (1969 in the case of labour), followed by a period of decreasing migration until recent years (Tables 1 and 8). The fact that migration began to decrease substantially prior to the Auslanderstopp was partly due to economic measures but it also suggests that the migration process for Greeks was occurring very rapidly. The rapid decline in Greek migration to West Germany in the early 1970s resulted in 1972 and 1973 in the negative net migration of labour, and the overall migration balance was also negative in 1973. Thus at a time when other nationalities were endeavouring to enter West Germany because of the impending ban, fewer Greeks were entering the country and out-migration was relatively high (Tables 1 to 4). The reasons for this were related to the political situation in Greece.

The high level of female migration has also been a major feature of Greek migration. Females comprised about 45 per cent of the total of in-migrants from as early as 1968 (Table 20) and only marginally fewer of out-migrants (Table 21). Thus by 1974, only 42 per cent of the Greek resident population were adult males, and by 1981 this proportion had fallen to 39 per cent (Table 75). Many of these females have been members of the labour force: as many as 80 per cent of female in-migrants were labour in the early 1960's compared to the average of 60 per cent (Tables 48 and 44), and females comprised 30 – 40 per cent of labour in-migrants prior to the Auslanderstopp (Table 48). This early migration of females many of whom were employees, has facilitated the early migration of dependant children. This is seen in the high proportion of dependants amongst migrants, even amongst males (Tables 48 and 49) and in the high ratios of dependant migrants to labour migrants (Tables 18 and 19). Thus by 1974, the Greek resident population contained the highest proportion (23 per cent) of children, and though this proportion is now second to that in the Turkish population, it has increased to 28 per cent (Table 75).

The reduction in in-migration as a result of the Auslanderstopp was not as great for Greeks as for other migrants, and-was seemingly the slightly inflated continuation of an existing trend (Tables 1 and 27). Out-migration was similarly inflated (Tables 3 and 4), and the negative balance of 1973 was increased substantially, such that the Greek net out-flow was almost as great as those from the much larger Turkish and Yugoslav populations (Tables 5 and 72). Indeed, the balance of dependant migration since 1973 has been greater than that for any other nationality with a negative flow (Table 1 7). The Greek resident population began to decrease in size in 1972, and apart from a temporary increase in 1973 (which does not tally with the migration data even if natural increase is taken into account) has declined steadily to 1979, after which there has been a very gradual increase.

For the Greek migrant population, therefore, the process of migration began early and occurred relatively rapidly. The flow of migrants has never been excessively dominated by males nor by labour, such that a much more balanced population developed at an early stage. For those that remain in West Germany, there is now relatively little in-migration of dependants (Tables 66 to 68) indicating that families have on the whole been reunited. Levels of out-migration, for both dependants and labour, are somewhat higher (Tables 15 and 16, 10 and 11) and until 1981, the Greek population was decreasing as a result of migration, though the level of out-migration has fallen (Table 3). Of the six migrant populations under consideration, the Greek population had by 1981 probably progressed furthest in the migration process. The level of net migration was by then very low and the population within West Germany was relatively well-balanced with respect to age and sex.

Spanish migration to West Germany reached a peak at a very early stage, in 1965, and never regained that level, though there was an increase after the 1966-7 recession (Table 1). This concentration of migration in the early years is reflected in the age structure of the 1981 resident population (Table 77). The Spanish population has, at least since 1967, always been smaller than the Greek population despite similar early in- migration patterns (Table 72). In fact, Spanish net migration has been considerably lower than Greek net migration since the early 1960's, and especially after 1967 (Table 5). This is also true of labour and of dependants (Tables 12 and 17). The difference in population sizes increased until the early 1970s, as Spanish migration remained at a relatively low level and f rom 1970 began to decline. After the Auslanderstopp, in-migration fell dramatically (Table 1) such that migration from Spain comprised only 1 - 2 per cent of total in-migration (Table 2). Out-migration, however, remained relatively high (Tables 3 and 4) resulting in levels of net out-migration that exceeded net in-migration in the 1968-73 period (Table 5). Many of these out-migrants were labour (Tables 7 and 1 2) especially during the 1974-5 recession. The initial response to the 1960 bi-lateral agreement between Spain and West Germany was thus short-lived and though migration continued and the Spanish resident population increased slowly to a peak in 1973, there has been a gradual decline in the population size. By 1981 the population was the same size as it was in the recession year 1967 (Table 72).

Compared to the Greek population, the Spanish population had a relatively high proportion of adult males in 1974, and this difference persists (Table 75). This is due to the high proportion of males among Spanish in-migrants (Table 20). In addition, a high proportion of Spanish male in-migrants and out-migrants were labour (Tables 50 and 51). Of the small proportion of migrants who were female about half were labour during the period 1968-1973 and about 70 per cent prior to the 1966-7 recession, rather fewer than among Greek female migrants. These relatively low levels of female migration and female labour force participation were accompanied by and contributed to relatively low numbers of dependant children, especially after 1967 (Tables 13, 14, 17 and 18), leading to smaller proportions of children amongst the Spanish resident population (Table 75). Prior to the Auslanderstopp, the Spanish population contained a high proportion of adult males, and though labour in-migration was diminishing, the in-migration of dependants was also decreasing so that the structure of the population was not becoming significantly more balanced. The Auslanderstopp led to a better demographic balance, however, primarily because of the massive exit of labour rather than the entry of dependants (Tables 10 to 14). Thus both the population size and number of employees declined considerably (Tables 58 and 72). The entry of dependants since the Auslanderstopp has been at a very slow rate with only one dependant per 26 or 27 employees entering West Germany per year including short-term movement (Table 66). The out-migration of dependants has been rather more frequent an occurrence (Table 69), leading to negative net dependant migration (Table 17). Both labour and dependant migration are now at very low levels (Tables 8 to 12, 13 to 17) and the population structure is relatively constant (Table 75). The migration process of the Spanish population is thus in its later stages, though a small negative migration balance continues to outweigh natural increase, and the population structure is relatively imbalanced (Table 75). It is this latter feature that will prolong the migration process in that the population will continue to be affected by its current demographic structure for some time.

The case of Portugal

In terms of its contribution to the migrant population and labour force, the Portuguese population is minute and has never made up more than 4 percent of the total (Tables 72, 58 and 59). The bi-lateral agreement with Portugal was signed in 1964 and had barely had time to take effect on migration levels before the 1966-7 recession caused many Portuguese people to leave West Germany (Tables 1 to 5). It was not until 1969 that migration from Portugal gathered strength, but even then it comprised only 2 per cent of the total flow, rising to 4.5 per cent in 1973 (Table 2). Though the proportion of labour amongst in-migrants was very high in 1964 and 1965, the entry of dependants reduced this somewhat after the recession (Table 52). Amongst males, however, the proportion of labour remained very high (Table 52), resulting by 1974 in a very male-dominated population structure and a notable absence of children (Table 75). This was also partly due to the low level of female participation in the labour force relative to other nationalities such as Greece and even Spain in the early years of migration (Table 29).

The Auslanderstopp put a premature end to labour migration from Portugal, though it must be acknowledged that the level of labour in-migration had fallen slightly in 1971 and 1972 but this was more than compensated for by the large increase in 1973 (Table 8). As for other nationalities, the net outflow of labour was considerable, and the number of Portuguese employees has decreased steadily with the exception of a slight rise in 1979 (Tables 12 and 58). In contrast to the older established populations of Greek and Spanish migrants and to the Italian population, the Auslanderstopp did not result in the immediate net exit of dependants (Table 17). In common with the other more recently migratory populations of Turks and Yugoslavs, the entry of dependants continued after 1973 because there were relatively few dependants then living in West Germany and for those migrant workers who made the decision to remain in West Germany, the process of family reunification began or was accelerated. As this process of family reunification progressed, fewer dependants entered the country (Tables 18 and 66) such that by 1981 the rate of entry per employee was as slow as that for the Spanish population (Tables 66 to 68). In terms of net migration, Portuguese dependants were leaving the country in relatively high numbers in 1980-1.

The effects of these migration flows are seen in the structure of the Portuguese resident population. The peaked adult age distribution is a result of the Auslanderstopp and the late start to migration and the absence of older people also reflects the late start (Table 77). The continued exit of labour after 1973 and the entry of dependants, except very recently, has reduced the excess of adult males in the population considerably. By 1981, the Portuguese population was almost as well balanced as the Greek (Table 75). In terms of population size, there has been a steady decline until 1979 as net migration remained negative (Table 5) but natural increase outweighed net out- migration in 1979 to produce a slight increase in 1980. The higher levels of dependant and labour out-migration in 1980 and 1981, however, resulted in a further decline in the 1981 population size (Tables 72, 10 and 15). For the Portuguese the process of migration has thus been brought to its later stages by the Auslanderstopp. The unaccompanied male employees have in the main either left the country or brought in their dependants such that the demographic structure of the population is relatively well-balanced. The time span from the onset of migration to a balanced population will thus be relatively short.

Continuing in-migration: the case of Turkey

Though migration from Turkey began to grow with the signing of the first bi-lateral agreement in 1961, and the level of migration was comparable with that from Greece and Spain in the mid-1960's, the full extent of the flow did not occur until after 1968 when the second bi-lateral agreement came into effect (Table 1). The 1966-7 recession had relatively little effect on the flow of Turkish in-migrants, especially dependants. Though labour in-migration was reduced, it was not until 1967 that the net flow became negative (Tables 8 and 12). Dependant in-migration was barely affected by the recession and though out-migration increased the total effect was not sufficient to produce a net outflow (Tables 13, 15 and 17). This is in contrast to the earlier established Greek and Spanish populations which suffered net labour outflows in the first year of the recession and sizeable net outflows of dependants (Tables 12 and 17).

Despite the fact that labour migration was increasing rapidly in the late 1960s, the proportion of dependants amongst migrants was also increasing, and by 1973 had reached about 50 per cent (Tables 54 and 55). The proportion of labour amongst male in-migrants was also low (Table 54) indicating the presence of male dependant children. This high rate of dependant migration in the period 1968 to 1973 (Tables 18 and 19) was not due to the earlier migration of females since males comprised about 85 per cent of Turkish migrants in the early 1960s (Tables 20 and 21). Of the females that did migrate in those early years, a relatively low proportion were labour (Table 29), and this proportion decreased considerably as dependant migration increased (Tables 54 and 55). Thus for Turks, the consolidation of the population began relatively soon after migration had become established, with high rates of dependant per labour migration (Tables 18 and 19). By 1974, the proportion of dependant children in the population was second only to that of the Greek population, but the proportion of female adults was low with an excess of male adults (Table 75).

The Auslanderstopp reduced the entry of new Turkish labour to a few thousand per year (Table 12A), though the level of movement of Turkish employees was considerably greater than this (Tables 8 and 10). Net labour migration was negative but after 1975 in-migration increased whilst out-migration decreased, resulting in positive balances in 1979 and 1980. This was due mainly to the use of political asylum as a means of entry to West Germany at least temporarily. With the restrictions on work permits and the introduction of visas for Turks in 1980, this positive balance again became negative in 1981 (Table 12). The number of Turkish employees in West Germany reflects these developments. Turkish employment reached a peak in 1974, and was slowly reduced to 88 percent of that level by 1978. The positive balance of labour and the continued entry of young Turks onto the labour market increased employment to almost its 1974 level in 1980, but the restrictions of that year marginally reduced the number of employees in 1981 (Table 58). Nevertheless, the Turkish proportion of migrant employees has increased steadily, not only since the Auslanderstopp but since migration began (Tables 59, 61 and 63).

Dependant migration increased in anticipation of the Auslanderstopp and again in the following year. It then resumed its former level and steadily increasing trend so that by 1979 and 1980 more dependants were entering West Germany per year than before the Auslanderstopp (Table 13) and Turks comprised fully two-thirds of dependant in-migration from the six recruitment countries combined (Table 14). Though out-migration of dependant Turks was comparatively common (Table 16), it was decreasing until 1981 at least (Table 15), and net migration has been positive since 1974 with an increasing trend over the period 1975 to 1980 (Table 17). The proportion of children in the population has thus increased considerably and in 1981 stood at 36 per cent (Table 75). This increase has not been accompanied by an increase in the proportion of women, but rather by a decrease in the proportion of men, which by 1981 was smaller than for any other nationality. In fact, the proportion of women has also decreased slightly and the imbalance in the sex ratio of Turkish adults persists (Table 75). This suggests that a large number of wives still remain in Turkey, many of whom also have children with them.

Though on balance migration between Turkey and West Germany has at times been negative, the Turkish resident population has steadily increased to its present level of 1,550,000 (Table 72), representing one third of the total foreign population resident in West Germany. Recent migration experience has shown that where possible Turks will continue to migrate to West Germany (Tables 12A, 8 and 17), giving no indication of a move away from the early stages of the migration process except by strictly enforced legislation. Even then, however, the fall in in-migration may be apparent rather than real, because illegal entry may be increasing (OECD, 1982, p. 126). Even without the entry of new workers, it is estimated that there are 600,000 Turkish dependants in Turkey waiting to go to West Germany, 350,000 of whom are children (OECD, 1982, p.130). The continuation of in-migration, and at increasing rates of entry (Table 66), is thus the natural progress of the migration process and as such Turkish migration is still at a relatively early stage of this process. Efforts on the part of the federal government to restrict the entry of new workers and the dependants of existing labour seek to bring the migration process of Turks to its later stage characterised by minimal migration and a more balanced resident population. To this end the authorities aim to severely limit the entry of dependants, and fearful that this might not be sufficient for their desires are also seeking to encourage migrants to return to their countries of origin (OECD, 1982; Castles, 1983).

The Yugoslav case

Yugoslavia has for many years been a source of labour to West Germany. In 1954, before any bi-lateral agreements were signed by West Germany, Yugoslavs (along with Italians) were numerous enough to be separately listed in the migration data. By 1965, Yugoslavs were entering West

Germany in numbers that rivalled those from countries with bi-lateral agreements, and during the 1966-7 recession Yugoslavs took the lead (Tables 1 and 8). It was not until 1968, however, that Yugoslavia signed a bi-lateral agreement with West Germany, after which her proportion of labour in-migration reached 28 percent (Table 9). In 1971, however, Yugoslav labour in-migration was reduced to a much greater extent than for other nationalities (Table 8) such that the net flow was only moderate and the restriction on the migration of highly skilled labour by the Yugoslav government resulted in further reductions in 1972 (Table 12). Prior to recruitment, about 85 per cent of migrants were labour, with about 94 per cent of males and about 60 per cent of females employed. These figures increased when recruitment began but in 1971 decreased substantially (Table 56). Though dependant in-migration was increasing at this time (Table 13) the net flow was constant (Table 17) such that the entire change in the composition of net migration was due to the reduction in labour. The low level of dependant migration relative to labour resulted in an extremely unbalanced demographic structure of the resident population by 1974. Only 11.5 per cent of the population were children and though as many as 32 per cent were women, 57 per cent were men (Table 75). The resident population had grown very rapidly and by 1969, only one year after recruitment began, exceeded each of the populations of Greeks, Spaniards and Turks (Table 72). With the reduction in labour migration, growth was more moderate, and the population reached a peak of 708,000 in 1974.

The Auslanderstopp caused an immediate decline in population size (Table 72). Net migration unlike that with Turkey, became negative (Table 5). Though net dependant migration was positive in 1974, net labour migration was negative and relatively large (Tables 17 and 12). By 1975, after the initial entry of dependants as a result of the Auslanderstopp (Table 13), dependant migration was also negative and continued to be so until 1981 (Table 17). The resident population thus decreased as a result of labour, and to a lesser extent dependant, net outflows until 1978 by which time the loss of labour had been reduced sufficiently for it to be more than counter-balanced by natural increase and the population grew over the period 1979 to 1981 (Tables 12 and 72). The concentration of males amongst out-migrants (Table 21) relative to in-migrants (Table 20) resulted in a reduction in the proportion of adult males in the resident population, but the proportion of adult females has not changed appreciably since 1974. Rather the increase has been among children, whose proportion has virtually doubled in the 7 year period since 1974 (Table 75). This is echoed in the number of employees, which has fallen annually since the Auslanderstopp (Table 58).

For Yugoslavs, then, migration has been heavily concentrated on labour migration especially in the early years of recruitment. Though some of this labour has left, the entry of dependants has never been great and the population structure continues to reflect the concentration of male labour migration. In recent years the balance of labour migration has been small, and in 1980 positive, due to reduced out-migration and increased in-migration (Tables 8, 10 and 12). This suggests that the permanent exit of labour has now virtually ceased. There is, however, a continued flow of several thousand new workers per year, which has been greater in recent years and suggest that there are Yugoslavs who are keen to work in West Germany, though not on the scale seen amongst Turks (Table 12A). The continued net outflow of dependants suggest that most of those families who wish to have already brought dependants into West Germany. The migration process has thus progressed relatively quickly with a move from the early stages of migration itself to the later stages of population development within West Germany. The imbalanced demographic structure of the population will, however, prolong this later stage.

Immigrants and guestworkers

It is clear that many of the migrants to West Germany have returned to their country of origin, and to this extent there have been elements who were temporary and who may be termed guestworkers. Some of these have no doubt left West Germany voluntarily, but many others have been forced to leave as a result of the economic and other measures taken by the federal government to encourage their return. Whether they were destined to return or to remain in West Germany, many migrant workers brought dependants into the country in the late sixties and early seventies. With economic recession and the Auslanderstopp, however, many workers and their dependants were compelled to leave and this was especially true of the older established migrant populations. Others brought in dependants since the Auslanderstopp forced them to decide between remaining in West Germany at least for the foreseeable future and thus establishing their families there or leaving their families in their country of origin and either joining them or visiting them only for vacations. With this decision having been made, the post-1973 population may be said to largely represent those who intend to remain in West Germany. Though most of the six nationalities have continued to lose members of their population through net out-migration, this trend has been generally reduced over time so that their current populations may be regarded as permanent. For the Turkish population, the balance between out-migration and in-migration has been positive for dependants indicating the intentions of Turkish migrants to remain in West Germany. Indeed, the recent entry of labour under asylum regulations indicates that many Turks would like to work and reside in West Germany. This reinforces the permanent nature of this population as immigrants. Only the Italian population currently contains large elements of temporary workers and residents as a result of Italy's membership of the EEC, but there are also many Italians who are permanent. In total, therefore, the migrant population in West Germany is best described as a permanent, immigrant population.

Tables to part II

Abbreviations

n.d	no data available
C(0–15)	children aged 0–15
W(16+)	women aged 16+
M(16+)	Men aged 16+

TABLE 1 The Number of In-migrants by Sending Country

Year	Total	Italy	Greece	Spain	Portugal	Turkey	Yugoslavia
1954	46853	2997	n.d.	n.d.	n.d.	n.d.	2018
1955	60368	5016	n.d.	n.d.	n.d.	n.d.	3043
1956	82505	16003	n.d.	n.d.	n.d.	n.d.	3532
1957	107418	21660	n.d.	n.d.	n.d.	n.d.	5798
1958	118282	29468	n.d.	n.d.	n.d.	n.d.	7464
1959	145919	49446	n.d.	n.d.	n.d.	n.d.	7411
1960	317685	143614	27317	31233	602	3614	7211
1961	411069	179071	37843	53967	1220	8781	13602
1962	488872	201474	53056	62561	1295	17559	34081
1963	498438	187528	64583	62134	2007	31025	26328
1964	625484	209653	81709	81818	4590	71256	31381
1965	716157	269012	78233	82324	11844	72476	51300
1966	632496	237268	55396	54363	10810	60488	74453
1967	330298	105961	20589	17012	3997	33106	37890
1968	589562	178296	53107	38042	8242	79711	95277
1969	909566	190571	87884	59273	15214	151142	220450
1970	976232	183980	94307	61318	22474	176972	238502
1971	870737	167570	71064	52434	23793	186955	159398
1972	787162	147207	51083	44540	24549	184549	134117
1973	869109	152545	36102	46234	39269	24969	151056
1974	538574	85591	29960	13760	13247	160750	72289
1975	366095	50907	18196	7606	8139	98562	45561
1976	387303	66361	16004	6269	5839	105758	40715
1977	422845	80230	15276	5641	4761	114515	38553
1978	456117	83037	15387	5277	4687	131019	38553
1979	545187	89292	14787	5049	4424	171880	40573
1980	631434	86138	15811	5402	3958	212254	41884
1981	501138	65044	18536	5674	3078	84052	33945

157

TABLE 2 The Percentage of In-migrants by Sending Country

Year	Total	Recruitment Countries	Italy	Greece	Spain	Portugal	Turkey	Yugoslavia
1954	46853	10.7	6.4	n.d	n.d	n.d	n.d	4.3
1955	60638	13.3	8.3	n.d	n.d	n.d	n.d	5.0
1956	82505	23.7	19.4	n.d	n.d	n.d	n.d	4.3
1957	107418	25.6	20.2	n.d	n.d	n.d	n.d	5.4
1958	118282	31.2	24.9	n.d	n.d	n.d	n.d	6.3
1959	1459.9	39.0	33.9	n.d	n.d	n.d	n.d	5.1
1960	317685	67.2	45.2	8.6	9.8	0.2	1.1	2.3
1961	411069	71.6	43.6	9.2	13.1	0.3	2.1	3.3
1962	488872	75.7	41.2	10.9	12.8	0.3	3.6	7.0
1963	498438	75.0	37.6	13.0	12.5	0.4	6.2	5.3
1964	625484	76.8	33.5	13.1	13.1	0.7	11.4	5.0
1965	716157	78.9	37.6	10.9	11.5	1.7	10.1	7.2
1966	632396	77.9	37.5	8.8	8.6	1.7	9.6	11.8
1967	330298	66.2	32.1	6.2	5.2	1.2	10.0	11.5
1968	589652	76.8	30.2	9.0	6.5	1.4	13.5	16.2
1969	909566	79.7	21.0	9.7	6.5	1.7	16.6	24.2
1970	976232	79.6	18.8	9.7	6.3	2.3	18.1	24.4
1971	870737	75.9	19.2	8.2	6.0	2.7	21.5	18.3
1972	787162	74.5	18.7	6.5	5.7	3.1	23.4	17.0
1973	869109	77.7	17.6	4.2	5.3	4.5	28.7	17.4
1974	538574	69.7	15.9	5.6	2.6	2.5	29.8	13.4
1975	366095	62.5	13.9	5.0	2.1	2.2	26.9	12.4
1976	387303	62.2	17.1	4.1	1.6	1.5	27.3	10.5
1977	422845	62.0	19.0	3.6	1.3	1.1	27.1	9.9
1978	456117	60.9	18.2	3.4	1.2	1.0	28.7	8.5
1979	545187	59.8	16.4	2.7	0.9	0.8	31.5	7.4
1980	631434	57.9	13.6	2.5	0.9	0.6	33.6	6.6
1981	501138	42.0	13.0	3.7	1.1	0.6	16.8	6.8

TABLE 3   The Number of Out-migrants by Sending Country

Year	Total	Italy	Greece	Spain	Portugal	Turkey	Yugoslavia
1954	28831	1990	n.d	n.d	n.d	n.d	788
1955	35548	2679	n.d	n.d	n.d	n.d	1234
1956	48221	8555	n.d	n.d	n.d	n.d	1524
1957	59292	11895	n.d	n.d	n.d	n.d	2391
1958	64011	16820	n.d	n.d	n.d	n.d	3511
1959	80630	27584	n.d	n.d	n.d	n.d	4060
1960	124441	57498	3033	3379	230	1003	3614
1961	181524	92249	8559	12118	335	1364	4758
1962	245066	130824	14002	20847	376	3565	9023
1963	344526	184628	23894	34095	630	6267	16168
1964	371448	165925	36369	40853	782	13820	21765
1965	412704	174334	44157	48641	1717	22682	24699
1966	535235	220263	58093	68890	3765	40368	36866
1967	527894	174320	73828	67725	6005	53890	40797
1968	332625	121607	29043	26643	2919	27740	30562
1969	368664	132097	24394	25609	3025	31622	54633
1970	434652	136531	30259	31939	5371	42355	88991
1971	500258	139040	40119	35924	8312	60883	107709
1972	514446	127472	48060	36124	8667	75008	97209
1973	526811	121463	48807	39203	10451	87094	91534
1974	580445	120317	48732	47574	17382	110825	101955
1975	600105	104498	65709	40077	14928	148475	100016
1976	515438	84755	58200	32780	12276	130354	74393
1977	542093	75396	48000	24543	9049	113531	58415
1978	405753	73925	36258	17447	6560	88080	50943
1979	366008	73931	29247	12139	5761	66256	44413
1980	385843	77429	22318	10001	7994	70583	41078
1981	415524	80728	15782	8899	7789	70905	40026

TABLE 4   The Percentage of Out-migrants by Sending Country

Year	Total	Recruitment Countries	Italy	Greece	Spain	Portugal	Turkey	Yugoslavia
1954	28831	9.6	6.9	n.d	n.d	n.d	n.d	2.7
1955	35548	11.0	7.5	n.d	n.d	n.d	n.d	3.5
1956	48221	20.9	17.7	n.d	n.d	n.d	n.d	3.2
1957	59292	24.1	20.1	n.d	n.d	n.d	n.d	4.0
1958	64011	31.8	26.3	n.d	n.d	n.d	n.d	5.5
1959	80630	39.2	34.2	n.d	n.d	n.d	n.d	5.0
1960	124441	55.3	46.2	2.4	2.7	0.2	0.8	2.9
1961	181524	65.8	50.8	4.7	6.7	0.2	0.8	2.6
1962	245066	72.9	53.4	5.7	8.5	0.2	1.5	3.7
1963	344526	77.1	53.6	6.9	9.9	0.2	1.8	4.7
1964	371448	75.2	44.7	9.8	11.0	0.2	3.7	5.9
1965	412704	76.6	42.2	10.7	11.8	0.4	5.5	6.0
1966	535235	80.0	41.2	10.9	12.9	0.7	7.5	6.9
1967	527894	78.9	33.0	14.0	12.8	1.1	10.2	7.7
1968	332625	71.7	36.6	8.7	8.0	0.9	8.3	9.2
1969	368664	73.6	35.8	6.6	6.9	0.8	8.6	14.8
1970	434652	77.2	31.4	7.0	7.3	1.2	9.7	20.5
1971	500258	78.4	27.8	8.0	7.2	1.7	12.2	21.5
1972	514446	76.3	24.8	9.3	7.0	1.7	14.6	18.9
1973	526811	75.7	23.1	9.3	7.4	2.0	16.5	17.4
1974	580445	77.0	20.7	8.4	8.2	3.0	19.1	17.6
1975	600105	78.9	17.4	10.9	6.7	2.5	24.7	16.7
1976	515438	76.2	16.4	11.3	6.4	2.4	25.3	14.4
1977	452093	72.8	16.7	10.6	5.4	2.0	25.1	12.9
1978	405753	67.3	18.2	8.9	4.3	1.6	21.7	12.6
1979	366008	63.3	20.2	8.0	3.3	1.6	18.1	12.1
1980	385843	59.5	20.1	5.8	2.6	2.1	18.3	10.6
1981	415524	53.9	19.4	3.8	2.1	1.9	17.1	9.6

TABLE 5 Net Migration by Sending Country

Year	Total	Italy	Greece	Spain	Portugal	Turkey	Yugoslavia
1954	18022	1007	n.d	n.d	n.d	n.d	1230
1955	24820	2337	n.d	n.d	n.d	n.d	1809
1956	34284	7448	n.d	n.d	n.d	n.d	2008
1957	48126	9765	n.d	n.d	n.d	n.d	3407
1958	54271	12648	n.d	n.d	n.d	n.d	3953
1959	65389	21862	n.d	n.d	n.d	n.d	3351
1960	193244	86116	24284	27854	372	2611	3597
1961	229545	86822	29284	41849	885	7417	8844
1962	243806	70650	39054	41714	919	13994	25058
1963	153912	2900	40689	28039	1377	24758	10160
1964	254036	43728	45340	40965	3808	57436	9616
1965	303453	94678	34076	33683	10127	49794	26601
1966	97261	17005	-2697	-14527	7045	20120	37587
1967	-197596	-68359	-53239	-50713	-2008	-20784	-2907
1968	256937	56689	24064	11399	5323	51971	64715
1969	540902	58474	63490	33664	12189	119520	165817
1970	541580	47449	64048	29379	17103	134617	149511
1971	370479	28530	30945	16510	15481	126072	51689
1972	272716	19735	3023	8416	15882	109541	36908
1973	342298	31082	-12705	7031	28818	162576	59522
1974	-41871	-34726	-18772	-33814	04135	49925	-29666
1975	-234010	-53591	-47513	-32471	-6789	-49913	-54455
1976	-128135	-18394	-42196	-26511	-6437	-24596	-33688
1977	-29248	4834	-32724	-18902	-4288	984	-16493
1978	50364	9112	-20871	-12170	-1873	42939	-12390
1979	179179	15361	-14460	-7090	-1337	105624	-3840
1980	245591	8709	-6507	-4599	-4036	141671	806
1981	85614	-15684	2754	-3225	-4711	13147	-6081

TABLE 6 Labour In-migrants as a Percentage of Total In-migrants by Sending Country

Year	Total	Italy	Greece	Spain	Portugal	Turkey	Yugoslavia
1962	84.6	93.9	90.0	86.4	72.2	81.9	87.7
1963	82.7	91.9	88.8	86.2	78.7	88.8	82.8
1964	83.4	91.6	88.2	88.2	86.8	91.5	83.7
1965	82.6	90.6	85.0	86.3	91.0	86.7	87.5
1966	79.6	87.5	79.9	82.7	86.2	82.1	88.6
1967	67.9	81.2	60.7	66.8	63.0	69.6	77.9
1968	74.9	81.7	71.3	79.0	71.4	75.2	89.7
1969	78.5	81.3	74.5	82.4	81.3	78.2	91.6
1970	75.9	79.2	69.1	80.5	86.9	69.6	88.2
1971	68.5	76.8	59.0	72.8	74.0	59.3	78.3
1972	62.6	73.7	52.3	66.7	67.8	49.8	71.9
1973	62.6	71.8	39.6	71.7	75.7	52.6	71.7
1974	40.3	62.1	22.8	30.7	17.9	18.0	45.6
1975	37.7	59.0	22.3	29.1	13.6	14.7	37.6
1976	39.5	64.2	27.6	33.7	14.2	14.1	32.6
1977	40.8	63.9	29.2	34.9	17.1	13.7	32.7
1978	42.0	64.3	31.6	34.8	15.7	15.9	35.0
1979	43.7	64.8	32.7	35.5	20.3	21.4	38.2
1980	47.3	63.3	35.3	40.6	24.6	29.9	42.9
1981	46.7	58.5	37.7	43.9	26.4	13.5	34.3

TABLE 7   Labour Out-migrants as a Percentage of Total Out-migrants by Sending Country

Year	Total	Italy	Greece	Spain	Portugal	Turkey	Yugoslavia
1962	84.4	95.3	84.6	88.8	72.6	73.9	74.6
1963	85.4	94.7	85.4	88.7	72.9	78.3	85.0
1964	84.0	94.3	85.9	89.2	75.6	89.0	87.7
1965	83.4	93.8	83.9	88.5	84.2	88.0	87.4
1966	82.8	91.5	80.6	86.3	90.3	88.7	88.5
1967	78.2	85.5	77.7	81.1	89.3	86.0	85.4
1968	72.9	84.2	68.9	74.9	79.5	78.3	81.8
1969	73.9	83.7	65.6	77.6	80.5	72.4	87.9
1970	75.1	82.2	65.6	80.1	85.2	69.4	88.2
1971	73.5	80.7	63.6	80.3	85.8	63.2	84.5
1972	68.8	76.8	58.2	76.7	81.7	56.8	79.4
1973	64.3	74.9	55.3	72.9	75.9	46.5	73.8
1974	61.6	68.9	54.1	70.3	74.7	46.3	71.6
1975	55.3	61.8	50.5	63.4	62.4	43.7	65.4
1976	48.6	58.3	47.6	56.2	51.6	34.2	56.3
1977	43.9	58.3	44.7	50.6	42.4	27.3	45.4
1978	41.9	56.3	43.3	48.6	42.1	26.2	39.9
1979	42.5	56.3	41.4	46.1	39.4	26.2	38.4
1980	47.0	56.5	40.0	45.5	43.7	41.0	38.2
1981	42.5	49.4	32.2	41.4	38.8	32.9	33.9

TABLE 8   Number of Labour In-migrants by Sending Country

Year	Total	Italy	Greece	Spain	Portugal	Turkey	Yugoslavia
1962	413354	189279	47737	54033	935	14385	29887
1963	412131	172428	57327	53551	1579	27542	21798
1964	521378	192120	72038	72198	3986	65211	26281
1965	591820	243691	66468	71029	10774	62854	44873
1966	503226	207728	44278	44953	9322	49683	65969
1967	224260	86076	12491	11358	2519	23055	29513
1968	441866	145651	37866	30052	5887	59945	85491
1969	714093	154975	65456	48846	12372	118201	201985
1970	741099	145801	65154	49383	19520	123094	210364
1971	596686	128633	41943	38175	17596	110940	124875
1972	492860	108540	26715	29699	16647	91997	96368
1973	544231	109530	14309	33170	29739	131437	108368
1974	217314	53185	6838	4223	2376	28967	32983
1975	137875	30025	4052	2217	1108	14527	17142
1976	153131	42633	4410	2113	831	14960	13271
1977	172642	51254	4458	1966	814	15727	13702
1978	191626	53425	4863	1835	735	20828	13503
1979	238469	57874	4833	1794	897	36817	15492
1980	298484	54530	5575	2194	975	63441	17956
1981	233836	38055	6995	2489	812	11333	11658

TABLE 9   Percentage of Labour In-migrants by Sending Country

Year	Total	Recruitment Countries	Italy	Greece	Spain	Portugal	Turkey	Yugoslavia
1962	413354	81.3	45.8	11.5	13.1	0.2	3.5	7.2
1963	412131	81.1	41.8	13.9	13.0	0.4	6.7	5.3
1964	521378	82.8	36.8	13.8	13.8	0.8	12.5	5.0
1965	591820	84.4	41.2	11.2	12.0	1.8	10.6	7.6
1966	503225	83.8	41.3	8.8	8.9	1.9	9.9	13.1
1967	224260	73.6	38.4	5.6	5.1	1.1	10.3	13.2
1968	441866	82.6	33.0	8.6	6.8	1.3	13.6	19.3
1969	714093	84.3	21.7	9.2	6.8	1.7	16.6	28.3
1970	741099	82.8	19.7	8.8	6.7	2.6	16.6	28.4
1971	596686	77.5	21.6	7.0	6.4	2.9	18.6	20.9
1972	492860	75.1	22.0	5.4	6.0	3.4	18.7	19.6
1973	544231	78.4	20.1	2.6	6.1	5.5	24.2	19.9
1974	217314	59.2	24.5	3.1	1.9	1.1	13.3	15.2
1975	137875	50.1	21.8	2.9	1.6	0.8	10.5	12.4
1976	153131	51.1	27.8	2.9	1.4	0.5	9.8	8.7
1977	172642	50.9	29.7	2.6	1.1	0.5	9.1	7.9
1978	191626	49.7	27.9	2.5	1.0	0.4	10.9	7.0
1979	238469	49.4	24.3	2.0	0.8	0.4	15.4	6.5
1980	298484	48.5	18.3	1.9	0.7	0.3	21.3	6.0
1981	233836	30.5	16.3	3.0	1.1	0.3	4.8	5.0

TABLE 10   Number of Labour Out-migrants by Sending Country

Year	Total	Italy	Greece	Spain	Portugal	Turkey	Yugoslavia
1962	206776	124626	11847	18508	273	2633	6734
1963	294172	174916	20406	30238	459	4907	13737
1964	312090	156470	31238	36453	591	12303	19095
1965	344207	163505	37029	43056	1445	19950	21575
1966	443149	201548	46842	59484	3399	35794	32630
1967	412727	148982	57394	54925	5365	46370	34824
1968	242625	102441	20001	19947	2320	21711	24995
1969	272590	110608	15989	19863	2436	22892	48034
1970	326364	112223	19836	25572	4578	29410	78470
1971	367901	112199	25499	28841	7133	38504	91034
1972	353735	97835	27982	27706	7085	42642	77151
1973	338806	90931	27014	28586	7935	40508	67513
1974	357421	82889	26375	33425	12991	51281	73018
1975	332125	64632	33183	25425	9322	64933	65365
1976	250740	49395	27675	18433	6339	44560	41887
1977	198654	43955	21470	12417	3840	30947	26522
1978	170007	41630	15685	8479	2763	23034	20343
1979	155556	41620	12011	5591	2270	17381	17070
1980	181438	43731	8938	4554	3493	28967	15693
1981	176550	39892	5075	3683	3021	23361	13579

TABLE 11 Percentage of Labour Out-migrants by Sending Country

Year	Total	Recruitment Countries	Italy	Greece	Spain	Portugal	Turkey	Yugoslavia
1962	206776	79.6	60.3	5.7	9.0	0.1	1.3	3.3
1963	294172	83.2	59.5	6.9	10.3	0.2	1.7	4.7
1964	312090	82.1	50.1	10.0	11.7	0.2	3.9	6.1
1965	344207	83.3	47.5	10.8	12.5	0.4	5.8	6.3
1966	443149	85.7	45.5	10.6	13.4	0.8	8.1	7.4
1967	412727	84.3	36.1	13.9	13.3	1.3	11.2	8.4
1968	242625	78.9	42.2	8.2	8.2	1.0	8.9	10.3
1969	272590	80.6	40.6	5.9	7.3	0.9	8.4	17.6
1970	326364	82.8	34.4	6.1	7.8	1.4	9.0	24.0
1971	367901	82.4	30.5	6.9	7.8	1.9	10.5	24.7
1972	353735	79.3	27.7	7.9	7.8	2.0	12.1	21.8
1973	338806	77.5	26.8	8.0	8.4	2.3	12.0	19.9
1974	357421	78.3	23.2	7.4	9.4	3.6	14.3	20.4
1975	332125	79.1	19.5	10.0	7.7	2.8	19.6	19.7
1976	250740	75.1	19.7	11.0	7.4	2.5	17.8	16.7
1977	198654	70.0	22.1	10.8	6.3	1.9	15.6	13.4
1978	170007	65.8	24.5	9.2	5.0	1.6	13.5	12.0
1979	155556	61.7	26.8	7.7	3.6	1.5	11.2	11.0
1980	181438	58.1	24.1	4.9	2.5	1.9	16.0	8.6
1981	176550	50.2	22.6	2.9	2.1	1.7	13.2	7.7

TABLE 12 Net Labour Migration by Sending Country

Year	Total	Italy	Greece	Spain	Portugal	Turkey	Yugoslavia
1962	206578	64653	35890	35525	662	11752	23153
1963	117959	-2488	36921	23313	1120	22635	8061
1964	209288	35650	40800	35745	3395	52908	7186
1965	247613	80186	29439	27973	9329	42904	23298
1966	60076	6180	-2564	-14531	5923	13889	33339
1967	-188467	-62906	-44903	-43567	-2846	-23315	-5311
1968	199241	43210	17865	10105	3567	38234	60496
1969	441503	44367	49467	28983	9936	95309	153951
1970	414735	33578	45318	23811	14942	93684	131894
1971	228785	16434	16444	9334	10463	72436	33841
1972	139125	10715	-1267	1993	9562	49355	19217
1973	205425	18599	-12705	4584	21804	90929	40855
1974	-140107	-29704	-19537	-29202	-10615	-22314	-40035
1975	-194250	-34607	-29131	-23208	-8214	-50406	-48223
1976	-97609	-6762	-23265	-16320	-5508	-29600	-28616
1977	-26012	7299	-17012	-10451	-3026	-15220	-12820
1978	21619	11795	-10822	-6644	-2028	-2206	-6840
1979	82913	16254	-7178	-3797	-1373	19436	-1578
1980	117046	10799	-3363	-2360	-2518	34474	2263
1981	57286	-1837	1920	-1194	-2209	-12028	-1921

TABLE 12a Migrant Workers newly entering West Germany by Sending Country

Year	Total	Greece	Spain	Portugal	Turkey	Yugoslavia
1968	390879	37248	31995	6709	62376	76782
1970	713882	64026	48836	20119	123626	202360
1972	479797	24606	28657	16476	96210	75501
1974	46321	1773	1206	494	6081	7653
1975	21906	660	546	244	1965	3037
1976	24140	831	659	138	2642	2067
1977	29700	1100	446	135	3317	2845
1978	19521	789	275	58	1480	2600
1979	37915	777	232	97	5676	5730
1980	82553	944	541	165	29219	7875
1981	43889	477	1137	135	3580	5129

Note: Italians are not included in these data since under EEC regulations they do not require work permits.

Source: Federal Republic of Germany. SOPEMI 1982.

TABLE 13 Number of Dependant In-migrants by Sending Country

Year	Total	Italy	Greece	Spain	Portugal	Turkey	Yugoslavia
1962	75518	12195	5319	8528	360	3174	4194
1963	86307	15100	7256	8583	428	3483	4530
1964	104106	17533	9671	9620	604	6045	5100
1965	124337	25321	11765	11295	1070	9622	6427
1966	129271	29540	11118	9410	1488	10805	8484
1967	106038	19885	8098	5654	1478	10051	8377
1968	147696	32645	15241	7990	2355	19766	9786
1969	195473	35596	22428	10427	2842	32941	18465
1970	235133	38179	29153	11935	2954	53878	28138
1971	274051	38937	29121	14259	6197	76015	34523
1972	294302	38667	24368	14843	7902	92552	37749
1973	324878	43015	21793	13064	9530	118233	42688
1974	321260	32406	23122	9537	10871	131783	39306
1975	228220	20882	14144	5389	7031	84035	28419
1976	234172	23728	11594	4156	5008	90798	27434
1977	250203	28976	10818	3675	3947	98788	28220
1978	264491	29612	10524	3442	3952	110191	25050
1979	306718	31418	9954	3255	3527	135063	25081
1980	332950	31608	10236	3208	2983	148813	23928
1981	267302	26989	11541	3185	2266	72719	22287

TABLE 14 Percentage of Dependant In-migrants by Sending Country

Year	Total	Recruitment Countries	Italy	Greece	Spain	Portugal	Turkey	Yugoslavia
1962	75518	44.7	16.1	7.0	11.3	0.5	4.2	5.6
1963	86307	45.6	17.5	8.4	9.9	0.5	4.0	5.2
1964	104106	46.7	16.8	9.3	9.2	0.6	5.8	4.9
1965	124337	52.7	20.4	9.5	9.1	0.9	7.7	5.2
1966	129271	54.8	22.9	8.6	7.3	1.2	8.4	6.6
1967	106038	50.5	18.8	7.6	5.3	1.4	9.5	7.9
1968	147696	59.4	22.1	10.3	5.4	1.6	13.4	6.6
1969	195473	62.8	18.2	11.5	5.3	1.5	16.9	9.4
1970	235133	69.8	16.2	12.4	5.1	1.3	22.9	12.0
1971	274051	72.6	14.2	10.6	5.2	2.3	27.7	12.6
1972	294302	73.4	13.1	8.3	5.0	2.7	31.4	12.8
1973	324878	76.4	13.2	6.7	4.0	2.9	36.4	13.1
1974	321260	76.9	10.1	7.2	3.0	3.4	41.0	12.2
1975	228220	70.1	9.1	6.2	2.4	3.1	36.8	12.5
1976	234172	69.5	10.1	5.0	1.8	2.1	38.8	11.7
1977	250203	69.7	11.6	4.3	1.5	1.6	39.5	11.3
1978	264491	69.1	11.2	4.0	1.3	1.5	41.7	9.5
1979	306718	67.9	10.2	3.2	1.1	1.1	44.0	8.2
1980	332950	66.3	9.5	3.1	1.0	0.9	44.7	7.2
1981	267302	52.0	10.1	4.3	1.2	0.8	27.2	8.3

TABLE 15 Number of Dependant Out-migrants by Sending Country

Year	Total	Italy	Greece	Spain	Portugal	Turkey	Yugoslavia
1962	38290	6198	2155	2339	103	932	2289
1963	50354	9712	3488	3857	171	1360	2431
1964	59358	9455	5131	4400	191	1517	2670
1965	68497	10829	7128	5585	272	2732	3124
1966	92086	18715	11251	9406	366	4574	4236
1967	115167	25338	16434	12800	640	7520	5973
1968	90000	19166	9042	6696	599	6029	5567
1969	96074	21489	8405	5746	589	8730	6599
1970	108288	24308	10423	6367	793	12945	10521
1971	132357	26841	14620	7083	1179	22379	16675
1972	160711	29637	20078	8418	1582	32366	20058
1973	188005	30532	21793	10617	2516	46586	24021
1974	223024	37428	22357	14149	4391	59544	28937
1975	267980	39866	32526	14652	5606	83542	34651
1976	264698	35360	30525	14347	5937	85794	32506
1977	253439	31441	26530	12126	5209	82584	31893
1978	235746	32295	20573	8968	3797	65046	30600
1979	210452	32311	17236	6548	3491	48875	27343
1980	204405	33698	13380	5447	4501	41616	25385
1981	238974	40836	10707	5216	4768	47544	26447

TABLE 16 Percentage of Dependant Out-migrants by Sending Country

Year	Total	Recruitment Countries	Italy	Greece	Spain	Portugal	Turkey	Yugoslavia
1962	38290	36.6	16.2	5.6	6.1	0.3	2.4	6.0
1963	50354	41.7	19.3	6.9	7.7	0.3	2.7	4.8
1964	59358	39.4	15.9	8.6	7.4	0.3	2.6	4.5
1965	68497	43.3	15.8	10.4	8.2	0.4	4.0	4.6
1966	92086	52.7	20.3	12.2	10.2	0.4	5.0	4.6
1967	115167	59.7	22.0	14.3	11.1	0.6	6.5	5.2
1968	90000	52.3	21.3	10.0	7.4	0.7	6.7	6.2
1969	96074	53.7	22.4	8.7	6.0	0.6	9.1	6.9
1970	108288	60.4	22.4	9.6	5.9	0.6	12.0	9.7
1971	132357	67.1	20.3	11.0	5.4	0.7	16.9	12.6
1972	160711	69.8	18.4	12.5	5.2	0.9	20.1	12.5
1973	188005	72.4	16.2	11.6	5.6	1.0	24.8	12.8
1974	223024	74.8	16.8	10.0	6.3	1.3	26.7	13.0
1975	267980	78.7	14.9	12.1	5.5	2.0	31.2	12.9
1976	264698	77.2	13.4	11.5	5.4	2.1	32.4	12.3
1977	253439	74.9	12.4	10.5	4.8	2.2	32.6	12.6
1978	235746	68.4	13.7	8.7	3.8	2.1	27.6	13.0
1979	210452	64.5	15.4	8.2	3.1	1.6	23.2	13.0
1980	204405	60.7	16.5	6.5	2.7	1.7	20.4	12.4
1981	238974	56.7	17.1	4.5	2.2	2.2	19.9	11.1

TABLE 17 Net Dependant Migration by Sending Country

Year	Total	Italy	Greece	Spain	Portugal	Turkey	Yugoslavia
1962	37228	5997	3164	6189	257	2242	1905
1963	35953	5388	3768	4726	257	2123	2099
1964	44748	8078	4540	5220	413	4528	2430
1965	55840	14492	4637	5710	798	6890	3303
1966	37185	10825	-133	4	1122	6231	4248
1967	-9129	-5453	-8336	-7146	838	2531	2404
1968	57696	13479	6199	1294	1756	13737	4219
1969	99399	14107	14023	4681	2253	24211	11866
1970	126845	13871	18730	5568	2161	40933	17617
1971	141694	12096	14501	7176	5018	53636	17848
1972	133591	9030	4290	6423	6320	60186	17691
1973	136873	12483	n.d	2447	7014	71647	18667
1974	98236	-5022	765	-4612	6480	72239	10369
1975	-39760	-18984	-18382	-9263	1425	493	-6232
1976	-30526	-11632	-18931	-10191	-929	5004	-5072
1977	-3236	-2465	-15712	-8451	-1262	16204	-3673
1978	28745	-2683	-10049	-5526	155	45145	-5550
1979	96266	-893	-7282	-3293	36	86188	-2262
1980	128545	-2090	-3144	-2239	-1518	107197	-1457
1981	28328	-13847	834	-2031	-2502	25175	-4160

TABLE 18   Dependant In-migrants per Labour In-migrant by Sending Country

Year	Total	Italy	Greece	Spain	Portugal	Turkey	Yugoslavia
1962	0.18	0.06	0.11	0.16	0.39	0.22	0.14
1963	0.21	0.09	0.13	0.16	0.27	0.13	0.21
1964	0.20	0.09	0.13	0.13	0.15	0.09	0.19
1965	0.21	0.10	0.18	0.16	0.10	0.15	0.14
1966	0.26	0.14	0.25	0.21	0.16	0.22	0.13
1967	0.47	0.23	0.65	0.50	0.59	0.44	0.28
1968	0.33	0.22	0.40	0.27	0.40	0.33	0.11
1969	0.27	0.23	0.34	0.21	0.23	0.28	0.09
1970	0.32	0.26	0.45	0.24	0.15	0.44	0.13
1971	0.46	0.30	0.69	0.37	0.35	0.69	0.28
1972	0.60	0.36	0.91	0.50	0.47	1.01	0.39
1973	0.60	0.39	1.52	0.39	0.32	0.90	0.39
1974	1.48	0.61	3.38	2.26	4.58	4.55	1.19
1975	1.66	0.70	3.49	2.43	6.35	5.78	1.66
1976	1.53	0.56	2.63	1.97	6.03	6.07	2.07
1977	1.45	0.57	2.43	1.87	4.85	6.28	2.06
1978	1.38	0.55	2.16	1.88	5.38	5.29	1.86
1979	1.29	0.54	2.06	1.81	3.93	3.67	1.62
1980	1.12	0.58	1.84	1.46	3.06	2.35	1.33
1981	1.14	0.71	1.65	1.28	2.79	6.42	1.91

TABLE 19 Dependant Out-migrants per Labour Out-migrant by Sending Country

Year	Total	Italy	Greece	Spain	Portugal	Turkey	Yugoslavia
1962	0.19	0.05	0.18	0.13	0.38	0.35	0.34
1963	0.17	0.06	0.17	0.13	0.37	0.28	0.18
1964	0.19	0.06	0.16	0.12	0.32	0.12	0.14
1965	0.20	0.07	0.19	0.13	0.19	0.14	0.14
1966	0.21	0.09	0.24	0.16	0.11	0.13	0.13
1967	0.28	0.17	0.29	0.23	0.12	0.16	0.17
1968	0.37	0.19	0.45	0.34	0.26	0.28	0.22
1969	0.35	0.19	0.53	0.29	0.24	0.38	0.14
1970	0.33	0.22	0.53	0.25	0.17	0.44	0.13
1971	0.36	0.24	0.57	0.25	0.17	0.58	0.18
1972	0.45	0.30	0.72	0.30	0.22	0.76	0.26
1973	0.55	0.34	0.81	0.37	0.32	1.15	0.36
1974	0.62	0.45	0.85	0.42	0.34	1.16	0.40
1975	0.81	0.62	0.98	0.58	0.60	1.29	0.53
1976	1.06	0.72	1.10	0.78	0.94	1.93	0.78
1977	1.28	0.72	1.24	0.98	1.36	2.67	1.20
1978	1.39	0.78	1.31	1.06	1.37	2.82	1.50
1979	1.35	0.78	1.44	1.17	1.54	2.81	1.60
1980	1.13	0.77	1.50	1.20	1.29	1.44	1.62
1981	1.35	1.02	2.11	1.42	1.58	2.04	1.95

TABLE 20 Male In-migrants as Percentage of Total In-migrants by Sending Country

Year	Total	Italy	Greece	Spain	Portugal	Turkey	Yugoslavia
1962	78.0	88.4	65.8	70.0	73.5	85.4	76.5
1963	75.5	86.1	65.8	69.0	73.0	85.9	68.9
1964	75.8	85.1	66.3	73.6	78.8	87.4	72.4
1965	73.2	83.4	57.9	71.4	84.1	76.1	71.8
1966	69.0	79.8	54.0	67.8	69.5	71.5	66.0
1967	63.1	75.0	53.9	58.9	55.0	67.5	60.8
1968	66.0	75.9	54.7	69.1	60.5	69.4	63.6
1969	68.2	75.5	55.8	74.9	70.5	73.0	69.0
1970	68.5	75.0	55.7	73.6	74.8	69.1	70.6
1971	66.5	74.0	54.1	68.7	65.4	66.5	66.0
1972	63.2	72.0	55.2	65.3	62.2	60.2	62.4
1973	63.8	71.2	53.7	70.4	68.9	61.8	63.1
1974	55.6	65.7	53.5	49.2	37.1	52.1	53.2
1975	53.9	62.9	53.5	50.2	42.3	51.8	50.3
1976	55.4	67.3	56.8	52.0	41.7	51.1	47.4
1977	56.3	66.8	56.5	49.4	42.2	51.7	47.5
1978	58.4	67.4	57.9	51.2	40.0	54.9	49.8
1979	61.9	67.8	57.6	50.7	47.4	61.8	53.6
1980	63.8	66.7	57.8	57.3	47.3	66.2	56.3
1981	60.1	63.6	60.2	60.3	48.3	58.5	53.5

TABLE 21 Male Out-migrants as Percentage of Total Out-migrants by Sending Country

Year	Total	Italy	Greece	Spain	Portugal	Turkey	Yugoslavia
1962	83.2	92.7	75.9	81.0	80.1	86.3	71.9
1963	82.1	90.9	71.3	78.3	74.9	85.2	77.9
1964	79.6	89.1	71.4	78.1	74.8	88.4	81.0
1965	78.8	88.6	69.2	77.9	82.4	85.9	80.2
1966	76.9	85.7	63.5	75.8	86.3	84.2	79.2
1967	70.5	78.2	58.6	67.9	83.1	81.4	72.5
1968	68.8	78.9	58.2	64.5	76.1	77.0	67.3
1969	70.2	78.9	58.3	70.6	78.4	74.4	72.2
1970	71.4	78.2	58.7	75.6	83.3	73.5	73.8
1971	71.8	77.6	58.9	76.5	84.2	74.3	73.4
1972	69.7	74.9	58.0	73.7	79.8	72.9	71.4
1973	67.9	73.9	57.3	71.4	75.0	69.0	69.6
1974	66.4	69.6	56.9	69.8	74.2	67.2	68.8
1975	62.6	64.3	55.4	63.8	63.9	64.3	65.5
1976	60.0	63.1	54.8	59.9	58.3	61.0	60.9
1977	59.0	65.0	54.5	56.5	54.5	59.6	56.6
1978	59.6	66.0	54.7	56.4	52.6	60.6	55.9
1979	60.4	66.2	54.7	57.6	51.2	62.2	55.7
1980	63.1	67.5	53.9	57.5	53.3	70.4	56.1
1981	63.6	65.5	58.0	58.8	53.5	69.3	58.1

TABLE 22 Male Labour In-migrants as percentage of Male In-migrants by Sending Country

Year	Total	Italy	Greece	Spain	Portugal	Turkey	Yugoslavia
1962	90.8	97.5	94.1	93.0	80.6	87.9	95.0
1963	89.6	96.4	93.0	92.8	86.1	92.7	92.4
1964	90.4	96.4	93.0	94.2	93.4	95.3	93.5
1965	89.9	95.9	89.4	93.0	96.4	92.0	94.9
1966	87.6	94.3	84.0	90.0	93.5	88.6	94.9
1967	79.1	90.7	67.9	78.3	79.2	80.1	89.5
1968	84.4	90.8	77.1	88.0	85.2	84.9	95.3
1969	86.9	90.6	80.1	90.7	90.5	87.0	96.3
1970	85.4	89.6	76.3	89.4	94.1	80.7	94.8
1971	80.6	88.4	68.1	84.9	86.9	73.6	90.5
1972	75.7	86.5	63.4	80.3	83.2	63.7	86.5
1973	76.1	85.1	50.1	84.4	88.7	66.8	86.5
1974	54.6	78.0	31.2	45.9	32.8	29.2	67.2
1975	51.2	75.7	31.0	43.2	22.1	24.7	58.4
1976	53.9	79.5	38.2	48.3	23.3	24.1	51.8
1977	55.3	79.7	40.8	50.0	27.3	23.1	52.6
1978	55.8	80.0	43.6	48.5	25.8	25.4	54.2
1979	56.6	80.5	45.0	49.6	30.6	32.0	57.5
1980	58.9	78.8	47.3	53.7	36.5	41.0	67.1
1981	58.3	74.3	51.2	60.1	38.9	20.2	53.0

179

TABLE 23   Number of Male In-migrants by Sending Country

Year	Total	Italy	Greece	Spain	Portugal	Turkey	Yugoslavia
1962	381496	178176	34932	43823	952	14990	26083
1963	376246	161553	42489	42869	1465	26661	18128
1964	474332	178368	54151	60243	3616	62277	22730
1965	524311	224342	45300	58777	9959	55185	36808
1966	436183	189440	29902	36878	7517	43275	49147
1967	208570	79513	11096	10017	2197	22330	23045
1968	389110	135306	29076	26283	4985	55320	60562
1969	620664	143809	49015	44409	10723	110408	152192
1970	668296	137968	52552	45132	16810	122259	168324
1971	578610	124033	38481	36017	15558	124361	105260
1972	497323	106043	28214	29071	15268	111013	83704
1973	554668	108687	19389	32529	27039	154249	95286
1974	299382	56224	16042	6774	4917	83778	38448
1975	197403	32027	9727	3821	3443	51097	22900
1976	214424	44637	9084	3260	2434	54001	19279
1977	237997	53557	8626	2785	2009	59200	19902
1978	266402	55955	8907	2701	1875	71986	19183
1979	337639	60501	8517	2558	2096	106236	21766
1980	403112	57450	9145	3093	1874	140485	23580
1981	300941	41370	11156	3420	1486	49143	18150

TABLE 24   Number of Male Out-migrants by Sending Country

Year	Total	Italy	Greece	Spain	Portugal	Turkey	Yugoslavia
1962	203926	121329	10627	16877	301	3077	6484
1963	282798	167806	17037	26688	472	5338	12600
1964	295591	147852	25961	31895	585	12213	17630
1965	325328	154446	30560	37908	1415	19490	19804
1966	411859	188686	36890	52205	3248	33989	29203
1967	372217	136251	43275	45995	4993	43866	29593
1968	228755	95913	16911	17178	2221	21357	20573
1969	258939	104186	14229	18087	2373	23542	39446
1970	310281	106743	17761	24158	4474	31142	65707
1971	359166	107883	23629	27489	6995	45210	79024
1972	358776	95492	27890	26608	6912	54653	69453
1973	357581	89784	27974	28004	7838	60064	63705
1974	385429	83726	27749	33195	12903	74521	70143
1975	375922	67220	36380	25558	9532	95493	65513
1976	309141	53456	31895	19651	7162	79577	45269
1977	266581	49012	26176	13855	4928	67641	33048
1978	241627	48778	19845	9832	3453	53333	28457
1979	221045	48909	16002	6989	2950	41228	24760
1980	243395	52238	12026	5751	4264	49713	23049
1981	264075	52885	9158	5229	4167	49160	23247

TABLE 25 Male Labour Out-migrants as Percentage of Male Out-migrants by Sending Country

Year	Total	Italy	Greece	Spain	Portugal	Turkey	Yugoslavia
1962	90.6	97.4	89.6	93.2	82.1	79.2	87.8
1963	91.7	97.6	90.1	94.3	81.1	84.2	94.0
1964	90.9	97.6	90.8	84.2	83.8	92.6	95.7
1965	90.3	97.2	89.2	94.2	90.9	92.3	95.5
1966	90.0	96.2	86.0	92.8	95.2	92.9	95.9
1967	86.9	93.0	82.6	89.1	95.0	91.4	94.3
1968	83.0	92.0	74.9	83.9	88.2	84.8	92.3
1969	83.7	91.5	72.5	86.5	89.1	80.1	95.1
1970	84.6	90.6	72.9	88.3	92.6	78.2	94.9
1971	83.6	89.9	70.8	88.7	93.0	73.8	93.3
1972	80.0	87.6	65.6	86.4	91.6	68.8	90.3
1973	76.0	86.3	62.0	83.8	88.0	58.1	86.7
1974	73.9	81.9	61.0	82.5	87.1	57.8	85.6
1975	68.2	76.5	56.9	76.4	77.4	55.7	80.7
1976	60.7	72.4	53.8	68.8	66.0	44.5	72.3
1977	55.5	71.8	51.4	63.7	56.6	36.4	60.5
1978	52.6	69.0	50.5	61.5	55.4	34.7	52.8
1979	53.9	69.5	47.9	58.3	51.9	35.7	52.1
1980	58.4	69.2	47.6	58.4	58.2	52.7	49.9
1981	53.3	61.6	39.1	52.6	51.5	43.2	45.3

TABLE 26 Net Male Migration by Sending Country

Year	Total	Italy	Greece	Spain	Portugal	Turkey	Yugoslavia
1962	177570	56847	24305	26946	651	11913	19599
1963	93448	-6253	25452	16181	993	21323	5528
1964	178741	30516	28190	28348	3031	50064	5100
1965	198983	69896	14740	20869	8544	35695	17004
1966	24324	754	-6988	-15327	4269	9286	19944
1967	-163647	-56738	-32179	-35978	-2796	-21536	-6548
1968	160355	39393	12165	9105	2764	33963	39989
1969	361725	39623	34786	26322	8350	86866	112746
1970	358015	31225	34791	20974	12336	91117	102617
1971	219444	16150	14852	8528	8563	79151	26236
1972	138547	10551	324	2463	8356	56360	14251
1973	197087	18903	-8585	4525	19201	94185	31581
1974	-86047	-27502	-11707	-26421	-7986	9257	-31695
1975	-178519	-35193	-26653	-21737	-6089	-44396	-42613
1976	-94717	-8819	-22811	-16391	-4728	-25576	-25990
1977	-28584	4545	-17550	-11070	-2919	-8441	-13146
1978	24775	7177	-10938	-7131	-1578	18653	-9274
1979	116594	11592	-7485	-4431	-854	65008	-2994
1980	159717	5212	-2881	-2658	-2390	90772	531
1981	36866	-11515	1998	-1809	-2681	-17	-5097

TABLE 27 Number of Female In-migrants by Sending Country

Year	Total	Italy	Greece	Spain	Portugal	Turkey	Yugoslavia
1962	107376	23298	18124	18738	343	2569	7998
1963	122192	25975	22094	19265	542	4364	8200
1964	151152	31285	27558	21575	974	8979	8651
1965	191846	44670	32933	25347	1885	17291	14492
1966	196313	47828	25494	17485	3293	17213	25306
1967	121728	26448	9493	6995	1800	10776	14845
1968	200452	42990	24031	11759	3257	24391	34715
1969	288902	46762	38869	14864	4491	40734	68258
1970	307936	46012	41755	16186	5664	54713	70178
1971	292127	43537	32583	16417	8235	62594	54138
1972	289839	41164	22869	15469	9281	73536	50413
1973	314441	43858	16713	13705	12230	95421	55770
1974	239192	29367	13918	6986	8330	76972	33841
1975	168692	18880	8469	3785	4696	47465	22661
1976	172879	21724	6920	3009	3405	51757	21426
1977	184848	26673	6650	2856	2752	55315	22020
1978	189715	27082	6480	2576	2812	59033	19370
1979	207548	28791	6270	2491	2328	65644	18807
1980	228322	28688	6666	2309	2084	71769	18304
1981	200197	23674	7380	2254	1592	34909	15795

TABLE 28 Number of Female Out-migrants by Sending Country

Year	Total	Italy	Greece	Spain	Portugal	Turkey	Yugoslavia
1962	41140	9495	3375	3970	75	488	2539
1963	61728	16822	6857	7407	158	929	3568
1964	75857	18073	10408	8958	197	1607	4135
1965	87376	19888	13597	10733	302	3192	4895
1966	123376	31577	21203	16685	517	6379	7663
1967	155677	38069	30553	21730	1012	10024	11204
1968	103870	25694	12132	9465	698	6383	9989
1969	109725	27911	10165	7522	652	8080	15187
1970	124371	29788	12498	7781	897	11213	23284
1971	141092	31157	16490	8435	1317	15673	28685
1972	155670	31980	20170	9516	1755	20355	27756
1973	169230	31679	20833	11199	2613	27030	27829
1974	195016	36591	20983	14379	4479	36304	31812
1975	224183	37278	29329	14519	5396	52982	34503
1976	206297	31299	26305	13129	5114	50777	29124
1977	185512	26384	21824	10688	4121	45890	25367
1978	164126	25147	16413	7615	3107	34747	22486
1979	144963	25022	13245	5150	2811	25028	19653
1980	142448	25191	10292	4250	3730	20870	18029
1981	151449	27843	6624	3670	3622	21745	16779

TABLE 29 Female Labour In-migrants as Percentage of Female In-migrants by Sending Country

Year	Total	Italy	Greece	Spain	Portugal	Turkey	Yugoslavia
1962	62.3	66.9	82.1	70.9	49.0	46.8	63.7
1963	61.5	64.4	80.5	71.4	58.5	65.1	61.5
1964	61.2	64.4	78.6	71.6	62.5	65.4	58.1
1965	62.8	63.8	78.9	69.6	62.3	70.0	68.7
1966	61.7	60.8	75.2	67.2	69.5	66.0	76.3
1967	48.6	52.6	52.2	50.2	43.3	47.9	59.9
1968	56.6	53.0	64.3	58.9	50.3	53.2	80.0
1969	60.5	52.8	67.4	57.8	59.5	54.4	81.2
1970	55.4	48.3	60.0	55.9	65.4	44.7	72.4
1971	44.7	43.5	48.3	46.3	49.5	31.0	54.7
1972	40.1	40.8	38.7	41.0	42.4	28.9	47.5
1973	38.9	38.7	27.5	41.7	47.0	29.8	46.5
1974	22.5	31.8	13.2	15.9	9.2	5.9	21.1
1975	21.8	30.6	12.3	14.9	7.4	4.0	16.6
1976	21.8	33.0	13.6	17.8	7.7	3.8	15.3
1977	22.2	32.2	14.1	20.1	9.6	3.7	14.7
1978	22.6	32.0	15.2	20.4	8.9	4.3	16.1
1979	22.9	31.9	16.0	21.0	11.0	4.3	15.8
1980	26.7	32.2	18.7	23.1	14.0	8.2	18.6
1981	29.2	31.0	17.3	19.3	14.7	4.0	12.9

TABLE 30   Female Labour Out-migrants as Percentage of Female Out-migrants by Sending Country

Year	Total	Italy	Greece	Spain	Portugal	Turkey	Yugoslavia
1962	53.7	68.2	88.7	70.1	34.7	40.0	40.9
1963	56.3	66.6	73.7	68.4	48.1	44.6	52.9
1964	57.2	67.4	73.7	71.6	51.3	61.7	53.7
1965	57.7	67.4	71.8	68.4	52.6	61.5	54.6
1966	58.6	63.6	71.4	66.3	59.4	66.2	60.3
1967	57.4	58.5	70.8	64.7	61.7	62.6	61.8
1968	50.7	55.2	60.4	58.5	51.6	56.5	60.1
1969	51.0	54.6	55.8	56.2	49.4	50.0	69.2
1970	51.4	52.1	55.2	54.6	48.3	45.2	69.3
1971	48.0	48.8	53.1	52.9	47.8	32.7	60.4
1972	42.9	44.4	48.0	49.6	43.0	24.7	52.1
1973	39.5	42.5	46.4	45.6	39.8	20.7	44.1
1974	37.2	39.1	45.0	41.9	39.0	22.7	40.8
1975	33.8	35.5	42.6	40.7	36.1	22.1	36.3
1976	30.6	34.2	40.0	37.4	31.5	18.0	31.4
1977	27.4	33.2	36.8	33.5	25.5	13.7	25.7
1978	26.1	31.8	34.5	31.9	27.4	13.0	23.6
1979	25.1	30.5	32.8	29.5	26.3	10.7	21.2
1980	27.7	30.2	31.3	28.1	27.2	13.3	23.2
1981	23.7	26.2	22.6	25.4	24.2	9.8	18.2

TABLE 31 Net Female Migration by Sending Country

Year	Total	Italy	Greece	Spain	Portugal	Turkey	Yugoslavia
1962	66236	13803	14749	14768	268	2081	5459
1963	60464	9153	15237	11858	384	3435	4632
1964	75295	13212	17150	12617	777	7372	4516
1965	104470	24782	19336	12814	1583	14099	9597
1966	72937	16251	4291	800	2776	10834	17643
1967	-33949	-11621	-21060	-14735	788	752	3641
1968	96582	17296	11899	2294	2559	18008	24726
1969	179177	18851	28704	7342	3839	32654	53071
1970	183565	16224	29257	8405	4767	43500	46894
1971	151035	12380	16093	7982	6918	46921	25453
1972	134169	9184	2699	5953	7526	53181	22657
1973	145211	12179	-4120	2506	9617	68391	27941
1974	44176	-7224	-7065	-7393	3851	40668	2029
1975	-55491	-18398	-20860	-10734	-700	-5517	-11842
1976	-33418	-9575	-19385	-10120	-1709	980	-7698
1977	-664	289	-15174	-7832	-1369	9425	-3347
1978	25589	1935	-9935	-5039	-295	24286	-3116
1979	62585	3769	-6975	-2659	-483	40616	-846
1980	85874	3497	-3626	-1941	-1646	50899	275
1981	48748	-4169	756	-1416	-2030	13164	-984

TABLE 32 Number of Female Labour In-migrants by Sending Country

Year	Total	Italy	Greece	Spain	Portugal	Turkey	Yugoslavia
1962	66925	15592	14873	13292	168	1202	5098
1963	75187	16730	17793	13749	317	2839	5046
1964	92486	20147	21665	15445	609	5872	5029
1965	120450	28508	25989	16389	1174	12103	9951
1966	121087	29060	19167	11746	2290	11356	19312
1967	59180	13918	4954	3514	780	5166	8889
1968	113556	22806	15460	6931	1639	12977	27778
1969	174913	24673	26197	8585	2673	22158	55424
1970	170512	22228	25063	9043	3703	24484	50823
1971	130476	18945	15745	7602	4080	19394	29638
1972	116309	16813	8839	6345	3938	21238	23939
1973	122272	16985	4599	5721	5748	28456	25946
1974	53735	9343	1837	1113	763	4517	7146
1975	36736	5786	1038	565	348	1909	3757
1976	37611	7168	940	537	263	1959	3285
1977	41110	8580	937	574	265	2074	3238
1978	42920	8669	984	526	251	2560	3114
1979	47435	9185	1004	524	256	2840	2969
1980	60989	9240	1245	534	291	5905	3411
1981	58497	7331	1278	434	234	1390	2040

TABLE 33 Percentage of Female Labour In-migrants by Sending Country

Year	Total	Recruitment Countries	Italy	Greece	Spain	Portugal	Turkey	Yugoslavia
1962	66925	75.0	23.3	22.2	19.9	0.3	1.8	7.6
1963	75187	75.1	22.3	23.7	18.3	0.4	3.8	6.7
1964	92486	74.4	21.8	23.4	16.7	0.7	6.3	5.4
1965	120450	78.1	23.7	21.6	13.6	1.0	10.0	8.3
1966	121087	76.7	24.0	15.8	9.7	1.9	9.4	15.9
1967	59180	62.9	23.5	8.4	5.9	1.3	8.7	15.0
1968	113556	77.1	20.1	13.6	6.1	1.4	11.4	24.5
1969	174913	79.9	14.1	15.0	4.9	1.5	12.7	31.7
1970	170512	79.4	13.0	14.7	5.3	2.2	14.4	29.8
1971	130476	73.1	14.5	12.1	5.8	3.1	14.9	22.7
1972	116309	69.7	14.5	7.6	5.5	3.4	18.3	20.6
1973	122272	71.5	13.9	3.8	4.7	4.7	23.3	21.2
1974	53735	46.0	17.4	3.4	2.1	1.4	8.4	13.1
1975	36736	36.5	15.8	2.8	1.5	0.9	5.2	10.2
1976	37611	37.6	19.1	2.5	1.4	0.7	5.2	8.7
1977	41110	38.1	20.9	2.3	1.4	0.6	5.0	7.9
1978	42920	37.5	20.2	2.3	1.2	0.6	6.0	7.3
1979	47435	35.4	19.4	2.1	1.1	0.5	6.0	6.3
1980	60989	33.8	15.2	2.0	0.9	0.5	9.7	5.6
1981	58497	21.7	12.5	2.2	0.7	0.4	2.4	3.5

TABLE 34 Number of Male Labour In-migrants by Sending Country

Year	Total	Italy	Greece	Spain	Portugal	Turkey	Yugoslavia
1962	346429	173687	32864	40741	767	13183	24789
1963	336944	155698	39534	39802	1262	24703	16752
1964	418892	171973	50373	56753	3377	59339	21252
1965	471370	215183	40479	54640	9600	50751	34922
1966	382138	178668	25111	33207	7032	38327	46657
1967	165080	72158	7537	7844	1739	17889	20624
1968	328310	122845	22406	23121	4248	46968	57713
1969	539180	130302	39259	40261	9699	96043	146561
1970	570587	123573	40091	40340	15817	98610	159541
1971	466210	109688	26198	30573	13516	91546	95237
1972	376551	91727	17876	23354	12709	70759	72429
1973	421959	92545	9710	27449	23991	102981	82422
1974	163579	43842	5001	3110	1613	24450	25837
1975	101139	24239	3014	1652	760	12618	13385
1976	115520	35465	3470	1576	568	13002	9986
1977	131532	42674	3521	1392	549	13653	10464
1978	148706	44756	3879	1309	484	18268	10389
1979	191034	48689	3829	1270	641	33977	12523
1980	237495	45290	4330	1660	684	57536	14545
1981	175339	30724	5717	2055	578	9943	9618

TABLE 35 Percentage of Male Labour In-migrants by Sending Country

Year	Total	Recruitment Countries	Italy	Greece	Spain	Portugal	Turkey	Yugoslavia
1962	346429	82.6	50.1	9.5	11.8	0.2	3.8	7.2
1963	336944	82.4	46.2	11.7	11.8	0.4	7.3	5.0
1964	428892	84.7	40.1	11.7	13.2	0.8	13.8	5.0
1965	471370	86.0	45.7	8.6	11.6	2.0	10.8	7.4
1966	382138	86.1	46.8	6.6	8.7	1.8	10.0	12.2
1967	165080	77.4	43.7	4.6	4.8	1.1	10.8	12.5
1968	328310	84.5	37.4	6.8	7.0	1.3	14.3	17.6
1969	539180	85.7	24.2	7.3	7.5	1.8	17.8	27.2
1970	570587	83.8	21.7	7.0	7.1	2.8	17.3	28.0
1971	466210	78.7	23.5	5.6	6.6	2.9	19.6	20.4
1972	376551	76.7	24.4	4.7	6.2	3.4	18.8	19.2
1973	421959	80.4	21.9	2.3	6.5	5.7	24.4	19.5
1974	163579	63.5	26.8	3.1	1.9	1.0	14.9	15.8
1975	101139	55.0	24.0	3.0	1.6	0.8	12.5	13.2
1976	115520	55.5	30.7	3.0	1.4	0.5	11.3	8.6
1977	131532	54.9	32.4	2.7	1.1	0.4	10.4	8.0
1978	148706	53.2	30.1	2.6	0.9	0.3	12.3	7.0
1979	191034	52.8	25.5	2.0	0.7	0.3	17.8	6.6
1980	237495	52.2	19.1	1.8	0.7	0.3	24.2	6.1
1981	175339	33.4	17.5	3.3	1.2	0.3	5.7	5.5

TABLE 36   Number of Female Labour Out-migrants by Sending Country

Year	Total	Italy	Greece	Spain	Portugal	Turkey	Yugoslavia
1962	22100	6477	2320	2782	26	195	1038
1963	34731	11207	5057	5063	76	414	1888
1964	43428	12186	7670	6411	101	992	2219
1965	50390	13401	9763	7345	159	1963	2672
1966	72277	20071	15130	11056	307	4222	4620
1967	89415	22265	21632	13944	624	6271	6923
1968	52687	14194	7331	5537	360	3607	6006
1969	55976	15230	5676	4224	322	4036	10502
1970	63913	15517	6895	4252	433	5071	16130
1971	67759	15207	8762	4465	629	5123	17338
1972	66846	14193	9683	4722	755	5035	14464
1973	66876	13474	9668	5108	1039	5598	12276
1974	72608	14310	9450	6031	1747	8245	12968
1975	75885	13229	12483	5908	1947	11729	12518
1976	63034	10715	10520	4904	1610	9124	9154
1977	50768	8762	8022	3585	1049	6295	6525
1978	42797	7988	5662	2428	850	4502	5316
1979	36356	7622	4347	1517	740	2667	4174
1980	39403	7599	3217	1193	1013	2781	4181
1981	35912	7308	1496	931	877	2121	3058

TABLE 37 Percentage of Female Labour Out-migrants by Sending Country

Year	Total	Recruitment Countries	Italy	Greece	Spain	Portugal	Turkey	Yugoslavia
1962	22100	58.1	29.3	10.5	12.6	0.1	0.9	4.7
1963	34731	68.3	32.3	14.6	14.6	0.2	1.2	5.4
1964	43428	68.1	28.1	17.7	14.8	0.2	2.3	5.1
1965	50390	70.1	26.6	19.4	14.6	0.3	3.9	5.3
1966	72277	76.7	27.8	20.9	15.3	0.4	5.8	6.4
1967	89415	80.1	24.9	24.2	15.6	0.7	7.0	7.7
1968	52687	70.3	26.9	13.9	10.5	0.7	6.8	11.4
1969	55976	71.4	27.2	10.1	7.5	0.6	7.2	18.8
1970	63913	75.6	24.3	10.8	6.7	0.7	7.9	25.2
1971	67759	76.0	22.4	12.9	6.6	0.9	7.6	25.6
1972	66846	73.1	21.2	14.5	7.1	1.1	7.5	21.6
1973	66876	70.5	20.1	14.5	7.6	1.6	8.4	18.4
1974	72608	72.7	19.7	13.0	8.3	2.4	11.4	17.9
1975	75885	76.2	17.4	16.4	7.8	2.6	15.5	16.5
1976	63034	73.0	17.0	16.7	7.8	2.6	14.5	14.5
1977	50768	67.4	17.3	15.8	7.1	2.1	12.4	12.9
1978	42797	62.5	18.7	13.2	5.7	2.0	10.5	12.4
1979	36356	57.9	21.0	12.0	4.2	2.0	7.3	11.5
1980	39403	50.7	19.3	8.2	3.0	2.6	7.1	10.6
1981	35912	44.0	20.3	4.2	2.6	2.4	5.9	8.5

TABLE 38 Number of Male Labour Out-migrants by Sending Country

Year	Total	Italy	Greece	Spain	Portugal	Turkey	Yugoslavia
1962	184676	118149	9527	15726	247	2438	5696
1963	259441	163709	15349	25175	383	4493	11849
1964	268662	144284	23568	30042	490	11311	16876
1965	293817	150104	27266	35711	1286	17987	18903
1966	370872	181477	31712	48428	3092	31572	28010
1967	323312	126717	35762	40981	4741	40099	27901
1968	189938	88247	12670	14410	1960	18104	18989
1969	216614	95378	10313	15639	2114	18856	37532
1970	262451	96706	12941	21320	4145	24339	62340
1971	300142	96992	16737	24376	6504	33381	73696
1972	286889	83642	18299	22984	6330	37607	62687
1973	271920	77457	17346	23478	6896	34910	55237
1974	284813	68579	16925	27394	11244	43036	60050
1975	256240	51403	20700	19517	7375	53204	52847
1976	187706	38680	17155	13529	4729	35436	32722
1977	147886	35193	13448	8832	2791	24652	19997
1978	127210	33642	10023	6051	1913	18532	15027
1979	119200	33998	7664	4074	1530	14714	12896
1980	142035	36132	5721	3361	2480	26186	11512
1981	140638	32584	3579	2752	2144	21240	10521

195

TABLE 39 Percentage of Male Labour Out-migrants by Sending Country

Year	Total	Recruitment Countries	Italy	Greece	Spain	Portugal	Turkey	Yugoslavia
1962	184676	82.2	64.0	5.2	8.5	0.1	1.3	3.1
1963	259441	85.2	63.1	5.9	9.7	0.1	1.7	4.6
1964	268662	84.3	53.7	8.8	11.2	0.2	4.2	6.3
1965	293817	85.5	51.1	9.3	12.2	0.4	6.1	6.4
1966	370872	87.4	48.9	8.6	13.1	0.8	8.5	7.6
1967	323312	85.4	39.2	11.1	12.7	1.5	12.4	8.6
1968	189938	81.3	46.5	6.7	7.6	1.0	9.5	10.0
1969	216614	83.0	44.0	4.8	7.2	1.0	8.7	17.3
1970	262451	84.5	36.8	4.9	8.1	1.6	9.3	23.8
1971	300142	83.9	32.3	5.6	8.1	2.2	11.1	24.6
1972	286889	80.7	29.2	6.4	8.0	2.2	13.1	21.9
1973	271930	79.2	28.5	6.4	8.6	2.5	12.8	20.3
1974	284813	79.8	24.1	5.9	9.6	3.9	15.1	21.1
1975	256240	80.0	20.1	8.1	7.6	2.9	20.8	20.6
1976	187706	75.8	20.6	9.1	7.2	2.5	18.9	17.4
1977	147886	70.9	23.8	9.1	6.0	1.9	16.7	13.5
1978	127210	67.0	26.4	7.9	4.8	1.5	14.6	11.8
1979	119200	62.8	28.5	6.4	3.4	1.3	12.3	10.8
1980	142035	60.1	25.4	4.0	2.4	1.7	18.4	8.1
1981	140638	51.8	23.2	2.5	2.0	1.5	15.1	7.5

TABLE 40 Female Labour In-migrants as Percentage of Total Labour In-migrants by Sending Country

Year	Total	Italy	Greece	Spain	Portugal	Turkey	Yugoslavia
1962	16.2	8.2	31.2	24.6	18.0	8.4	17.1
1963	18.2	9.7	31.0	25.7	20.1	10.3	23.1
1964	17.7	10.5	30.1	21.4	15.3	9.0	19.1
1965	20.4	11.7	39.1	23.1	10.9	19.3	22.2
1966	24.1	14.0	43.3	26.1	24.6	22.9	29.3
1967	26.4	16.2	39.7	30.9	31.0	22.4	30.1
1968	25.7	15.7	40.8	23.1	27.8	21.6	32.5
1969	24.5	15.9	40.0	17.6	21.6	18.7	27.4
1970	23.0	15.2	38.5	18.3	19.0	19.9	24.2
1971	21.9	14.7	37.5	19.9	23.2	17.5	23.7
1972	23.6	15.5	33.1	21.4	23.7	23.1	24.8
1973	22.5	15.5	32.1	17.2	19.3	21.6	23.9
1974	24.7	17.6	26.9	26.4	32.1	15.6	21.7
1975	26.6	19.3	25.6	25.5	31.4	13.1	21.9
1976	24.6	16.8	21.3	25.4	31.6	13.1	24.8
1977	23.8	16.7	21.0	29.2	32.6	13.2	23.6
1978	22.4	16.2	20.2	28.7	34.1	12.3	23.1
1979	19.9	15.9	20.8	29.2	28.5	7.7	19.2
1980	20.4	16.9	22.3	24.3	29.8	9.3	19.0
1981	25.0	19.3	18.3	17.4	28.8	12.3	17.5

TABLE 41 Female Labour Out-migrants as Percentage of Total Labour Out-migrants by Sending Country

Year	Total	Italy	Greece	Spain	Portugal	Turkey	Yugoslavia
1962	10.7	5.2	19.6	15.0	9.5	7.4	15.4
1963	11.8	6.4	24.8	16.7	16.6	8.4	13.7
1964	13.9	7.8	24.6	17.6	17.1	8.1	11.6
1965	14.6	8.2	26.4	17.1	11.0	9.8	12.4
1966	16.3	10.0	32.3	18.6	9.0	11.8	14.2
1967	21.7	14.9	37.7	25.4	11.6	13.5	19.9
1968	21.7	13.9	36.7	27.8	15.5	16.6	24.0
1969	20.5	13.8	35.5	21.3	13.2	17.6	21.9
1970	19.6	13.8	34.8	16.6	9.5	17.2	20.6
1971	18.4	13.6	34.4	15.5	8.8	13.3	19.0
1972	18.9	14.5	34.6	17.0	10.7	11.8	18.7
1973	19.7	14.8	35.8	17.9	13.1	13.8	18.2
1974	20.3	17.3	35.8	18.0	13.4	16.1	17.8
1975	22.8	20.5	37.6	23.2	20.9	18.1	19.2
1976	25.1	21.7	38.0	26.6	25.4	20.5	21.9
1977	25.6	19.9	37.4	28.9	27.3	20.3	24.6
1978	25.2	19.2	36.1	28.6	30.8	19.5	26.1
1979	23.4	18.3	36.2	27.1	32.6	15.3	24.5
1980	21.7	17.4	36.0	26.2	29.0	9.6	26.6
1981	20.3	18.3	29.5	25.3	29.0	9.1	22.5

TABLE 42   Net Female Labour Migration by Sending Country

Year	Total	Italy	Greece	Spain	Portugal	Turkey	Yugoslavia
1962	44825	9115	12553	19510	142	1007	4060
1963	40456	5523	12736	8686	241	2425	3158
1964	49058	7961	13995	9034	508	4880	2810
1965	70060	15107	16226	9044	1015	10140	7279
1966	48810	8989	4037	690	1983	7134	14692
1967	-30235	-8347	-16678	-10430	156	-1105	1966
1968	60869	8612	8129	1394	1279	9370	21772
1969	118937	9443	20521	4361	2351	18122	44922
1970	106599	6711	18168	4791	3270	19413	34693
1971	62717	3738	6983	3137	3451	14271	12300
1972	49463	2620	-844	1623	3183	16203	9475
1973	55396	3511	-5069	613	4709	22858	13670
1974	-18873	-4967	-7613	-4918	-984	-3728	-5822
1975	-39149	-7443	-11445	-5343	-1599	-9820	-8761
1976	-25423	-3547	-9580	-4367	-1347	-7166	-5869
1977	-9658	-182	-7085	-3011	-784	-4221	-3287
1978	123	681	-4678	-1902	-599	-1942	-2202
1979	11079	1563	-3343	-993	-484	173	-1205
1980	21586	1641	-1972	-659	-722	3124	-770
1981	22585	23	-218	-497	-643	-731	-1018

TABLE 43 Net Male Labour Migration by Sending Country

Year	Total	Italy	Greece	Spain	Portugal	Turkey	Yugoslavia
1962	161753	55538	23337	25015	520	10745	19093
1963	77503	-8011	24185	14627	879	20210	4903
1964	160230	27689	26805	26711	2887	48028	4376
1965	177553	65079	13213	18929	8314	32764	16019
1966	11266	-2809	-6601	-15221	3940	6755	18647
1967	-158232	-54559	-28225	-33137	-3002	-22210	-7277
1968	138372	34598	9736	8711	2288	28864	38724
1969	322566	34924	28946	24622	7585	77187	109029
1970	308136	26867	27150	19020	11672	74271	97201
1971	166068	12696	9461	6197	7012	58165	21541
1972	89662	8085	-423	370	6379	33152	9742
1973	150029	15088	-7636	3971	17095	68071	27185
1974	-121234	-24737	-11924	-24284	-9631	-18586	-34213
1975	-155101	-27164	-17686	-17865	-6615	-40586	-39462
1976	-72186	-3215	-13685	-11953	-4161	-22434	-22747
1977	-16354	7481	-9927	-7440	-2242	-10999	-9533
1978	21496	11114	-6144	-4742	-1429	-264	-4638
1979	71834	14691	-3835	-2804	-889	19263	-373
1980	95460	9158	-1391	-1701	-1796	31350	3033
1981	34701	-1860	2138	-697	-1566	-11297	-903

TABLE 44 Labour In-migration from all Foreign Countries

Year	L/T	ML/L	ML/M	FL/F
1962	84.6	83.8	90.8	62.3
1963	82.7	81.8	89.6	61.5
1964	83.4	82.3	90.4	61.2
1965	82.6	79.6	89.9	62.8
1966	79.6	75.9	87.6	61.7
1967	67.9	73.6	79.1	48.6
1968	74.9	74.3	84.4	56.6
1969	78.5	75.5	86.9	60.5
1970	75.9	77.0	85.4	55.4
1971	68.5	78.1	80.6	44.7
1972	62.6	76.4	75.7	40.1
1973	62.6	77.5	76.1	38.9
1974	40.3	75.3	54.6	22.5
1975	37.7	73.4	51.2	21.8
1976	39.5	75.4	53.9	21.8
1977	40.8	76.2	55.3	22.2
1978	42.0	77.6	55.8	22.6
1979	43.7	80.1	56.6	22.9
1980	47.3	79.6	58.9	26.7
1981	46.7	75.0	58.3	29.2

Note:

F – Female Migrants

ML – Male Labour Migrants

FL – Female Labour Migrants

All figures are percentages

T – Total Migrants

L – Labour Migrants

M – Male Migrants

TABLE 45 Labour Out-migration to all Foreign Countries

Year	L/T	ML/L	ML/M	FL/F
1962	84.4	89.3	90.6	53.7
1963	85.4	88.2	91.7	56.3
1964	84.0	86.1	90.9	57.2
1965	83.4	85.4	90.3	57.7
1966	82.8	83.7	90.0	58.6
1967	78.2	78.3	86.9	57.4
1968	72.9	78.3	83.0	50.7
1969	73.9	79.5	83.7	51.0
1970	75.1	80.4	84.6	51.4
1971	73.5	81.6	83.6	48.0
1972	68.8	81.1	80.0	42.9
1973	64.3	80.3	76.0	39.5
1974	61.6	79.7	73.9	37.2
1975	55.3	77.2	68.2	33.8
1976	48.6	74.9	60.7	30.6
1977	43.9	74.4	55.5	27.4
1978	41.9	74.8	52.6	26.1
1979	42.5	76.6	53.9	25.1
1980	47.0	78.3	58.4	27.7
1981	42.5	79.7	53.3	23.7

Note: See Table 44

TABLE 46 Labour In-migration from Italy

Year	L/T	ML/L	ML/M	FL/F
1962	93.9	91.8	97.5	66.9
1963	91.9	90.3	96.4	64.4
1964	91.6	89.5	96.4	64.4
1965	90.6	88.3	95.9	63.8
1966	87.5	86.0	94.3	60.8
1967	81.2	83.8	90.7	52.6
1968	81.7	84.3	90.8	53.0
1969	81.3	84.1	90.6	52.8
1970	79.2	84.8	89.6	48.3
1971	76.8	85.3	88.4	43.5
1972	73.7	84.5	86.5	40.8
1973	71.8	84.5	85.1	38.7
1974	62.1	82.4	78.0	31.8
1975	59.0	80.7	75.7	30.6
1976	64.2	83.2	79.5	33.0
1977	63.9	83.3	79.7	32.3
1978	64.3	83.8	80.0	32.0
1979	64.8	84.1	80.5	31.9
1980	63.3	83.1	78.8	32.2
1981	58.5	80.7	74.3	31.0

Note: See Table 44

TABLE 47 Labour Out-migration to Italy

Year	L/T	ML/L	ML/M	FL/F
1962	95.3	94.8	97.4	68.2
1963	94.7	93.6	97.6	66.6
1964	94.3	92.2	97.6	67.4
1965	93.8	91.8	97.2	67.4
1966	91.5	90.0	96.2	63.6
1967	85.5	85.1	93.0	58.5
1968	84.2	86.1	92.0	55.2
1969	83.7	86.2	91.5	54.6
1970	82.2	86.2	90.6	52.1
1971	80.7	86.4	89.9	48.8
1972	76.8	85.5	87.6	44.4
1973	74.9	85.2	86.3	42.5
1974	68.9	82.7	81.9	39.1
1975	61.8	79.5	76.5	35.5
1976	58.3	78.3	72.4	34.2
1977	58.3	80.1	71.8	33.2
1978	56.3	80.8	69.0	31.8
1979	56.3	81.7	69.5	30.5
1980	56.5	82.6	69.2	30.2
1981	49.4	81.7	61.6	26.2

Note: See Table 44

TABLE 48 Labour In-migration from Greece

Year	L/T	ML/L	ML/M	FL/F
1962	90.0	68.8	94.1	82.1
1963	88.8	69.0	93.0	80.5
1964	88.2	69.9	93.0	78.6
1965	85.0	60.9	89.4	78.9
1966	79.9	56.7	84.0	75.2
1967	60.7	60.3	67.9	52.2
1968	71.3	59.2	77.1	64.3
1969	74.5	60.0	80.1	67.4
1970	69.1	61.5	76.3	60.0
1971	59.0	62.5	68.1	48.3
1972	52.3	66.9	63.4	38.7
1973	39.6	67.9	50.1	27.5
1974	22.8	73.1	31.2	13.2
1975	22.3	74.4	31.0	12.3
1976	27.6	78.7	38.2	13.6
1977	29.2	79.0	40.8	14.1
1978	31.6	79.8	43.6	15.2
1979	32.7	79.2	45.0	16.0
1980	35.3	77.7	47.3	18.7
1981	37.7	81.7	51.2	17.3

Note: See Table 44

TABLE 49 Labour Out-migration to Greece

Year	L/T	ML/L	ML/M	FL/F
1962	84.6	80.4	89.6	68.7
1963	85.4	75.2	90.1	73.7
1964	85.9	75.4	90.8	73.7
1965	83.9	73.6	89.2	71.8
1966	80.6	67.7	86.0	71.4
1967	77.7	62.3	82.6	70.8
1968	68.9	63.3	74.9	60.4
1969	65.5	64.5	72.5	55.8
1970	65.6	65.2	72.9	55.2
1971	63.6	65.6	70.8	53.1
1972	58.2	65.4	65.6	48.0
1973	55.3	64.2	62.0	46.4
1974	54.1	64.2	61.0	45.0
1975	50.5	62.4	56.9	42.6
1976	47.6	62.0	53.8	40.0
1977	44.7	62.6	51.4	36.8
1978	43.3	63.9	50.5	34.5
1979	41.1	63.8	47.9	32.8
1980	40.0	64.0	47.6	31.3
1981	32.2	70.5	39.1	22.6

Note: See Table 44

TABLE 50 Labour In-migration from Spain

Year	L/T	ML/L	ML/M	FL/F
1962	86.4	75.4	93.0	70.9
1963	86.2	74.3	92.8	71.4
1964	88.2	78.6	94.2	71.6
1965	86.3	76.9	93.0	69.6
1966	82.7	73.9	90.0	67.2
1967	66.8	69.1	78.3	50.2
1968	79.0	76.9	88.0	58.9
1969	82.4	82.4	90.7	57.8
1970	80.5	81.7	89.4	55.9
1971	72.8	80.1	84.9	46.3
1972	66.7	78.6	80.3	41.0
1973	71.7	82.8	84.4	41.7
1974	30.7	73.6	45.9	15.9
1975	29.1	74.5	43.2	14.9
1976	33.7	74.6	48.3	17.8
1977	34.9	70.8	50.0	20.1
1978	34.8	71.3	48.5	20.4
1979	35.5	70.8	49.6	21.0
1980	40.6	75.7	53.7	23.1
1981	43.9	82.6	60.1	19.3

Note: See Table 44

TABLE 51 Labour Out-migration to Spain

Year	L/T	ML/L	ML/M	FL/F
1962	88.8	85.0	93.2	70.1
1963	88.7	83.3	94.3	68.4
1964	89.2	82.4	94.2	71.6
1965	88.5	82.9	94.2	68.4
1966	86.3	81.4	92.8	66.3
1967	81.1	74.6	89.1	64.2
1968	74.9	72.2	83.9	58.5
1969	77.6	78.7	86.5	56.2
1970	80.1	83.4	88.3	54.6
1971	80.3	84.5	88.7	52.9
1972	76.7	83.0	86.4	49.6
1973	72.9	82.1	83.8	45.6
1974	70.3	82.0	82.5	41.9
1975	63.4	76.8	76.4	40.7
1976	56.2	73.4	68.8	37.4
1977	50.6	71.1	63.7	33.5
1978	48.6	71.4	61.5	31.9
1979	46.1	72.9	58.3	29.5
1980	45.5	73.8	58.4	28.1
1981	41.4	74.7	52.6	25.4

Note: See Table 44

TABLE 52 Labour In-migration from Portugal

Year	L/T	ML/L	ML/M	FL/F
1962	72.2	82.0	80.6	49.0
1963	78.7	79.9	86.1	58.5
1964	86.8	84.7	93.4	62.5
1965	91.0	89.1	96.4	62.3
1966	86.2	75.4	93.5	69.5
1967	63.0	69.0	79.2	43.3
1968	71.4	72.2	85.2	50.3
1969	81.3	78.4	90.5	59.5
1970	86.9	81.0	94.1	65.4
1971	74.0	76.8	86.9	49.5
1972	67.8	76.3	83.2	42.4
1973	75.7	80.7	88.7	47.0
1974	17.9	67.9	32.8	9.2
1975	13.6	68.6	22.1	7.4
1976	14.2	68.4	23.3	7.7
1977	17.1	67.4	27.3	9.6
1978	15.7	65.9	25.8	8.9
1979	20.3	71.5	30.6	11.0
1980	24.6	70.2	36.5	14.0
1981	26.4	71.2	38.9	14.7

Note: See Table 44

TABLE 53 Labour Out-migration to Portugal

Year	L/T	ML/L	ML/M	FL/F
1962	72.6	90.5	82.1	34.7
1963	72.9	83.4	81.1	48.1
1964	75.6	82.9	83.8	51.3
1965	84.2	89.0	90.9	52.6
1966	90.3	91.0	95.2	59.4
1967	89.3	88.4	95.0	61.7
1968	79.5	84.5	88.2	51.6
1969	80.5	86.8	89.1	49.4
1970	85.2	90.5	92.6	48.3
1971	85.8	91.2	93.0	47.8
1972	81.7	89.3	91.6	43.0
1973	75.9	86.9	88.0	39.8
1974	74.7	86.6	87.1	39.0
1975	62.4	79.1	77.4	36.1
1976	51.6	74.6	66.0	31.5
1977	42.4	72.7	56.6	25.5
1978	42.1	69.2	55.4	27.4
1979	39.4	67.4	51.9	26.3
1980	43.7	71.0	58.2	27.2
1981	38.8	71.0	51.5	24.2

Note: See Table 44

TABLE 54 Labour In-migration from Turkey

Year	L/T	ML/L	ML/M	FL/F
1962	81.9	91.6	87.9	46.8
1963	88.8	89.7	92.7	65.1
1964	91.5	91.0	95.3	65.4
1965	86.7	80.7	92.0	70.0
1966	82.1	77.1	88.6	66.0
1967	69.6	77.6	80.1	47.9
1968	75.2	78.4	84.9	53.2
1969	78.2	81.3	87.0	54.5
1970	69.6	80.1	80.7	44.7
1971	59.3	82.5	73.6	31.0
1972	49.8	76.9	63.7	28.9
1973	52.6	78.4	66.8	29.8
1974	18.0	84.4	29.2	5.9
1975	14.7	86.9	24.7	4.0
1976	14.1	86.9	24.1	3.8
1977	13.7	86.8	23.1	3.7
1978	15.9	87.7	25.4	4.3
1979	21.4	92.3	32.0	4.3
1980	29.9	90.7	41.0	8.2
1981	13.5	87.7	20.2	4.0

Note: See Table 44

TABLE 55 Labour Out-migration to Turkey

Year	L/T	ML/L	ML/M	FL/F
1962	73.9	92.6	79.2	40.0
1963	78.3	91.6	84.2	44.6
1964	89.0	91.9	92.6	61.7
1965	88.0	90.2	92.3	61.5
1966	88.7	88.2	92.9	66.2
1967	86.0	86.5	91.4	62.6
1968	78.3	83.4	84.8	56.5
1969	72.4	82.4	80.1	50.0
1970	69.4	82.8	78.2	45.2
1971	63.2	86.7	73.8	32.7
1972	56.8	88.2	68.8	24.7
1973	46.5	86.2	58.1	20.7
1974	46.3	83.9	57.8	22.7
1975	43.7	81.9	55.7	22.1
1976	34.2	79.5	44.5	18.0
1977	27.3	79.7	36.4	13.7
1978	26.2	80.5	34.7	13.0
1979	26.2	84.7	35.7	13.0
1980	41.0	90.4	52.7	10.7
1981	32.9	90.9	43.2	9.8

Note: See Table 44

TABLE 56 Labour In-migration from Yugoslavia

Year	L/T	ML/L	ML/M	FL/F
1962	87.7	82.9	95.0	63.7
1963	82.8	76.9	92.4	61.5
1964	83.7	80.9	93.5	58.1
1965	87.5	77.8	94.9	68.7
1966	88.6	70.7	94.9	76.3
1967	77.9	69.9	89.5	59.9
1968	89.7	67.5	95.3	80.0
1969	91.6	72.6	96.3	81.2
1970	88.2	75.8	94.8	72.4
1971	78.3	76.3	90.5	54.7
1972	71.9	75.2	86.5	47.5
1973	71.7	76.1	86.5	46.5
1974	45.6	78.3	67.2	21.1
1975	37.6	78.1	58.4	16.6
1976	32.6	75.2	51.8	15.3
1977	32.7	76.4	52.6	14.7
1978	35.0	76.9	54.2	16.1
1979	38.2	80.8	57.5	15.8
1980	42.9	81.0	61.7	18.6
1981	34.3	82.5	53.0	12.9

Note: See Table 44

TABLE 57 Labour Out-migration to Yugoslavia

Year	L/T	ML/L	ML/M	FL/F
1962	74.6	84.6	87.8	40.9
1963	85.0	86.3	94.0	52.9
1964	87.7	88.4	95.7	53.7
1965	87.4	87.6	95.5	54.6
1966	88.5	85.8	95.9	60.3
1967	85.4	80.1	94.3	61.8
1968	81.8	76.0	92.3	60.1
1969	87.9	78.1	95.1	69.2
1970	88.2	79.4	94.9	69.3
1971	84.5	81.0	93.3	60.4
1972	79.4	81.3	90.3	52.1
1973	73.8	81.8	86.7	44.1
1974	71.6	82.2	85.6	40.8
1975	65.4	80.8	80.7	36.3
1976	56.3	78.1	72.3	31.4
1977	45.4	75.4	60.5	25.7
1978	39.9	73.9	52.8	23.6
1979	38.4	75.5	52.1	21.2
1980	38.2	73.4	49.9	23.2
1981	33.9	77.5	45.3	18.2

Note: See Table 44

TABLE 58   Number of Employees by Country of Nationality

Year	Total	Italy	Greece	Spain	Portugal	Turkey	Yugoslavia
1954	72906	6509	548	411	n.d	n.d	1801
1955	79607	7461	637	486	n.d	n.d	2085
1956	98818	18597	953	698	n.d	n.d	2297
1957	108190	19096	1822	967	n.d	n.d	2778
1958	127083	25609	2838	1494	n.d	n.d	4846
1959	166829	48809	4089	2150	n.d	n.d	7310
1960	279390	121685	13005	9454	261	2495	8826
1961	507419	218003	43948	50976	n.d	n.d	n.d
1962	655463	265978	69146	87327	1421	15318	23608
1963	811213	299235	106152	117494	2284	27144	44428
1964	932932	289252	143859	144256	3463	69211	53057
1965	1164364	359773	181658	180572	10509	121121	64060
1966	1314031	399154	196247	185336	19802	157978	96675
1967	1023747	274249	146817	129126	18519	137081	97725
1968	1014774	287440	136191	111982	18743	139336	99660
1969	1372059	340244	174348	135546	26379	212951	226290
1970	1838859	374981	229379	165854	40222	327985	388953
1971	2168766	405092	261592	183636	55214	424374	469173
1972	2316980	422220	269689	183960	63128	497296	471892
1973	2595000	450000	250000	190000	n.d	605000	535000
1974	2331173	340939	234718	158936	82400	617531	473203
1975	2070735	297079	203629	129817	70520	553217	418745
1976	1937134	276367	178800	111006	63579	527483	390079
1977	1888585	281224	162495	100311	60160	517467	377206
1978	1869294	288648	146792	92586	58771	514694	369506
1979	1933651	300442	140139	89992	59145	540471	367301
1980	2071658	309226	132980	86547	58780	590623	357427
1981	1929737	291066	123767	81845	55085	580868	340573

Note: 1973 figures are estimates

208

TABLE 59 Percentage of Employees by Country of Nationality

Year	Total	Recruitment Countries	Italy	Greece	Spain	Portugal	Turkey	Yugoslavia
1954	72906	12.7	8.9	0.8	0.6	n.d	n.d	2.5
1955	79607	13.4	9.4	0.8	0.6	n.d	n.d	2.6
1956	98818	22.8	18.8	1.0	0.7	n.d	n.d	2.3
1957	108190	22.8	17.7	1.7	0.9	n.d	n.d	2.6
1958	127083	27.4	20.2	2.2	1.2	n.d	n.d	3.8
1959	166829	37.4	29.3	2.5	1.3	n.d	n.d	4.4
1960	279390	55.7	43.6	4.7	3.4	0.1	0.9	3.2
1961	507419	61.7	43.0	8.7	10.0	n.d	n.d	n.d
1962	655463	70.6	40.6	10.5	13.3	0.2	2.3	3.6
1963	811213	73.6	36.9	13.1	14.5	0.3	3.3	5.5
1964	932932	75.4	31.0	15.4	15.5	0.4	7.4	5.7
1965	1164364	78.8	30.9	15.6	15.5	0.9	10.4	5.5
1966	1314031	80.3	30.4	14.9	14.1	1.5	12.0	7.4
1967	1023747	78.5	26.8	14.3	12.6	1.8	13.4	9.5
1968	1014774	78.2	28.3	13.4	11.0	1.8	13.7	9.8
1969	1372059	81.3	24.8	12.7	9.9	1.9	15.5	16.5
1970	1838859	83.1	20.4	12.5	9.0	2.2	17.8	21.2
1971	2168766	83.0	18.7	12.1	8.5	2.5	19.6	21.6
1972	2316980	82.4	18.2	11.6	7.9	2.7	21.5	20.4
1973	2595000	78.2	17.3	9.6	7.3	n.d	23.3	20.6
1974	2331173	81.8	14.6	10.1	6.8	3.5	26.5	20.3
1975	2070735	80.8	14.3	9.8	6.3	3.4	26.7	20.2
1976	1937134	79.9	14.3	9.2	5.7	3.3	27.2	20.1
1977	1888585	79.4	14.9	8.6	5.3	3.2	27.4	20.0
1978	1869294	78.7	15.4	7.9	5.0	3.1	27.5	19.8
1979	1933651	77.4	15.5	7.2	4.7	3.1	28.0	19.0
1980	2071658	74.1	14.9	6.4	4.2	2.8	28.5	17.3
1981	1929737	76.3	15.1	6.4	4.2	2.9	30.1	17.6

Note: See Table 58

209

TABLE 60   Number of Male Employees by Country of Nationality

Year	Total	Italy	Greece	Spain	Portugal	Turkey	Yugoslavia
1959	135295	44425	3560	1755	n.d	n.d	5936
1960	236197	113866	11479	7808	224	2295	7169
1961	n.d	n.d	n.d	n.d	n.d	n.d	n.d
1962	538196	242089	49113	66047	1219	14045	19299
1963	643234	265315	71171	84131	1864	24167	35130
1964	726004	249389	96107	102422	2677	62280	41915
1965	895438	305750	115890	128728	8898	105566	49617
1966	981681	330089	118420	128526	16564	131853	71204
1967	728272	214938	85322	83615	14098	111692	65523
1968	715243	223902	78983	71431	13655	109167	63458
1969	969336	262348	100261	91391	18779	165954	152120
1970	1305352	286811	131977	116181	28949	255949	269240
1971	1553874	309715	150381	129668	40010	333009	331098
1972	1641259	318939	153076	128637	44225	383771	326188
1973	n.d	n.d	n.d	n.d	n.d	n.d	n.d
1974	1605571	249193	132655	109037	56854	457547	310771
1975	1417576	216821	116219	87883	47889	409606	267990
1976	1328849	202442	102980	75211	42833	392589	249096
1977	1299743	207927	94168	68383	40296	383471	239788
1978	1290246	215152	85835	63299	39145	379680	234652
1979	1339794	224462	82472	61684	39032	397720	232479
1980	1429952	229345	78627	59154	38019	437016	224427
1981	1340257	215435	74220	56297	35683	429809	214170

Note: n.d = No Data

210

TABLE 61 Percentage of Male Employees by Country of Nationality

Year	Total	Recruitment Countries	Italy	Greece	Spain	Portugal	Turkey	Yugoslavia
1959	135295	41.2	32.8	2.6	1.3	0.0	0.0	4.4
1960	236197	60.5	48.2	4.9	3.3	0.1	1.0	3.0
1961	n.d	n.d	n.d	n.d	n.d	n.d	n.d	n.d
1962	538196	72.8	45.0	9.1	12.3	0.2	2.6	3.6
1963	643234	74.9	41.2	11.1	13.1	0.3	3.8	5.5
1964	726004	76.4	34.4	13.2	14.1	0.4	8.6	5.8
1965	895438	79.8	34.1	12.9	14.4	1.0	11.8	5.5
1966	981681	81.2	33.6	12.1	13.1	1.7	13.4	7.3
1967	728272	79.0	29.5	11.7	11.5	1.9	15.3	9.0
1968	715243	78.4	31.3	11.0	10.0	1.9	15.3	8.9
1969	969336	81.6	27.1	10.3	9.4	2.1	17.1	15.7
1970	1305352	83.4	22.0	10.1	8.9	2.2	19.6	20.6
1971	1553874	83.3	19.9	9.7	8.3	2.6	21.4	21.3
1972	1641257	82.5	19.4	9.3	7.8	2.7	23.4	19.9
1973	n.d	n.d	n.d	n.d	n.d	n.d	n.d	n.d
1974	1605571	82.0	15.5	8.3	6.8	3.5	28.5	19.4
1975	1417576	80.9	15.3	8.2	6.2	3.4	28.9	18.9
1976	1328849	80.2	15.2	7.7	5.7	3.2	29.5	18.7
1977	1299743	79.6	16.0	7.2	5.3	3.1	29.5	18.4
1978	1290246	78.9	16.7	6.7	4.9	3.0	29.4	18.2
1979	1339794	77.5	16.8	6.2	4.6	2.9	29.7	17.4
1980	1429952	74.6	16.0	5.5	4.1	2.7	30.6	15.7
1981	1340257	76.5	16.1	5.5	4.2	2.7	32.1	16.0

Note: See Table 60

TABLE 62   Number of Female Employees by Country of Nationality

Year	Total	Italy	Greece	Spain	Portugal	Turkey	Yugoslavia
1959	31534	4384	529	395	n.d	n.d	1374
1960	43193	7819	1526	1646	37	200	1657
1961	m.d	n.d	n.d	n.d	n.d	n.d	n.d
1962	117267	23889	20033	21280	202	1273	4309
1963	167979	33920	34981	33363	420	2977	9298
1964	206928	39863	47752	41834	786	6931	11142
1965	268926	54023	65768	51844	1611	15555	14443
1966	332350	69065	77827	56810	3238	26125	25471
1967	295475	59311	61495	45511	4421	25389	32202
1968	299531	63538	57208	40551	5088	30169	36202
1969	402723	77896	74087	44155	7600	46997	74170
1970	533507	88170	97402	49673	11273	72036	119713
1971	614892	95377	111211	53968	15204	91365	138075
1972	675723	103281	116613	55323	18903	113525	145704
1973	n.d	n.d	n.d	n.d	n.d	n.d	n.d
1974	725602	91746	102063	49899	25546	159984	162432
1975	653159	80258	87410	41934	22631	143611	150755
1976	608285	73925	75820	35795	20746	134894	140983
1977	588842	73297	68327	31928	19864	133996	137418
1978	579048	73496	60957	29287	19626	135014	134854
1979	593857	75980	57667	28308	20113	142751	134822
1980	641706	79881	54353	27393	20761	153607	133000
1981	589480	75631	49547	25548	19402	151059	126403

Note: See Table 60

212

TABLE 63 Percentage of Female Employees by Country of Nationality

Year	Total	Recruitment Countries	Italy	Greece	Spain	Portugal	Turkey	Yugoslavia
1959	31534	21.2	13.9	1.7	1.3	n.d	n.d	4.4
1960	43193	29.8	18.1	3.5	3.8	0.1	0.5	3.8
1961	n.d	n.d	n.d	n.d	n.d	n.d	n.d	n.d
1962	117267	60.5	20.4	17.1	18.1	0.2	1.1	3.7
1963	167979	68.4	20.2	20.8	19.9	0.3	1.8	5.5
1964	206928	71.7	19.3	23.1	20.2	0.4	3.3	5.4
1965	268926	75.6	20.1	24.5	19.3	0.6	5.8	5.4
1966	332350	77.8	20.8	23.4	17.1	1.0	7.9	7.7
1967	295475	77.3	20.1	20.8	15.4	1.5	8.6	10.9
1968	299531	77.7	21.2	19.1	13.5	1.7	10.1	12.1
1969	402723	80.7	19.3	18.4	11.0	1.9	11.7	18.4
1970	533507	82.1	16.5	18.3	9.3	2.1	13.5	22.4
1971	614892	82.2	15.5	18.1	8.8	2.5	14.9	22.5
1972	675723	81.9	15.3	17.3	8.2	2.8	16.8	21.6
1973	n.d	n.d	n.d	n.d	n.d	n.d	n.d	n.d
1974	725602	81.5	12.6	14.1	6.9	3.5	22.0	22.4
1975	653159	80.6	12.3	13.4	6.4	3.5	22.0	23.1
1976	608285	79.3	12.2	12.5	5.9	3.4	22.2	23.2
1977	588842	78.9	12.4	11.6	5.4	3.4	22.8	23.3
1978	579048	78.3	12.7	10.5	5.1	3.4	23.3	23.3
1979	593857	77.4	12.8	9.7	4.8	3.4	24.0	22.7
1980	641706	73.1	12.4	8.5	4.3	3.2	23.9	20.7
1981	589480	75.9	12.8	8.4	4.3	3.3	25.6	21.4

Note: See Table 60

213

TABLE 64 Ratio of Employees per In-migrant by Sending Country

Year	Total	Italy	Greece	Spain	Portugal	Turkey	Yugoslavia
1954	1.6	2.2	n.d	n.d	n.d	n.d	0.9
1955	1.3	1.5	n.d	n.d	n.d	n.d	0.7
1956	1.2	1.2	n.d	n.d	n.d	n.d	0.7
1957	1.0	0.9	n.d	n.d	n.d	n.d	0.5
1958	1.1	0.9	n.d	n.d	n.d	n.d	0.6
1959	1.1	1.0	n.d	n.d	n.d	n.d	1.0
1960	0.9	0.8	0.5	0.3	0.4	0.7	1.2
1961	1.2	1.2	1.2	0.9	n.d	n.d	n.d
1962	1.3	1.3	1.3	1.4	1.1	0.9	0.7
1963	1.6	1.6	1.6	1.9	1.1	1.0	1.7
1964	1.5	1.4	1.8	1.8	0.8	1.7	1.2
1965	1.6	1.3	2.3	2.2	0.9	2.6	1.3
1966	2.1	1.7	3.5	3.4	1.8	4.1	2.6
1967	3.1	2.6	7.1	7.6	4.6	1.7	1.0
1968	1.7	1.6	2.6	2.9	2.3	1.4	1.0
1969	1.5	1.8	2.0	2.3	1.7	1.9	1.6
1970	1.9	2.0	2.4	2.7	1.8	2.3	2.9
1971	2.5	2.4	3.7	3.5	2.3	2.7	3.5
1972	2.9	2.9	5.3	4.1	2.6	2.4	3.5
1973	3.0	2.9	6.9	4.1	n.d	3.8	6.5
1974	4.3	4.0	7.8	11.6	6.2	5.6	9.2
1975	5.7	5.8	11.2	17.1	8.7	5.0	9.6
1976	5.0	4.2	11.2	17.7	10.9	4.5	9.0
1977	4.5	3.5	10.6	17.8	12.6	3.9	9.6
1978	4.1	3.5	9.5	17.5	12.5	3.1	9.1
1979	3.5	3.4	9.5	17.8	13.4	2.8	8.5
1980	3.3	3.6	8.4	16.0	14.9	6.9	8.5
1981	3.9	4.5	6.7	14.4	17.9	6.9	10.0

Note: See Table 60

TABLE 65 Ratio of Employees per Out-migrant by Sending Country

Year	Total	Italy	Greece	Spain	Portugal	Turkey	Yugoslavia
1954	2.5	3.3	n.d	n.d	n.d	n.d	2.3
1955	2.2	2.8	n.d	n.d	n.d	n.d	1.7
1956	2.0	2.2	n.d	n.d	n.d	n.d	1.5
1957	1.8	1.6	n.d	n.d	n.d	n.d	1.2
1958	2.0	1.5	n.d	n.d	n.d	n.d	1.4
1959	2.1	1.8	n.d	n.d	n.d	n.d	1.8
1960	2.2	2.1	4.3	2.8	1.1	2.5	2.4
1961	2.8	2.4	5.1	4.2	n.d	n.d	n.d
1962	2.7	2.0	4.9	4.2	3.8	4.3	2.6
1963	2.4	1.6	4.4	3.4	3.6	4.3	2.7
1964	2.5	1.7	4.0	3.5	4.4	5.0	2.4
1965	2.8	2.1	4.1	3.7	6.1	5.3	2.6
1966	2.5	1.8	3.4	2.7	5.3	3.9	2.6
1967	1.9	1.6	2.0	1.9	3.1	2.5	2.4
1968	3.1	2.4	4.7	4.2	6.4	5.0	3.3
1969	3.7	2.6	7.1	5.3	8.7	6.7	4.1
1970	4.2	2.7	7.6	5.2	7.5	7.7	4.4
1971	4.3	2.9	6.5	5.1	6.6	7.0	4.4
1972	4.5	3.3	5.6	5.1	7.3	6.6	4.9
1973	4.9	3.7	5.1	4.8	n.d	6.9	5.8
1974	4.0	2.8	4.8	3.3	4.7	5.6	4.6
1975	3.5	2.8	3.1	3.2	5.2	3.7	4.2
1976	3.8	3.3	3.1	3.4	6.6	4.0	5.2
1977	4.2	3.7	3.4	4.1	6.6	4.6	6.5
1978	4.6	3.9	4.0	5.3	9.0	5.8	7.3
1979	5.3	4.1	4.8	7.4	10.3	8.2	8.3
1980	5.4	4.0	6.0	8.7	7.4	8.4	8.7
1981	4.6	3.6	7.8	9.2	7.1	8.2	8.5

Note: See Table 60

215

TABLE 66   Ratio of Employees per Dependant In-migrant by Sending Country

Year	Total	Italy	Greece	Spain	Portugal	Turkey	Yugoslavia
1962	8.7	21.8	13.0	10.2	3.9	4.8	5.6
1963	9.4	19.8	14.6	13.7	5.3	7.8	9.8
1964	9.0	16.5	14.9	15.0	5.7	11.4	10.4
1965	9.4	14.2	15.4	16.0	9.8	12.6	10.0
1966	10.2	13.5	17.7	19.7	13.3	14.6	11.4
1967	9.7	13.8	18.1	22.8	12.5	13.6	11.7
1968	6.9	8.8	8.9	14.0	8.0	7.0	10.2
1969	7.0	9.6	7.8	13.0	9.3	6.5	12.3
1970	7.8	9.8	7.9	13.9	13.6	6.1	13.8
1971	7.9	10.4	9.0	12.9	8.9	5.6	13.6
1972	7.9	10.9	11.1	12.4	8.0	5.4	12.5
1973	8.0	10.5	11.5	14.5	n.d	5.1	12.5
1974	7.3	10.5	10.2	16.7	7.6	4.7	12.0
1975	9.1	14.2	14.4	24.1	10.0	6.6	14.7
1976	8.3	11.6	15.4	26.7	12.7	5.8	14.2
1977	7.5	9.7	15.0	27.3	15.2	5.2	13.4
1978	7.1	9.7	13.9	26.9	14.9	4.7	14.8
1979	6.3	9.6	14.1	27.6	16.8	4.0	14.6
1980	6.2	9.8	13.0	27.0	19.7	4.0	14.9
1981	7.2	10.8	10.7	25.7	24.3	8.0	15.3

Note: See Table 60

216

TABLE 67 Ratio of Female Employees per Dependant In-migrant by Sending Country

Year	Total	Italy	Greece	Spain	Portugal	Turkey	Yugoslavia
1962	1.6	2.0	3.8	2.5	0.6	0.4	1.0
1963	1.9	2.2	4.8	3.9	1.0	0.9	2.1
1964	2.0	2.3	4.9	4.3	1.3	1.1	2.2
1965	2.2	2.1	5.6	4.6	1.5	1.6	2.2
1966	2.6	2.3	7.0	6.0	2.2	2.4	3.0
1967	2.8	3.0	7.6	8.0	3.0	2.5	3.8
1968	2.0	1.9	3.8	5.1	2.2	1.5	3.7
1969	2.1	2.2	3.3	4.2	2.7	1.4	4.0
1970	2.3	2.3	3.3	4.2	3.8	1.3	4.3
1971	2.2	2.4	3.8	3.8	2.5	1.2	4.0
1972	2.3	2.7	4.8	3.7	2.4	1.2	3.9
1973	0.0	0.0	0.0	0.0	0.0	0.0	0.0
1974	2.3	2.8	4.4	5.2	2.3	1.2	4.1
1975	2.9	3.8	6.2	7.8	3.2	1.7	5.3
1976	2.6	3.1	6.5	8.6	4.1	1.5	5.1
1977	2.4	2.5	6.3	8.7	5.0	1.4	4.9
1978	2.2	2.5	5.8	8.5	5.0	1.2	5.4
1979	1.9	2.4	5.8	8.7	5.7	1.1	5.4
1980	1.9	2.5	5.3	8.5	7.0	1.0	5.6
1981	2.2	2.8	4.3	8.0	8.6	2.1	5.7

Note: See Table 60

217

TABLE 68 Ratio of Male Employees per Dependant In-migrant by Sending Country

Year	Total	Italy	Greece	Spain	Portugal	Turkey	Yugoslavia
1962	7.1	19.9	9.2	7.7	3.4	4.4	4.6
1963	7.5	17.6	9.8	9.8	4.4	6.9	7.8
1964	7.0	14.2	9.9	10.6	4.4	10.3	8.2
1965	7.2	12.1	9.9	11.4	8.3	11.0	7.7
1966	7.6	11.2	10.7	13.7	11.1	12.2	8.4
1967	6.9	10.8	10.5	14.8	9.5	11.1	7.8
1968	4.8	6.9	5.2	8.9	5.8	5.5	6.5
1969	5.0	7.4	4.5	8.8	6.6	5.0	8.2
1970	5.6	7.5	4.5	9.7	9.8	4.8	9.6
1971	5.7	8.0	5.2	9.1	6.5	4.4	9.6
1972	5.6	8.2	6.3	8.7	5.6	4.1	8.6
1973	0.0	0.0	0.0	0.0	0.0	0.0	0.0
1974	5.0	7.7	5.7	11.4	5.2	3.5	7.9
1975	6.2	10.4	8.2	16.3	6.8	4.9	9.4
1976	5.7	8.5	8.9	18.1	8.6	4.3	9.1
1977	5.2	7.2	8.7	18.6	10.2	3.9	8.5
1978	4.9	7.3	8.2	18.4	9.9	3.4	9.4
1979	4.4	7.1	8.3	19.0	11.1	2.9	9.3
1980	4.3	7.3	7.7	18.4	12.7	2.9	9.4
1981	5.0	8.0	6.4	17.7	15.7	5.9	9.6

Note: See Table 60

TABLE 69 Ratio of Employees per Dependant Out-migrant by Sending Country

Year	Total	Italy	Greece	Spain	Portugal	Turkey	Yugoslavia
1962	17.1	42.9	32.1	37.3	13.8	16.4	10.3
1963	16.1	30.8	30.4	30.5	13.4	20.0	18.3
1964	15.7	30.6	28.0	32.8	18.1	45.6	19.9
1965	17.0	33.2	25.5	32.3	38.6	44.3	20.5
1966	14.3	21.3	17.4	19.7	54.1	34.5	22.8
1967	8.9	10.8	8.9	10.1	28.9	18.2	16.4
1968	11.3	15.0	15.1	16.7	31.3	23.1	17.9
1969	14.3	15.8	20.7	23.6	44.8	24.4	34.3
1970	17.0	15.4	22.0	26.0	50.7	25.3	37.0
1971	16.4	15.1	17.9	25.9	46.8	19.0	28.1
1972	14.4	14.2	13.4	21.9	39.9	15.4	23.5
1973	13.8	14.7	11.5	17.9	0.0	13.0	22.3
1974	10.5	9.1	10.5	11.2	18.8	10.4	16.4
1975	7.7	7.5	6.3	8.9	12.6	6.6	12.1
1976	7.3	7.8	5.9	7.7	10.7	6.1	12.0
1977	7.5	8.9	6.1	8.3	11.5	6.3	11.8
1978	7.9	8.9	7.1	10.3	15.5	7.9	12.1
1979	9.2	9.3	8.1	13.7	16.9	11.1	13.4
1980	10.1	9.2	9.9	15.9	13.1	14.2	14.1
1981	8.1	7.1	11.6	15.7	11.6	12.2	12.9

Note: See Table 60

TABLE 70 Ratio of Female Employees per Dependant Out-migrant by Sending Country

Year	Total	Italy	Greece	Spain	Portugal	Turkey	Yugoslavia
1962	3.1	3.9	9.3	9.1	2.0	1.4	1.9
1963	3.3	3.5	10.0	8.6	2.5	2.2	3.8
1964	3.5	4.2	9.3	9.5	4.1	4.6	4.2
1965	3.9	5.0	9.2	9.3	5.9	5.7	4.6
1966	3.6	3.7	6.9	6.0	8.8	5.7	6.0
1967	2.6	2.3	3.7	3.6	6.9	3.4	5.4
1968	3.3	3.3	6.3	6.1	8.5	5.0	6.5
1969	4.2	3.6	8.8	7.7	12.9	5.4	11.2
1970	4.9	3.6	9.3	7.8	14.2	5.6	11.4
1971	4.6	3.6	7.6	7.6	12.9	4.1	8.3
1972	4.2	3.5	5.8	6.6	11.9	3.5	7.3
1973	0.0	0.0	0.0	0.0	0.0	0.0	0.0
1974	3.3	2.5	4.6	3.5	5.8	2.7	5.6
1975	2.4	2.0	2.7	2.9	4.0	1.7	4.4
1976	2.3	2.1	2.5	2.5	3.5	1.6	4.3
1977	2.3	2.3	2.6	2.6	3.8	1.6	4.3
1978	2.5	2.3	3.0	3.3	5.2	2.1	4.4
1979	2.8	2.4	3.3	4.3	5.8	2.9	4.9
1980	3.1	2.4	4.1	5.0	4.6	3.7	5.2
1981	2.5	1.9	4.6	4.9	4.1	3.2	4.8

Note: See Table 60

TABLE 71 Ratio of Male Employees per Dependant Out-migrant by Sending Country

Year	Total	Italy	Greece	Spain	Portugal	Turkey	Yugoslavia
1962	14.1	39.1	22.8	28.2	11.8	15.1	8.4
1963	12.8	27.3	20.4	21.8	10.9	17.8	14.5
1964	12.2	26.4	18.7	23.3	14.0	41.1	15.7
1965	13.1	28.2	16.3	23.0	32.7	38.6	15.9
1966	10.7	17.6	10.5	13.7	45.3	28.8	16.8
1967	6.3	8.5	5.2	6.5	22.0	18.1	11.0
1968	7.9	11.7	8.7	10.7	22.8	18.1	11.4
1969	10.1	12.2	11.9	15.9	31.9	19.0	23.1
1970	12.1	11.8	12.7	18.2	36.5	19.8	25.6
1971	11.7	11.5	10.3	18.3	33.9	14.9	19.9
1972	10.2	10.8	7.6	15.3	28.0	11.9	16.3
1973	n.d	n.d	n.d	n.d	n.d	n.d	n.d
1974	7.2	6.7	5.9	7.7	12.9	7.7	10.7
1975	5.3	5.4	3.6	6.0	8.5	4.9	7.7
1976	5.0	5.7	3.4	5.2	7.2	4.6	7.7
1977	5.1	6.6	3.5	5.6	7.7	4.6	7.5
1978	5.5	6.7	4.2	7.1	10.3	5.8	7.7
1979	6.4	6.9	4.8	9.4	11.2	8.1	8.5
1980	7.0	6.8	5.9	10.9	8.4	10.5	8.8
1981	5.6	5.3	6.9	10.8	7.5	9.0	8.1

Note: See Table 60

TABLE 72   Number of Residents by Sending Country

Year	Total	Italy	Greece	Spain	Portugal	Turkey	Yugoslavia
1951	506000	23500	3300	1600	---	1300	23700
1952	466200	24500	3400	1700	---	1300	21200
1953	489700	26000	3600	1800	---	1500	22100
1954	481900	25600	3600	1900	---	1500	21000
1955	484800	25800	3800	2100	---	1700	21000
1961	686200	196700	42100	44200	800	6700	16400
1967	1806653	412777	200951	177033	23966	172439	140553
1968	1924229	454216	211764	174989	26889	205354	169130
1969	2381061	514552	271313	206895	37474	322421	331576
1970	2976497	573648	342891	245530	54386	469160	514476
1971	3438711	589825	394949	270350	75241	652812	594284
1972	3526568	581699	389426	267248	84671	712289	608646
1973	3966200	630735	407614	287021	111969	910525	701588
1974	4127366	629628	406394	272676	121533	1027770	707771
1975	4089594	601405	390455	247447	118536	1077097	677863
1976	3948337	567984	353733	219427	113720	1079300	640380
1977	3948278	570825	328465	201429	110977	1118041	630027
1978	3981061	572522	305523	188937	109924	1165119	610184
1979	4143836	594424	296803	182155	109843	1268307	620649
1980	4453308	617895	297518	179952	112270	1462442	631842
1981	4629779	624505	299303	176955	109417	1546311	637313

Source: Korte (1980): Bevölkerung und Erwerbstätigkeit. Fachserie 1. Reihe 1.4, Ausländer: 1961 Census.

TABLE 73 Number of Female Residents by Sending Country

Year	Total	Italy	Greece	Spain	Portugal	Turkey	Yugoslavia
1974	1588900	223900	187900	106200	47300	366600	265800
1975	1614700	221700	183200	100900	50500	407100	269600
1976	1614400	211400	166300	91300	50300	419600	264500
1977	1628600	211900	152900	84000	49900	443100	263200
1978	1650900	215100	143000	79100	50000	472700	262300
1979	1633300	223800	140900	77300	50400	522000	271700
1980	1834100	222300	138300	76100	51800	586200	273400
1981	1919500	238400	138800	75100	50700	630400	276700

Source: Bevolkerung und Erwerbstatigkeit, Fachserie 1, Reihe 1.4, Auslander.

TABLE 74 Number of Male Residents by Sending Country

Year	Total	Italy	Greece	Spain	Portugal	Turkey	Yugoslavia
1974	2519400	405700	218500	166500	74200	661200	441900
1975	2427800	379700	207200	146600	68000	670000	408300
1976	2311200	356600	187400	128100	63500	659700	375800
1977	2319700	358900	175500	117400	61100	674900	366800
1978	2304800	357400	162500	109900	59900	692500	347900
1979	2266700	370600	155900	104900	59400	746300	348900
1980	2619200	385600	159200	103900	60500	876200	358400
1981	2710200	386100	160500	101800	58700	915800	360600

Source: See Table 73

TABLE 75 Proportions of Children, Women and Men by Country of Nationality

Year	Group	Total	Italy	Greece	Spain	Portugal	Turkey	Yugoslavia
1974	C(0-15)	18.6	21.4	22.6	19.0	16.4	22.0	11.5
	W(16+)	30.1	25.0	35.4	30.0	31.0	26.6	31.8
	M(16+)	51.3	53.6	42.1	51.0	52.7	51.4	56.7
1978	C(0-15)	23.9	23.3	27.0	23.0	25.8	33.5	19.2
	W(16+)	30.7	26.0	33.7	31.0	32.8	26.2	33.4
	M(16+)	45.4	50.7	39.3	46.0	41.4	40.2	47.4
1981	C(0-15)	25.2	23.3	27.8	22.4	27.0	35.9	22.3
	W(16+)	29.9	26.6	32.9	31.9	33.1	25.4	32.3
	M(16+)	44.9	50.1	39.3	45.7	39.8	38.7	45.4

Source: See Table 73

TABLE 76 Age Structure of the Total Foreign Population

Age	1974	1978	1981
0-5	9.1	10.5	8.8
6-9	4.9	6.6	7.1
10-14	4.4	6.6	7.8
15-17	3.1	3.2	4.7
18-20	5.0	4.0	4.6
21-24	10.3	7.1	7.1
25-29	16.9	13.0	10.8
30-34	14.7	14.0	13.1
35-39	11.8	11.7	10.9
40-44	8.1	8.8	9.2
45-49	4.8	5.7	6.3
50-54	2.9	3.5	3.8
55-59	1.2	2.1	2.4
60-64	1.0	1.0	1.2
65+	1.7	2.1	2.1
Total	100.0	100.0	100.0

Source: See Table 73

TABLE 77   Age Structure of Minority Populations by Country of Nationality, 1978

Year	Italy	Greece	Spain	Portugal	Turkey	Yugoslavia
0-5	9.6	10.7	8.4	10.3	15.7	10.7
6-9	6.3	8.0	6.2	7.1	9.1	5.5
10-14	7.0	8.8	7.4	7.2	8.2	3.8
15-17	4.1	3.6	3.7	3.5	3.9	1.7
18-20	6.6	4.0	3.8	2.9	4.2	1.8
21-24	10.7	5.1	5.2	3.8	5.9	5.1
25-29	13.1	8.1	10.2	9.3	8.9	18.3
30-34	10.7	12.3	12.8	18.8	13.5	17.5
35-39	88	11.3	10.3	15.6	14.1	13.0
40-44	7.6	12.3	11.3	10.7	9.4	10.0
45-49	5.9	8.5	10.1	6.1	4.7	6.8
50-54	4.4	4.6	6.1	2.7	1.5	3.3
55-59	2.7	1.4	2.9	1.0	0.4	1.5
60-64	1.2	0.6	0.9	0.3	0.1	0.4
65+	1.3	0.7	0.7	0.4	0.3	0.6
	100.0	100.0	100.0	100.0	100.0	100.0

Source: See Table 73

TABLE 78 Age Structure of the Foreign and Total Populations, 1981

Age	Foreign	Total
0-4	7.1	4.8
5-14	16.6	13.1
15-44	60.4	44.6
45-64	13.8	22.1
65+	2.1	15.5
Total	100.0	100.0

Source: OECD SOPEMI 1982; Statistisches Jahrbuch 1982.

TABLE 79 Dependency Ratios per Thousand Adult Population and per Thousand Labour Force by Age, Total and Foreign Populations, 1981

Age of dependants	Population 15 to 44		Population 15 to 64		Labour Force	
	total	foreign	total	foreign	total	foreign
0-4	107	117	72	95	105	140
5-14	293	275	196	224	288	329
0-14	400	391	268	319	393	469
65+	347	35	232	29	341	42
0-14; 65+	747	427	499	348	734	511
All dependants	---	---	---	---	1203	979

Source: OECD   SOPEMI 1982; Statistisches Jahrbuch 1982

TABLE 80 Length of Stay in West Germany by Country of Nationality, 1981

Year	Total	Italy	Greece	Spain	Portugal	Turkey	Yugoslavia
-1	5.7	5.2	2.5	1.8	2.0	4.1	2.8
1-3	19.4	17.1	8.0	5.5	9.6	24.1	10.3
4-5	8.3	7.9	5.6	4.3	8.6	10.4	6.3
6-7	9.6	7.2	8.1	6.8	16.3	12.8	8.8
8-9	14.1	11.0	12.5	14.0	26.2	18.3	16.7
10-14	27.5	29.4	38.6	34.7	28.9	24.5	46.9
15-19	8.7	14.0	19.0	24.9	7.7	5.2	6.1
20+	6.6	8.2	5.8	8.0	0.8	0.6	2.1
Total	100.0	100.0	100.0	100.0	100.0	100.0	100.0

Source: Bevolkerung und Erwerbstatigkeit, Fachserie 1, Reihe 1.4. Auslander, 1981.

Bibliography

Abadan-Unat, N. (1977) 'Implications of migration on emancipation and pseudo-emancipation of Turkish women', International Migration Review, XI, no. 1, pp 31-57

Adelstein, A. et al (1980) Perinatal and Infant Mortality: Social and Biological Factors 1975-1977, OPCS Studies on Medical and Population Subjects, no. 41, HMSO, London

Bagley, C. (1972) 'Interracial marriage in Britain – some statistics', New Community, I, no. 4

Benjamin, B. (1982) 'Variation of mortality in the United Kingdom with special reference to immigrants and minority groups', in Coleman, 1982

Booth, H. (1982) 'On the role of demography in the study of post-war migration to Western Europe', European Demographic Information Bulletin, XVIII, no. 4, pp 161-71

Booth, H. (1983a) 'Ethnic and racial questions in the census: the Home Affairs Committee report', New Community, XI, nos 1/2, pp 83-91

Booth, H. (1983b) 'The 'ethnic question': a critique of the Home Affairs Commmittee report', Radical Statistics, no. 28, pp 19-22

Booth, H. (1985a) Second-Generation Migrants in Western Europe: Demographic Data Sources and Needs, Statistical paper no. 1, Centre for Research in Ethnic Relations, University of Warwick

Booth, H. (1985b) The Availability and Relevance of Demographic Data on Second-Generation Migrants in Several Countries in Western Europe, UNDP/ILO European Regional Project for Second-Generation Migrants, Working Paper, ILO, Geneva

Booth, H. (1985c) 'Which 'ethnic question'? The development of questions identifying ethnic origin in official statistics', Sociological Review, 33, no. 2, pp 254-74

Booth, H. (1988) 'Identifying ethnic origin: the past, present and future of official data production', in Radical Statistics Race Group, Britain's Black Population, second edition, Gower, Aldershot

Brass, W. (1977) 'Welcome and keep out... the two signs on Britain's door', The Listener, 15 September

Brown, C. (1984) Black and White Britain: The Third PSI Survey, Heinemann Educational Books, London

Bundesinstitut fur Bevolkerungsforschung (1974) 'Systems of registration of international migrations: permanent registration (the case of the Federal Republic of Germany)', in International Migration: Proceedings of a Seminar on Demographic Research in Relation to International Migration, Buenos Aries, 5-11 March, CICRED, Paris

Bundesminister fur Arbeit und Sozialordnung (1977) Vorschlage der Bund-Lander-Kommission Zur Forentwicklung einer umfassenden Konzeption der Auslanderbeschaftigungspolitik, Bonn

Cartwright, A. (1978) Recent Trends in Family Building and Contraception, OPCS Studies in Medical and Population Subjects, no. 34, HMSO, London

Castles, S. (1980) 'The social time-bomb: education of an underclass in West Germany', Race and Class, XXI, no. 4

Castles, S. (1983) 'West German government plans mass repatriation', Searchlight, no. 97, pp 17-18

Castles, S. and Kosack, G. (1973) Immigrant Workers and Class Structure in Western Europe, Oxford University Press, London

Castles, S. with Booth, H. and Wallace, T. (1984) Here for Good: Western Europe's New Ethnic Minorities, Pluto Press, London

Chamberlain, R. et al (1975) British Births 1970, Volume 1: The First Week of Life, Heinemann Medical Books, London

Coleman, D. A. (ed.)(1982) Demography of Immigrants and Minority Groups in the United Kingdom, Academic Press, London

Council of Europe (1980) Recent Demographic Developments in the Member States of the Council of Europe, Strasbourg

Department of Employment (quarterly) Employment Gazette, HMSO, London

Department of the Environment (1978) National Dwelling and Housing Survey, HMSO, London

Department of the Environment (1980) National Dwelling and Housing Survey, Phases II and III, HMSO, London

Duffield, M. R. (1988) Black Radicalism and the Politics of De-industrialisation: The Hidden History of Indian Foundry Workers, Avebury, Aldershot

Eversley, D. and Sukdeo, F. (1989) The Dependants of the Coloured Commonwealth Population of England and Wales, Institute of Race Relations, London

Federal Republic of Germany (1982) 'SOPEMI 1982', unpublished report submitted to the OECD for summarisation in the OECD SOPEMI 1982 report

File, N. and Power, C. (1981) Black Settlers in Britain 1555-1955, Heinemann Educational Books, London

Foner, N. (1979) Jamaica Farewell, Jamaican Migrants in London, Routledge and Kegan Paul, London

Froebel, F., Heinrichs, J. and Kreye, O. (1980) The New International Division of Labour, Cambridge University Press, Cambridge

Fryer, P. (1984) Staying Power: The History of Black People in Britain, Pluto Press, London

Hiemenz, U. and Schatz, K. W. (1979) Trade in Place of Migration, ILO, Geneva

Home Affairs Committee (1981) Immigration from the Indian Sub-Continent, Minutes of Evidence, HMSO, London

Home Affairs Committee (1982) Immigration from the Indian Sub-Continent, HMSO, London

Home Affairs Committee (1983) Ethnic and Racial Questions in the Census, vols I, II, III, HMSO, London

Home Office (1977) A Register of Dependants, report of the Parliamentary Group on the feasibility and usefulness of a Register of Dependants, HMSO, London, cmnd 6698

Home Office (annual) Control of Immigration, United Kingdom, HMSO, London

Home Office (quarterly) Statistical Bulletin, HMSO, London

Honekopp, E. and Ullman, H. (1980) 'The effect of immigration on social structures, Federal Republic of Germany', UNESCO, Paris

Iliffe, L. (1978) 'Estimated fertility rates of Asian and West Indian immigrant women in Britain, 1969–1974', Journal of Biosocial Science, 10, pp 189–97

Jones, P. R. (1984) 'Ethnic intermarriage in Britain: a further assessment', Ethnic and Racial Studies, 7, no. 3, pp 398–405

Joshua, H. and Wallace, T. with the assistance of Booth, H. (1983) To Ride the Storm: The 19S0 Bristol 'Riot' and the State, Heinemann Educational Books, London

Killian, L. M. (1983) 'The collection of official data on ethnicity and religion: the US experience', New Community, XI, nos 1/2, pp 74–82

Korte, H. (1980) 'The development and significance of labour migration and employment of foreigners in the Federal Republic of Germany between 1950 and 1979', paper presented at the World Peace Foundation Conference on Temporary Labour Migration in Europe: Lessons for the American Policy Debate, Elkridge, 12–14 June

Kraus, R. (1983)"Asylum seekers in the Federal Republic of Germany: analysis of the situation – elements of a solution', International Migration, XXI, no.2, pp 230–37

Lomas. G. B. G. (1973) Census 1971: The Coloured Population of Great Britain, Runnymede Trust, London

Macfarlane, A. and Mugford, M. Birth Counts, Statistics of Pregnancy and Childbirth, HMSO, London

Marmot, M., Adelstein, A. and Bulusu, L. 'Immigrant mortality in England and Wales 1970–78', Population Trends, no. 33

New Community (1980) VIII, nos 1/2

O'Loughlin, J. (1980) 'Distribution and migration of foreigners in German cities', Geographical Review, 70, no.3

OECD (annual) SOPEMI, continuous reporting system on migration, OECD, Paris

OPCS, Immigrant Statistics Unit (1976) 'Country of birth and colour 1971–4', Population Trends, no. 2

OPCS, Immigrant Statistics Unit (1977) 'New Commonwealth and Pakistani population estimates', Population Trends, no. 9

OPCS, Immigrant Statistics Unit (1978a) 'Marriage and birth patterns among the New Commonwealth and Pakistani population', Population Trends, no. 11

OPCS (1978b) Occupational Mortality 1970–72, decennial supplement, Series DS, no.1, HMSO, London

OPCS (1979) 'Population of New Commonwealth and Pakistani ethnic origin: new projections', Population Trends, no.16

OPCS, Monitor CEN 80/2 (1980a) Tests of an Ethnic Question, HMSO, London, 20 March

OPCS, Monitor CEN 80/3 (1980b) The Government's Decision on an Ethnic Question in the 1981 Census, HMSO, London, 2 April

OPCS, Monitor PP1 82/1 (1982a) Sources of Statistics on Ethnic Minorities, HMSO, London, 22 June

OPCS (1982b) Mortality Statistics, Perinatal and Infant: Social and Biological Factors 197S, 1979, Series DH3, no. 7, HMSO, London

OPCS (1982c) Labour Force Survey 1981, HMSO, London

OPCS, Monitor LFS 83/1 (1983a) Labour Force Survey 1981: Country of Birth and Ethnic Origin, HMSO, London, 22 February

OPCS (1983b) 1980 Mortality Statistics: Perinatal and Infant: Social and Biological Factors, Series DH3, no. 9, HMSO, London

OPCS (1983c) Immigrant Mortality, Studies on Medical and Population Subjects, no. 47, HMSO, London

OPCS (1983d) Census 1981: Country of Birth : Great Britain, HMSO, London

OPCS, Monitor LFS 84/2 (1984) Labour Force Survey: Country of Birth, Ethnic origin, Nationality and Year of Entry, HMSO, London, 18 December

OPCS (1985a) 1981 Mortality Statistics: Perinatal and Infant: Social and Biological Factors, Series DH3, no. 13, HMSO, London

OPCS (1985b) 1982 Mortality Statistics: Perinatal and Infant: Social and Biological Factors, Series DH3, no. 14, HMSO, London

OPCS Monitor DH3 85/1 (1985c) Infant and Perinatal Mortality: Birthweight, HMSO, London

OPCS, Monitor DH3 86/1 (1986) Infant and Perinatal Mortality: Birthweight, HMSO, London

OPCS International Migration, Series MN, HMSO, London

OPCS, Monitor FM1 Series Birth by Birthplace of Parents, HMSO, London

OPCS, Monitor DH1 Series Deaths by Birthplace of Deceased, HMSO, London

OPCS (occasional) Census 1981 County Reports, HMSO, London

OPCS (annual) Mortality Statistics: Perinatal and Infant: Social and Biological Factors, Series DH3, HMSO, London

OPCS and General Register Office Scotland (1974) Census 1971, Great Britain, Country of Birth Tables, HMSO, London

Overton, E. (1980) 'The fertility of the population of New Commonwealth and Pakistani ethnic origin: some recent estimates', Policy Studies, 1, Part I

Peach, C. (1968) West Indian Migration to Britain: A Social Geography, Oxford University Press for the Institute of Race Relations, London

Peach, C. and Winchester, S. W. C. (1974) 'Birthplace, ethnicity and the under-enumeration of West Indians, Indians and Pakistanis in the censuses of 1966 and 1971', New Community, 3, pp 386-93

Power, J. (1979) Migrant Workers in Western Europe and the United States, Pergamon, Oxford

Rist, R. C. (1979) 'Guestworkers and post-World War II European Migrations', Studies in Comparative International Development, 14, no.2, New Brunswick, NJ

Robinson, V. (1982) 'The assimilation of South and East African Asian immigrants in Britain', in Coleman

Rose, E. J. B. et al ((1969) Colour and Citizenship: A Report on British Race Relations, Oxford University Press for the Institute of Race Relations, London, Part III

Royal Commission on Population (1949) Report, HMSO, London, cmnd 7695

Runnymede Trust and Radical Statistics Group (1980) Britain's Black Population, lst edition, Heinemann Educational Books, London

Saunders, C. (1978) Census 1981 - Question on Racial and Ethnic Origin, briefing paper, The Runnymede Trust, London

Sillitoe, K. (1978a) 'Ethnic origin: the search for a question', Population Trends, no. 13

Sillitoe, K. (1978b) Ethnic Origins 1, OPCS Occasional Paper no. 8, HMSO, London

Sillitoe, K. (1978c) Ethnic Origins 2, OPCS Occasional Paper no. 9, HMSO, London

Sillitoe, K. (1978d) Ethnic Origins 3, OPCS Occasional Paper no. 10, HMSO, London

Sillitoe, K. (1981) Ethnic Origins 4. An Experiment in the Use of a Direct Question About Ethnicity for the Census, OPCS Occasional Paper no. 24, HMSO, London

Smith, D. J. (1976) The Facts of Racial Disadvantage: A National Survey, Political and Economic Planning, London

Smith, T. E. (1981) Commonwealth Migration: Flows and Policies, Macmillan, London

Statistisches Bundesamt (annual) Bevolkerung und Erwerbstatigkeit, Fachserie 1, Reihe 1.4, Auslander

Statistisches Bundesamt (bi-annual) Bevolkerung und Erwerbstatigkeit, Fachserue 1, Reihe 1.S.2, Ausgewahlte Strukturdaten fur Auslander

Thompson, J. H. (1982) 'Differential fertility among ethnic minorities' in Coleman

United Nations (1979) Labour Supply and Migration in Europe: Demographic Dimensions 1950-1975 and Prospects, United Nations, New York

Visaria, P. M. (1967) 'Sex ratios at birth in territories with a relatively complete registration', Eugenics Quarterly, 14, no. 2, pp 134–5

Volker, G. E. (1975) 'Labour migration: aid to the West German economy?', in Krane, R. E. (ed.) Manpower Mobility Across Cultural Boundaries: Social, Economic and Legal Aspects: The Case of Turkey and West Germany, E J Brill, Leiden

Weidacher, A. (1983) 'Policy with respect to aliens and migration research in the Federal Republic of Germany 1973–1983', International Migration, XXI, no. 4, pp 463–87

White Paper (1965) Immigration from the Commonwealth, HMSO, London, cmnd 2739

White Paper (1978) 1981 Census of Population, HMSO, London cmnd 7146

White, R. (1979) 'What's in a name? Problems in official and legal usages of 'race' ', New Community, VII, no. 3, pp 333–49

Wilpert, C. (1983) 'From guestworkers to immigrants: migrant workers and their families in the FRG', New Community, XI, nos 1/2, pp 137–42